The Palace of Justice

The Palace of Justice

A Colombian Tragedy

ANA CARRIGAN

Four Walls Eight Windows
NEW YORK / LONDON

A FOUR WALLS EIGHT WINDOWS FIRST EDITION

Copyright 1993 by Ana Carrigan

Published by
FOUR WALLS EIGHT WINDOWS
39 West 14th Street, room 503
New York, N.Y. 10011

First printing October 1993

Library of Congress Cataloging-in-Publication Data
Carrigan, Ana.
The Palace of Justice: a Colombian tragedy / by Ana Carrigan.—1st ed.
p.   cm.
ISBN 0-941423-82-4 : $22.95
1.Colombia—Politics and government—1974- 2. Palacio de Justicia (Bogotá,
Colombia)—Siege, 1985. 3. M-19 (Colombian guerrilla group) 4. Terrorism—
Colombia—History—20th century. 5. Hostages—Colombia—History—20th
century. 6. Bogotá (Colombia)—History. I. Title.
F2279.C365   1993
986.106'32—dc20   93-8704
CIP
Designed by Cindy LaBreacht

Printed in the U.S.A.

To the memory of my uncle Rafael,
who opened my eyes to the Latin world,
with love and sorrow

ACKNOWLEDGEMENTS

This book grew from an unpublished article for *The New York Times Sunday Magazine* in 1986. I owe a special debt to Mark Uhlig and Mark Danner, who worked on the manuscript at the time, and whose faith in the story gave me the impetus to pursue it further.

The largest debt I owe to all those in Colombia who took personal risks to help me tell this story. To those among them who must remain anonymous, and most particularly to "Gabriel," "Felipe," "Juan," and "Mauricio," my profoundest graditude.

My debts to friends, family and colleagues in three hemispheres are too numerous to list individually, but among them I owe a particular debt to Andrew Cockburn, for his uniquely generous response upon reading the manuscript; to Alistair Beaton, who read various unfinished drafts and whose support and advice were invaluable; in Bogotá, Germán Castro Caycedo, Ramón Jimenez and Juan Manuel Lopez Caballero guided me through the mass of disinformation; so did Carlos Jiménez Gómez, Juan Guillermo Ríos and Juan Vincente Peña. To the Gaona family, for much kindness and hospitality, my grateful thanks.

Robert Weiner of the Lawyers Committee in New York helped me find my way through the maze of the Colombian justice system. Rosario Barreto in Bogotá and Ivan Rada in New York helped me find important photographs. Chris Weicher in New York and Coleyn Thompson Moore in Ireland provided generous assistance in printing out the manuscript at crucial stages.

At the offices of my publisher, special thanks to Chris Holbrook, Cindy LaBreacht, John Oakes, and to my editor, Dan Simon, whose contribution to this book has been large and from whom I have learned much. To A.W., who didn't have to do anything and has done a lot; and to my mother—who does not approve, but never withdrew her support—thank you.

Finally, I am deeply grateful to the J. Roderick MacArthur Foundation, the Center for Investigative Reporting and the Fund for Investigative Journalism, which together made it possible for me to return to Colombia in 1991 to bring my research up to date.

A.C.
Dublin, Ireland
August 1993

Contents

"Esta casa aborrece la maldad, ama la paz, castiga los delitos, conserva los derechos, honra la virtud."

—*Inscription from the lobby of the Palace of Justice*

(This house abhors evil, loves peace, punishes crimes, protects rights, honors virtue).

Foreword

The Palace of Justice is an enthralling narrative, poignant and surrealistic at the same time. Ana Carrigan is clearly herself haunted by the events she has been impelled to reconstruct with such meticulous care and in riveting prose. She is herself Colombian, on her mother's side, and the love she felt for the country of her childhood underlies the horror inspired in her by the events in and around the Palace of Justice in November 1985, and the political and juridical sequels to those events.

Corruption is present, in varying degrees and at various levels, in all governments, but in Colombia it has attained the proportions of an eerie epic which is unable to stop. It is not mainly financial corruption, though that is abundantly present. It is mainly the corruption of hypocrisy; the facade of democratic institutions masking the reality of arbitrary and brutal military power. The events of November 1985, destroyed the credibility of that facade, but the facade itself has been assiduously preserved with a neurotic and pedantic punctilio.

As Ana Carrigan says, Colombia is not a military dictatorship. Things there might be marginally better if it were. Under a military dictatorship, the generals have to take responsibility for failures, as the Galtieri junta had to do in Argentina. But in a pseudo-democracy, like Colombia, the military have power without responsibility, which is just how they like it. At the time of the massacre in the Palace of Justice, and habitually, the military leadership depicted itself, and was described by the admiring media and politicians, as the defenders of democracy. And they are indeed the designated defenders of the particular version of democracy they defend with such ferocity.

The Palace of Justice is a chilling but fascinating exploration of the realities that underlie the copious rhetoric of a pseudo-democracy. This book will always haunt the imagination of all who read it.

—Conor Cruise O'Brien

Prologue

BOGOTÁ, TUESDAY, APRIL 9, 1991. My first evening back in Bogotá after five years. That particular fragrance in the air: A mix of eucalyptus trees and the red earth of the Andes in the thin mountain air. Unmistakeable. Put me down blindfolded and with my ears plugged and I will tell you within five seconds where I am. I have known this unique fragrance of Bogotá since I was a small child. Breathing it in now takes me back, not five years to my last visit, but all the way back to that first childhood encounter with my mother's country.

The pavements then were cleaner, and also a lot safer. The Indian women arrived in the morning with their donkeys heaped with fruit and vegetables and parked themselves in the shade to sell their produce. "AGUACAATE! PAPAS FRESCAS! FRIJOLES..." If I shut my eyes I can still hear the cadences of their high-pitched cries, calling out to the cooks along the street outside my aunt's house. On that morning long ago, my first ever in a tropical, Latin country, they woke me up. The first thing I saw when I jumped out of bed and ran to the window was the Indian woman, with her long, black, thick and shiny plait under her felt hat, and her small grey donkey padding ahead of her up the street. I thought that I was truly in a land of magic. Never had I seen a sky so blue, or mountain peaks towering so close, so high above me, and the red and purple of the bougainvillia blossoms in my aunt's garden were of a deeper richer hue than I had ever known existed. Then, that night, musicians came to serenade my mother under her window, welcoming her home to the town she had left so many years ago to marry my father. Tradition forbade us to put on the light or to look out. Under cover of darkness the fiction of the anonymity of her admirers had to be strictly maintained. Crouched beneath the open window we could hear the serenaders rustling and whispering in the dark before the first rhythmic notes of the guitars sounded, followed by male voices rising in passionate lamentations to broken hearts, lost loves, rejected dreams. Those male voices in the Bogotá night, those liquid guitars, brought another culture, another world of romance and mystery to my childhood.

Was it ever like that? I thought so.

Were the Indian women who spread their ample forms under the eucalyptus trees beside their vibrant loads of oranges and limes, melons and chirimoyas, happier and more prosperous than the gaunt figures who drag their donkeys through the Bogotá traffic today, going from restaurant to restaurant collecting yesterday's left-overs and shovelling them into buckets harnessed to their donkeys' backs? I think they were.

People tell me that the women are collecting garbage for the pigs that they keep in their shacks which cling to the mountain's side, just across the new super highway that circles the city from north to south, separating the penthouses of the latest skyscrapers from the mountain's shantytown. I fear the pigs are a fiction. Every time I drive along the highway I look out for them but I have yet to see one.

Yet it is not, of course, the physical landscape of my childhood alone that has changed. In recent times the international perception of Colombia reflects the image of a country and a society that has run amok. A place of drug barons and guerrillas where violence has become an accepted way of life, and a rich, sophisticated and resourceful country of almost 30 million people seems condemned to stagger convulsively from one trauma to the next. In 1985, I happened to be in Bogotá to witness one such convulsion, a tragedy whose legacy has affected every facet of political life in Colombia ever since. On a November morning of that year, thirty-five heavily armed guerrillas of the M-19 Revolutionary Movement invaded the Palace of Justice in the heart of Bogotá's historic Plaza

Bolívar, and the government of the day stood aside as the Colombian Army responded with an all out military assault involving tanks, armored cars and over two thousand troops. When the guerrillas attacked, there were over three hundred people within the great building that was home to the Colombian Supreme Court and the Council of State, including the hierarchy of the Colombian judiciary and their staff, among whom the guerrillas seized over one hundred hostages. The combat between the army and the guerrillas lasted, almost without a break, for twenty-seven straight hours. When it ended, at 2:30 pm on the following afternoon, over one hundred people, including eleven Supreme Court Justices, lay dead. One army lieutenant and eight policemen—many killed by the army's own "friendly fire"—had also died. An unknown number of people had "disappeared." And the interior of the Palace of Justice had been reduced to rubble by explosives and fire. When it ended, in time-honored fashion, the "official version" of these events was hurriedly assembled and rushed to press.

In the process of rewriting the history of those November days, it was of course necessary to weave multiple disguises around the real events, as they had occurred in real time, in one physical location in the heart of the nation's capital, with real bodies and missing people, real eyewitness survivors, and that left behind the incinerated remains of a once great building. The fact that throughout the two days that the battle lasted, these real events had all taken place under the glare of the television lights and the cameras, created a special challenge to the scriptwriters of the official scenario. Nevertheless, as history shows, it was a challenge they were well equipped to handle. Today many aspects of the official version, in particular the central one about the core involvement of the drug mafia, have survived virtually intact.

It is rare that a single event can illuminate an entire epoch. Yet the tragedy at the Palace of Justice provided a microcosm in which the three mythic figures of every Latin conflict of the last fifty years—the Rebel, the General, and the President—acted out their appointed roles without benefit of the usual, self-protective, camouflage. In the years since, from beneath the palimpsest of invention and distortion engraved upon the facts by the promoters of the official version, bits and pieces of the untold story have insistently risen to the surface. Jagged, harsh, disconnected, like the fragments of a vivid, chaotic nightmare, these brief glimpses of the truth of what happened and why continue to haunt me. Today I have returned to Bogotá, for the second time since the assault on the Palace, in search of an understanding of the whole truth which still eludes me.

Tonight, just after nightfall, I walked back alone from Clara's apartment to my cousin's house testing the lay of the land. It's easy to see that the people who live in this part of town never walk. Picking one's way among the pot-holes and fissures in the broken pavement is a hazardous occupation. Even outside the luxury apartment buildings, skyscrapers with names like "Torre Ejecutivo" and "Torre Presidencial," the red sand brought down from the mountain in every torrential rainfall turns to rivers of mud in the wet season, and cars drive right onto the sidewalk to park haphazardly across a pedestrian's path.

Clara says Bogotá is quieter now. Not like last year when the war on drugs had brought to the capital a taste of the nightly bombings and assassinations that have been daily fare in the provincial city of Medellín for the past four years. Yet at eight o'clock in the evening, there are no people on the streets except the ubiquitous security guards. On the corner of every block, outside the supermarket, at the entrance to each apartment building, uniformed guards carrying shotguns loom in the dark. A private army patrolling the enclave of the rich. When I reach my cousin's house he is appalled that I have walked twelve blocks alone. From now on, he insists, I must call a taxi to take me door to door.

My cousin has earned the right to be nervous. My cousin, who is not very rich, was kidnapped last year by people who thought he was. For a month he was chained to a tree deep in the mountains. Since I was here last, kidnapping has become a national industry worth hundreds of millions of dollars annually, with its own infrastructure of accountants and lawyers, professional negotiators and, of course, an army of young, professionally trained kidnappers and guards. My cousin was in the country, having a cup of coffee on the veranda of his farm at about six o'clock one evening when he was seized, in front of his wife and his son. Maybe they were guerrillas and maybe they were common criminals. He will never know and nor will the police. The entire time that he was held captive his guards never removed their masks, never permitted him to enter into conversation with them.

My cousin is a lucky man to be alive, changed and scarred though he is. In the end the secret police, helped by his son to track the blackmailing phone calls, came close enough to his captors' mountain camp to spook them, and as they fled my cousin managed somehow to negotiate his survival and regain his freedom. He lost the farm, of course, that had been my grandfather's and my uncle's before him. He lost a way of life in a wildly beautiful, tropical region of the country that he loved. But he doesn't complain. During the entire time that he was held captive it was the rainy season, and his terror, standing chained under the torrential, tropical rains during daily thunder storms, was that he'd be incinerated by a bolt of lightning attracted by the chain that held him prisoner. Every day, sometimes every hour, he had to endure this torture alone. Today we talked about it. "I don't stay too long in the shower," he said, "it makes me think too much and it all comes back." Then he laughed. I remember his laugh the way it used to be: rich, bellowing waves of sound, as uninhibited as a child's, reverberating through my aunt's house. I wonder how long it will be before he laughs like that again.

Then too there is something else, another sadness resulting from my cousin's ordeal that no one talks about, but that he, his wife, his sons, and his wife's family, have had to register in silence. In this small society where everyone knows everyone else, the trauma of his disappearance brought the prevailing anarchy of Colombian life inside the intimate circle of a large group of people, the traditional extended Latin family. Yet with a few, remarkable exceptions, when violence struck, the members of the familial circle were unavailable. Danger hovered around my cousin and his household like an unpleasant smell. When he did escape, he came home to people who hadn't wanted to know, people for whom the illusionary comfort provided by their denial of a reality

beyond their control was more important than the acknowledge-
ment or recognition of his ordeal. "So how is he?" a relative asks
me, when we meet. "You know I haven't called him since he got
back. I don't know what to say." I had not realized that the disintegration of this society had gone so far. I did not know that fear had
reached so deeply into the fabric of everyday life that even that last
bastion of solidarity, the extended Latin family, had crumbled
under the pressure.

BOGOTÁ, WEDNESDAY, APRIL 10. *"Aquí no pasa nada."*
"Nothing happens here." The obligatory pause in the conversation, the look that waits to see whether the listener knows the reference. The moment's pause to let the quotation marks sink in. I
know the passage well. It's from the García Márquez classic, *One
Hundred Years of Solitude*. The book that a former *Commandante
Supremo* of the M-19 Revolutionary Movement—Alvaro Fayad—
used to say was the only text where a Colombian could recover the
history of his country, the only required reading for a Colombian
revolutionary.

I am lunching with Juan Manuel Lopez Caballero, the son and
the grandson of two former Colombian Presidents, and we are
talking about recent Colombian history. And about myth. And
about how the biggest, most enduring myth of all in this chaotic
country remains that dense and tangled fiction known as
Colombian democracy.

"Aquí no pasa nada." As in the massacre of striking banana
workers in the small coastal town of Cienega in 1928. Hundreds of
United Fruit banana workers and their wives and children were
killed that year, when an army regiment was brought in from
Bogotá by United Fruit to settle the strike. The troops set up their
machine guns on the roofs of the low buildings at the corners of
the main square, closed off the access streets, and opened fire into
a dense Sunday crowd of workers and their wives and children who
had gathered, after Sunday Mass, to wait in the tropical sun for an
anticipated address from the boss of United Fruit.

The way García Márquez tells the story, the sole survivor of
the massacre escapes from a pile of bodies heaped onto the freight

train that is ferrying the corpses out of town to dump them into the sea. He returns to Cienega to find all traces of the slaughter have vanished. In the kitchens of the small houses the women are preparing the evening meal. The children play peacefully outside in the patios. And it is not only the physical evidences of the previous day's horror that have been erased. All memory of the killings has evaporated from the consciousness of the village inhabitants. In the sleepy police station the police chief looks up in amazement: Massacre? What massacre is he talking about? He must have been dreaming. Nothing has happened here. Nothing has ever happened in Macondo and nothing ever will. This is a happy town.

I am lunching with a man who knows his subject well. His vast book-lined, penthouse apartment affords spectacular views onto the nearby mountains, across the city and beyond, all the way northwards up the fertile plain that stretches the full length of this Andean plateau where the Spanish Conquistadors built their capital of Nueva Granada, the City of the Holy Faith—Santa Fe de Bogotá. After an excellent meal, Juan Manuel conducts me in his private elevator to the floor below, which he converted into a suite of offices that serve as the headquarters of his privately established Foundation for The Clarification of the Events in The Palace of Justice.

Juan Manuel's father, the ex-President, is still a Jefe of the largest of the two traditional parties, the Gran Partido Liberal. His brother is editor and publisher of the most influential weekly news magazine. Today, and for all of Colombia's yesterdays going back at least to the thirties, the Lopez family, directly or by marriage, has been at the center of political and economic power in this country. But in terms of the rigid, unchanging ways of this caste society, Juan Manuel is a maverick. In a society where all dissent is confined to the middle and lower classes, Juan Manuel is an alienated, disenchanted, pessimistic member of the elite. Not by any means a radical. But someone who has looked with a cold, clear eye into the complacent self-interest that motivates his own caste and turned away with distaste. In Bogotá society, where his own people are still frantically absorbed in patching together new alliances, spinning new fantasies, weaving the webs of denial and oblivion on which they depend to keep their system going, most of Juan Manuel's relatives and associates think he is crazy.

But then Juan Manuel has lived in Europe for many years. And when he returned to Bogotá in 1986, he found that everyone around him in the *clase dirigente*, within and without government circles, was committed to covering up and distorting what had happened during the attack on the Colombian Supreme Court by guerrillas of the M-19 some months previously. To Juan Manuel the local climate of denial and repression was stultifying. He became obsessed with establishing and clarifying the truth.

The brutal results of the attack were not, could not be questioned. But the truth of what actually transgressed, minute by minute, within and around the besieged building—while the Palace of Justice and many of its most illustrious inhabitants were being immolated beneath the shells and the bombs—that truth was only decipherable in the details. And it was precisely those details that were rendered mysterious, unfathomable—and, it was hoped, unknowable—by the scriptwriters of the official scenario of these events.

Juan Manuel says it took him eight months to listen to all of the tapes, screen all the videos, read all the news reports and interviews, and study all the official speeches: those of the President—Belisario Betancur—in the National Cathedral and the Senate, and those of the Ministers of Defense, of Justice and of the Interior. He spent weeks studying the Congressional debates, and poring over the endless testimonies that the soldiers and the survivors gave to the investigators of the official Commission of Inquiry. But only when he finally listened to a tape of the voice of the President of the Supreme Court, Chief Justice Alfonso Reyes Echandia, talking live on radio by telephone from his office inside the Court, just hours before his death, did Juan Manuel discover the full extent of the manipulations of the "official version." "The voice of the Chief Justice, when I heard it," he says, "was not the voice of a coward screaming for help, the way people had described it to me. The man was magnificent. His voice, his message, was the very essence of rationality."

Listening to Juan Manuel takes me back to where this story begins. For of course I cannot forget the impact of that voice either. Like the rest of the population of Bogotá on that awful November afternoon in 1985, I too was listening to the live radio reporting from the scene of the battle when the President of the Supreme Court, speaking by telephone to a reporter from his fourth floor office in the very epicenter of the battle, told a trans-fixed nation that he had been unable to make contact by phone with the President of the Republic, Belisario Betancur, and that unless someone in authority gave the order to the army to hold their fire, to permit him to negotiate with the guerrillas who were holding him hostage, there was going to be a massacre. And I know precisely what Juan Manuel means, because I can still not forget and never will, that what moved me most about that dra-matic moment, beyond the terrifying implications of the judge's message, was precisely the self-control and innate courtesy of the man that voice revealed.

Just two days later, when the establishment had re-grouped themselves around President Betancur, and were busily providing excuses for his failure to pick up the phone and answer his Chief Justice's repeated calls for help, one of the first targets on which they focused their outrage was this four-minute broadcast. The memory of this serious and urgent voice which they could not silence had to be distorted, discredited. So yes, I remember well the irritation of all those Bogotános who had accepted the official version of the massacre. "*Ay que Horror*" they told each other. "A Supreme Court Judge... Ay! that poor man... Can you imagine? For a judge to be so hysterical... Of course he was crazed! But then those *animales* had a gun to his head... They were forcing him to say what he did."

While Juan Manuel and I share an obsession with the events of those dreadful November days, he is less focused than I am on the details of what actually happened, the specifics of how and when and where and by whose hand eleven Justices of the Supreme Court and the Council of State and over a hundred other people met their death. What torments Juan Manuel are the historical consequences, the implications of the blanket legal immunity that has thus far protected all of the participants; the official arguments that have enshrined political necessity above the rule of law, and in so doing, have legitimized the savagery of a dirty war that has raged unchecked throughout the country ever since.

The bookshelves of Juan Manuel's office are lined from ceiling to floor with the accumulated evidence to support the terrible logic of his premise: if you annihilate the Palace of Justice and all of its innocent inhabitants, and reward the butchers, it must of necessity follow that the entire country will be condemned to become a slaughterhouse. Since I was here last, in the spring of 1986, the leadership and membership of one political party, the Unión Patriótica, has been systematically eliminated. That means over two thousand dead people, including congressmen, mayors, town councillors, three Presidential Candidates, countless grassroots activists and their families, friends, and supporters. Massacres of unarmed peasants and workers have become a weekly event. At night, in the major cities, police in mufti operate death squads, roaming the streets on forays known as "social clean-up." "Social clean-up" entails killing any beggars, prostitutes, street kids or homosexuals they find.

If you ask Juan Manuel precisely when the police realized that Bogotános would accept such a drastic solution to the vexing disturbance of street kids ambushing the windscreens of their shining Mercedes and BMWs at every traffic light armed with buckets and wash rags, he will answer: after the Palace of Justice. Today the street kids, Bogotá's gamines, who had been a historic presence on the streets of the city since the nineteenth century, are no more. Like the nonexistent beggars, like the poor in the slums, they have become invisible. Those who survive "social clean-up" live below ground, in the city's sewer system.

"Do you believe" asks Juan Manuel, "that the extermination of an entire political party in the last five years would have been possible without the support, or at the very least, the silent complicity of the government?" He points out that the statistics of the political violence contained in his files document the fact that more opponents of the status quo have been killed in Colombia in each of the past three years than died during the entire sixteen years of the Pinochet dictatorship in Chile. Or put another way: more people have been killed and disappeared, since I was last here in May 1986, than died in the ten years of the Contra War in Nicaragua.

For most people in this town, these statistics don't exist. "In Colombia," says Juan Manuel, "we have developed a deadly spiritual disease, a 'culture of tolerance' for the intolerable." Our conversation has come full circle. "*Aquí no pasa nada.*" "Nothing happens here." This is a happy country.

* * * * *

I am having trouble finding people. Everyone I need to see has apparently changed their telephone numbers. Some have moved to more secure buildings. Many are no longer in the same jobs. A number of the best informed, independent journalists who helped me when I was last here have had to leave the country since. In New York, I would see their names crop up on the macabre "death lists," copies of which began to circulate through the Colombian community as long ago as the summer of 1987. Identified as "subversives" by the American Embassy and the Colombian military intelligence agencies, most were unable to get visas to the States. So they left, and re-built their lives in exile far from access to the American media, far from the congressional opponents of United States aid for the Colombian Army's counter-insurgency war. They went to Mexico, to Spain, or to Canada, and their story, the story of what was really going on inside Colombia, remained untold.

Since I was here last, Colombians have invented a new word—*magnicidio*—to describe the slaughter of their great and would-be great men. Those who step onto the public stage to offer a glimmer of hope and are instantly characterized by yet another Colombian phenomenon whose popular name comes from García Márquez. They enter the ranks of the "*Muertes Anunciadas,*" the assassinations waiting to happen, as in his chilling novel of that title. Inexorably, inevitably, their "deaths foretold" keep patient, watchful company despite the squads of bodyguards, the bullet-proof limousines, the barricaded entrances, windows, and exits of their homes and offices. All the ultimately futile paraphernalia of security.

During the twelve months preceding the last elections in 1990, the killings succeeded each other so swiftly, the rage and despair at the heavily attended funerals of these lost leaders swept so repetitively through the scarred streets of Bogotá, that a certain fogginess about details is understandable. Was it the amnestied, former M-19 *Commandante* and first Presidential candidate of the M-19 Democratic Alliance, Carlos Pizzarro, who was killed in his seat on a commercial flight? And Unión Patriótica candidate Bernardo Jaramillo who was cut down in a hail of bullets in the departure lounge of the airport? Is it reform Liberal candidate Luis Carlos Galán's hit man who is in jail, or Pizzarro's, or both? Was it the witness to the planning of Galán's murder who was shot dead a week ago on the sidewalk in a fashionable, residential area of Bogotá?

Because, of course, Juan Manuel is right. The killers also disappear. But rarely into jail. Never into a court of law. Among the alienated who live outside the self-contained, high security enclaves of the elite, everyone "knows," or thinks they "know," the identities of those "dark forces" in the background who plan and organize the elimination of Colombia's fragile hopes. Fewer people each year believe that the drug mafia is behind every bullet aimed at the heads of those, nationally and locally, who have emerged to offer a program for a cleansing of the political landscape. After each new major assassination the most cynical among Bogotá observers watch the newspapers closely for the notices of new appointments to foreign embassies and consulates. This may be unfair, but in the climate of institutionalized legal immunity it is understandable.

Since I was here last, the war against subversion, against the organized left and its sympathisers, has spread to include ordinary people, people without any political allegiances. In the vastness of the remote hinterland, the committed warriors of the various factions—the guerrilla forces, the paramilitaries of the newest landowning class, the mafia, and the troops of the National Army— conduct their indiscrimminate and bloody wars while unarmed villagers and peasants, who have the misfortune to live in these areas, die. In *El Tiempo* this morning, under the caption "Massacres in Cauca" there is a photograph on the front page of the bodies of fourteen young men and three young women slain over the weekend. Their bodies lie side by side, almost touching one another, face down by the side of the road. The hands of the young man lying nearest to the camera are still clasped in prayer, stretched out in supplication on the grassy verge. A dark stain spreads from the back of his head into his white shirt. Studying the photograph more closely, I see that the same stain, an ugly, dark, newsprint smudge, is repeated down the whole line of white-shirted, barefoot young bodies.

According to the story, relegated to page three, the dead were coffee pickers from the locality, travelling to town early on Sunday evening, when their bus was intercepted by armed men. All of the passengers were ordered out, forced to lie down by the side of the road, and shot, execution style, in the back of the head with high caliber bullets. Identification of the dead was difficult the reporter notes because some had been shot two or three times and their faces had been partially or wholly blown away. Furthermore, local people, who passed along the road later that same Sunday evening, "considered it was too dangerous to go and inspect the scene of the shootings for fear of reprisals." So the bodies, exposed to the tropical heat of this coffee-growing region until Monday morning were already partially decomposed. Nevertheless, the report continues, "by their clothes local officials deduced that they were all peasants."

According to *El Tiempo* local officials blame a guerrilla force belonging to the ELN for the massacre of the coffee-pickers. The ELN—(The National Army of Liberation)—is a small, radical offshoot of the largest and oldest guerrilla force in Latin America, The FARC, (The Armed Revolutionary Forces of Colombia). It was the FARC's shortlived truce with President Betancur's government in 1984 that resulted in the formation of the doomed Unión Patriótica Party. The ELN by contrast has never signed any pact with any Colombian government. It is small, highly disciplined, and it spends most of its energies in a campaign of economic sabotage directed against the multi-national oil companies, blowing up oil wells and pipelines. In the process it is also creating ecological disaster areas in the fabulous virgin forests and the great plains, endless oceans of grass that spread into Venezuela along Colombia's North Eastern frontier. Since when have the ELN started killing unarmed peasants? The answer to that question depends on whom you ask. What is certain is that Colombian peasants, trapped between the guerrillas, the army and private paramilitary bands, lead excessively dangerous, unpleasant lives.

* * * * *

In my cousin's house on this Wednesday evening there is a party. I can feel the waves of apprehension and discomfort circulating through this family gathering as my Colombian cousins come to welcome my return. *Por Díos!* Why are you interested in the Palace of Justice? they ask. Such a dreadful story! "I understand it was all about drugs," the millionaire insurance executive who is married to a distant cousin says. "So and so was in the Presidential Palace at the time and knows all about it. It appears those bandits of the M-19 were paid by the mafia to go in and murder the judges because of the extradition cases." Someone else asks if I had heard this version, adding that, "It sounds very probable." Yes, I say, I've heard it.

Of course. It's The Official Story. The one peddled by the government, the army, the American Embassy and the State Department from the first moment after the battle to retake the great building from the guerrillas ended. It was also the first, succesful salvo in the campaign to remove the political significance from the violence and to transform the drug problem into the national scapegoat. Nevertheless, it is amazing that six years later anyone in this city still believes it. Even the President's own Commission of Inquiry could find no proof of any mafia involvement, and said so.

My cousin is too kind and too polite to voice his unease about my activities directly, but a message is transmitted to me by one of his young grand nephews. What a pity, the child is reported to have said, that his cousin doesn't write about some of the beautiful things in Colombia. I wonder what my young cousin considers beautiful.

Last Sunday, *El Tiempo* devoted half of its magazine section— six full pages, complete with color photographs—to the results of a poll on the attitudes, aspirations, tastes, ideas, fears, values and lifestyles of Colombia's upper class thirteen to eighteen year-olds. According to the paper's findings, this future *clase dirigente* is conservative, optimistic, and contented. They get along well with their parents (seventy-eight percent), and while, as *El Tiempo* puts it, "given the grave situation in the country at large, these young people conclude that the country is going badly," yet they insist that "for them personally everything is going well. Eighty-three percent are happy with their lives."

Their solution for the country's ills? Eighty percent of the young women and seventy-seven percent of the boys believe the answer lies in more repression. They want their government to "put on their trousers," to use "the iron fist."

Their aspirations? To become professionals and make lots of money. Their major preoccupations? Sex and fashion. The world figures they most admire? George Bush and Pope John Paul. Hussein, the butcher of the Kurds, is up there on their list too. Hussein is a "*macho*." Seventy-two percent of the young women believe in preserving their virginity, versus thirty-eight percent of their male companions. Fifty-four percent of both sexes would like to leave Colombia and live in a foreign country. "They have their own exclusive centers of activity. Bars that specialize in exotic cocktails and pop music, ice cream parlors with bizarre names, executive buses to take them to school at seven in the morning and bring them home at two or seven o'clock in the evening. They have clothing stores that sell the brand names they prefer, they have their favorite pizzarias, hamburger joints and hair cutting saloons.... Many look as though they have just stepped out of an American movie, and the rest dream of imitating them.... Nothing wrong in that," concludes *El Tiempo*.

Will my young cousin, living within this Latin American island of the self-satisfied consumer society, ever be exposed to a García Márquez novel, I wonder? Or look at a Botero painting and understand the rage and the tenderness that consume his vision of this society? Or wander down the narrow, decayed streets of the *Candelaria* section of Bogotá, just sixty or seventy blocks to the south of his high security apartment skyscraper in the enclave that alienated locals call "Miami," and open his imagination to the way life used to be lived in its gracious, simple, eighteenth century interiors? Is he ever to have the chance of meeting a young rebel Indian leader from the vast, unknown and glorious interior of his country, and would he notice the dignity of his bearing, or marvel at the clarity of his gaze? Will he, as my brother and I used to do, ever be able to gallop with the cowboys down a mountain slope behind a herd of wild horses in the blue-black-purple dusk of the high Andes? Will he, in short, ever get to know that wild and beautiful, volatile land beyond the confines of his own isolated world of privilege, saturated with the values of a foreign culture?

I know the world my young cousin lives in well. I lived in it myself once. The life I remember then in the Colonial Haciendas and airy townhouses, with their troops of servants, gardeners, and chauffeurs, was also light years removed from indigenous Colombian culture. As I turn the pages of my mother's family album I find in the black and white snapshots the generations-old images that evoke my own more recent childhood memories. The long weekend gatherings of our large extended family, picnics and flirting, dances and horseback riding, all set against the background of spacious, poorly heated, uncomfortable Colonial Haciendas, whose architecture, plumbing and sparse furnishings had changed very little since the days of the wars of Liberation.

My mother's family are descended from the adventurers who sailed with Columbus and their more recent ancestors fought with the great Liberator himself, Simón Bolívar, to wrest these rich and fabulous territories away from the tyranny of the Spanish King. In my mother's generation the history of Conquest and the history of Liberation were both equally present. That history formed part of a felt legacy of romance and achievement that accompanied their sense of identity. Before the Second World War they sent their sons to France and England for their education, bought their clothes and jewellery in London's Saville Row and Bond Street, or in Paris on the Fauburg St. Honoré and the Champs Elysée. The intellectuals among them read Proust and Cervantes. Life was leisurely; they played a lot of bridge and gin rummy; the women, driven everywhere by their chauffeurs, did good works in Church-related charities; the men had their *petites amies*, set up in their *garconières* downtown, and spent much leisure time in their exclusively male clubs and bars discussing women, money and politics. They had remained colonials in their own country, in a country that they, their friends and associates, ruled as they did their own private estates.

I was twelve when I first met this world. Too old to become a part of it, old enough to observe its tribal rituals with astonishment. It has taken me many years to piece together an understanding of its ethos. Three institutions governed my relatives' lives: the family, the Liberal Party and the Catholic Church—in that order. Uncritical devotion to "the family" went far beyond the normal loyalties of a group of individuals united by common lineage and history. This was family perceived as immutable entity, center of gravity, and sacred icon. The Liberal Party came a close second in influence and rank, for it was the natural, tribal extension of the family. In the small, hermetic world of Bogotá society, all opposition to "our" Liberal clan came from its mirror image— the Conservative clan. Like Montagues and Capulets, Conservative families and Liberal families, the heirs of the civil war that followed Independence, stood toe to toe in the competition for power and patronage in a city that resembled a Latin American Verona. European to the core, my family's world view was innocent, unquestioning and untroubled by any of the complexities or tragedies of the twentieth century. Their lives were graceful, full of generosity, charm and good intentions. They were untroubled by the gathering storm outside the hacienda gate.

For beyond this insulated circle lay a disorderly country with a growing and hungry population. This was many decades before guerrillas or drugs appeared on the scene. Already in my childhood life for the rich was too pleasant, too easy. Life for the poor was too hard. Colombian society today is no longer rooted in its European past. In the American century it has embraced the

American way. New York, Beverly Hills, Houston and Miami have replaced London and Paris as the centers of attraction, the beckoning lodestars of Colombian desires. Meanwhile Colombian society remains structurally committed to ignoring the lengthy succession of national disasters that have led, inexorably, to its present collapse. The Colombian pursuit of the American Dream has neatly sidestepped the Jeffersonian principles of democracy and human rights. Aided considerably in the last decade by two billion dollars a year of laundered drug profits, this elite has succeeded in managing the Colombian economy superbly for their own ten percent of the population. While their Colombia prospers, they do not see the endemic social ills that fester and poison the nation at large. On the pages of the newspapers that they own and control, on the screens of their television sets, in the streets of their enclaves, the poor are miraculously invisible. The violent are always the other.

My young cousin's generation, the members of the next *clase dirigente* cannot be blamed for being happy with their lives. Citizens of the enclave in *el Norte*, "for them personally everything is going well." The survival skills of their elders have protected and perpetuated their future. Until now.

BOGOTÁ, THURSDAY, APRIL 11. I have managed to find an old friend—Hermán. One of the best informed investigative journalists still around, Hermán now writes books for the history shelves of the future, but he is still one of the most respected and knowledgeable men in town. And he still has the old glint in his eyes that betrays the fact he is up to some chicanery. Now he proposes to put me in touch with the contact man for the Basque priest who leads the ELN, the Cura Pérez, and send me—with his personal guarantee of safety—to interview Pérez in his jungle sanctuary. I remember that it was on just such a clandestine trip to meet the Cura Pérez that the journalist daughter of a former President, Diana Turbay, was kidnapped by drug boss Pablo Escobar. She subsequently met her death when troops of the *Cuerpo Elite* arrived with guns blazing to rescue her. Through waves of sudden terror I hear Hermán's voice at its most persuasive, most dangerous, offering the journalistic scoop of the month. The Cura Pérez truly knows a thing or two about the reality of this country, Hermán is saying. It will only take you six days: two to arrive, two to spend with the ELN, and two to return... Sorry Hermán. I have become a coward since I was here last. I am growing too old for Colombian style revolutionary journalism, or too fond of life, or something...

Hermán too is depressed. "Colombians have a great talent, a vocation, for war. It's endemic," he says. He points out another nugget in the day's newspaper: The government's solution for the dirty war is to give twenty million dollars to the Army to improve the training and integration of all the official intelligence agencies under one command and provide more money to buy "better intelligence." "Where's the accountability for how the money is spent?" he rages. "Nowhere. It's a gringo solution. A slush fund for corrupt generals that will only lead to more deaths, more cruelty, as more innocent peasants are drawn into the fight between the Army and the guerrillas."

*   *   *   *   *

Waiting to see the former M-19 guerrilla leader, now Co-President of the Constituent Assembly, Antonio Navarro Wolf, I make a scribbled note: "Antonio Navarro's secretary has bought a new outfit." Is it frivolous to find meaning in the expensive clothes and fashionable haircut of a former guerrilla fighter, now secretary-receptionist of Colombia's newest man of the hour? Years of dealing with Bogotá bureaucrats who protect their little fiefdoms with arrogance and contempt for ordinary Colombian mortals who have the misfortune to need a stamp, or a form, have made me allergic to the species. When Antonio Navarro Wolf's elegant secretary waves her red fingernails in the direction of a distant chair and tells me curtly to "wait over there," while she resumes her flirtation with one of Navarro's armed and black-leather-jacketed bodyguards, I register alarm. This newly powerful secretary of the former guerrilla leader is every bit as arrogant and uninterested as any government functionary in this town.

Antonio Navarro comes to the door himself, preceded by a phalanx of young men who are his bodyguards, and to judge from the paperwork spread all over his desk, also his close aides and advisors. These men, who have not yet shed their rough edges, inject the incongruous aura of clandestine existence into the atmosphere. Their boss, by contrast, wears his city suit with elegant casualness. Behind the fashionable spectacles, his pale grey eyes aren't giving away anything. Navarro projects coolness, and control. Under his leadership the M-19's transformation from clandestinity has been smoother and more successful than could have been dreamed possible, and Navarro himself has made the transition from defeated guerrilla leader to power broker with apparent ease. In Bogotá today he is courted by some of the most important businessmen and political operators in town. He breakfasts and lunches with them, listens calmly to their analyses of the country's problems and needs, and calculates their offers of financial support against the favors they expect from him in return. Of the M-19's ambitions he says simply: "We are not talking about upheaval. We are talking about a transfer of some of the power. About participation. We are talking about opening up the boards of directors of the financial institutions of this country to new forces."

A mention of the Palace of Justice and Navarro becomes edgy, irritable. Now that their agenda has changed the M-19 wants the entire episode buried in oblivion even more than the army does. However, unlike many of his followers, Navarro, who was the number two in command of the M-19 Revolutionary Movement when the attack took place, wastes no breath trying to justify the Palace seizure. "An immense mistake" he says dismissively. Navarro was out of the country at the time the Palace attack was conceived, recovering in a Cuban hospital from a grenade attack on his life. Still, in solidarity with the dead leaders who planned and executed that mistake, he also says, with disarming honesty, that had he been around at the time he feels sure "the *compañeros*" would have persuaded him to go along.

The M-19 Democratic Alliance represents a new phenomenon in Colombian politics. A moderate Colombian version of

Sandinismo for the nineties. But in this cynical town of Bogotá, there are few who consider them committed to left wing ideals, and many who doubt their avocation for democracy. Inside the offices of The Foundation for Peace and Reconciliation, the M-19's public relations arm, I asked the young woman in charge how she explained the contrast between their experience of the last nine months and the fate of the Unión Patriótica. I was poorly prepared for her answer: "Those people of the Unión Patriótica were stupid," she declared. "Every time they opened their mouths they insulted the army. What did they expect? You don't have to walk around with a crucifix painted on your back and a sign saying shoot me!" So much for reconciliation and revolutionary solidarity.

Still, the M-19, which had been reduced to some 800 men and women under arms before the 1989 negotiations that earned them a blanket amnesty and legal political participation, learned a lot from the Unión Patriótica's experience. When they decided to give up 'the armed struggle,' they approached the army directly and their negotiations began, not with the government, but with the generals. The M-19 is not saying what deals were cut, what assurances were given. But this implicit recognition of the complex web of complicity that unites civilian and military authority and underwrites, more, guarantees all civilian power in Colombia, has served them well. The M-19, or the "Emme," as they are affectionately known by their friends and supporters, are on the inside track to power now. Antonio Navarro has every intention of riding that track all the way to the Presidential Palace, and like every other ambitious civilian politician, he has no objection to cutting deals with the generals along the way.

I first came into contact with M-19 circles in the spring of 1986. Like many Colombians who yearned to see the hegemony of the ruling parties broken, I used to be attracted to them. I think that if I had gone to university in Bogotá I would have been the perfect recruit for their flamboyant, middleclass, happy-go-lucky approach. *"la Revolucíon es una Fiesta,"* Jaime Bateman, founder and *Commandante* of the M-19, used to say: "The revolution is not just about having enough to eat, it's about being able to eat what we like..."

"We are no longer the Apostles. The M-19 is Colombia, and Colombia is the M-19." I don't remember which of the *Commandantes* said that, but I do remember that when they came out of hiding the first time, in 1984, and filled the plazas of Colombia with their ebullient followers, that is what they said and believed. For a short time a lot of other Colombians believed it too. Before the Palace of Justice. Everyone seemed to be "Emme" in those days: the chauffeurs and the maids, the security guards and the bank employees, the secretaries and the civil servants, and, of course, the students.

"We stand at the center of the contradictions between the oligarchy and the people." I remember when Rafael, handsome, bearded, bespectacled, the very picture of a thoughtful Latin American revolutionary, said that in 1986, earnestly pounding on the table in Sanbourne's fast food restaurant in Mexico City. I was investigating the Palace of Justice story for *The New York Times* then, and Rafael had been deputized to check me out for introductions to the few *compañeros* who were still underground in Bogotá. When the exiled revolutionaries reminisced about past exploits everything glowed with remembered excitement, everything was a cause for laughter. A mood of unscarred optimism sustained the carefree certainty that they were on the right track.

In my notebook for that weekend I find the following scribble: "They make the revolution sound like a game. They are like children playing at being revolutionaries."

During that weekend Rafael invited me to his house, which was full of books and music and paintings and electronic communications equipment. He introduced me to his warm and lovely wife, cooked a marvellous meal, and told sexist jokes with great relish and humor. We drank Colombian coffee and Doble XX beer and he talked for hours; with his hands, with his eyes, his whole body conveying enthusiasm and energy, conviction and passion, all for the cause of Colombian democracy.

The ruins of the Palace of Justice lay darkly between us. And something else, less concrete, harder to define, something to do with ends and means, and consequences. The lie at the heart of the M-19's world view was different from the lies of their antagonists in the elites, but no less fatal. Theirs was the lie of the pure at heart, of the true believers with all the answers; of men who practice a different kind of flight from reality, yet who share with their enemy one all-encompassing priority: the pursuit of power.

In my Mexican City notebook I also find this quote: "Flee from all the prophets; from all those who are ready to die for the truth; for they will also provide the death of many others before their own." (Umberto Eco.) A fitting epitaph for the Palace of Justice. A middle-aged epitaph.

* * * * *

John Agudelo Ríos, the conservative lawyer who led the peace negotiations with the M-19 for President Betancur in 1984 and '85, says that none of the leaders he got to know ever did grow up. Agudelo Ríos also says that no two of the M-19 leaders ever shared any common political ideology. There were right-wingers and Marxists, anarchists and a few lonely social democrats, and they could never agree on a program. They still can't. "I hate programs," says Antonio Navarro Wolf. "There is nothing more deadly than programs. Those sacred texts that people hang around their necks like the doctrinaire dogmas of the Catholic Church."

Neither the long march through the political institutions nor years of guerrilla warfare in the distant mountains was ever the M-19 style. From the moment they burst upon the scene in 1974 with the theft of one of the nation's most prized possessions, the sword of Simon Bolivar, through the high-jacking of several tons of weapons from the army's crack, XIIIth Brigade Bogotá headquarters over New Year's Eve in 1979, to the seizure of the Dominican Embassy while the entire Bogotá diplomatic corps were celebrating the Day of Dominican Independence in 1980, their specialty was always the "*golpe revolucionario publicitario*," designed to effect the maximum destabilization of the system. They were children of the media age, long on imagination and daring, short on discipline, and they believed their own high-flown rhetoric.

The M-19 always got good press from Colombian journalists desperate for an alternative with which they could identify, and for many of these middleclass supporters, their lack of revolutionary seriousness had its own appeal. It combined two images beloved by Latin societies: the macho rebel and the playboy, the weaver of exotic fantasies. Many Colombians forgave the M-19 a certain incoherence, because their romantic image, and their nationalism, protected them from the twin spectres of totalitarianism and foreign tutelage that had always hovered around the committed, serious men who led the decades-long, peasant-based insurgency of the FARC.

But in November 1985 the M-19 were in deep trouble. Across the country, their return to "total" war with the government of President Betancur had been badly received. Even their own constituency blamed M-19 intransigence and poor judgement for the collapse of a peace accord that the guerrillas had signed with hugely unrealistic expectations in August of the previous year. With their popular support ebbing the leadership believed they needed a public forum from which to address and inform the nation of the truth as they saw it. They needed to produce the proofs of their innocence, unmask the perfidy of an army that had used dirty war tactics against them, and the treachery, as they rated it, of a President who had betrayed the spirit and letter of the peace pact.

The M-19 leaders talked only to each other, listened only to those who agreed with them. "A hazard of the clandestine existence," says Navarro. With their backs to the wall, cut off from other more objective, more skeptical sources of information, the M-19's seizure of the Palace of Justice was conceived as a revolutionary spectacle. A publicity coup designed to set the historical record straight, impeach the President and his government, and project themselves into power on the wave of the popular acclaim that must follow.

The reality of those turbulent days was more complex. The relationship between the members of the army high command and the civilians in government hung poised on a knife's edge of tension and insecurity. From the military perspective, in dealing with the subversives of the M-19 and other guerrilla forces, President Betancur and his cabinet were guilty of betraying the Constitution. Nor were the army alone in their unhappiness. The traditional Colombian Right too was angered by government policies of "treachery," and were all too ready to incite the demoralised military leaders. But neither of these factors played any role in the M-19's deliberations.

Early one morning, in the spring of 1986, the telephone woke me in my hotel room and a voice said, "This is Miguel (not his real name). I'm parked across the street. If you can, come now." I struggled into some clothes and walked out through the nearly deserted lobby, conscious of the suspicious stare of the night porter boring a hole in my back as I crossed the street to where an ancient Volkswagon was parked at the curb. Miguel is not in the M-19, but his father participated in the assault on the Palace, and for two weeks Miguel had been promising to arrange an introduction for me to someone from the leadership. However, ever since the murder in Bogotá some weeks earlier of the M-19's Commander in Chief, Álvaro Fayad, all contacts with the M-19 underground had been suspended. Now, Miguel said, the leadership had changed its mind. They wanted to talk to me.

We drove in circles through some of the poorest sections of the inner city for half an hour, until Miguel was satisfied we had not been followed. Then he stopped in an abandonned lot in the center of the city and we started walking, down a steep and narrow street which at that early hour was still deserted. After four blocks, Miguel stopped and rang a doorbell. It was bitterly cold waiting for that door to open and my mind fixated on the ambush of Alvaro Fayad. I had seen the newsreel footage when the police turned in his body to the morgue. According to the police communique, he had died in a shoot-out when the police surrounded the house he was visiting. But those who had examined the body said that Fayad had seventeen bullet-holes in his back. The woman he had come to Bogotá to see, in whose house he was found, was also killed. An American press card, I thought gloomily, was not going to impress the Bogotá police when they erupted into this house seeking the person we had come to meet. The Bogotá authorities had never been too keen about leaving witnesses behind.

Finally, the sound of someone fumbling with a chain broke the silence, and the door was partially opened by a surly, bloated, middle-aged man, still groggy with sleep. "We have come to meet with Rosa," Miguel told him, and he opened the door, just enough to let us in. "You'll have to wait, he hasn't arrived yet," he mumbled, and motioned us up a narrow staircase leading from the filthy lobby of a house that smelt of rotting food and unwashed dishes, into a dank second floor bedroom. After about twenty minutes we heard low voices on the landing outside the room and a dark young man, who introduced himself as "Pedro," a member of "The National Directorate" came into the room.

He handed me a copy of the statement the M-19 had brought out a week or so after the tragedy:

"We sought the opportunity before this honorable Court to explain our reasons and to hold a public trial of the violation of the truce accords and the social reforms; to put this regime on trial for the violation of the National Constitution, for the surrender of economic and legal sovereignty, and for betraying the hope of the nation... We presented ourselves to the Supreme Court invoking our rights as citizens, because as an army of the people we embrace the defense of the Constitution and fight for its existence... We seized the Palace of Justice for truth and democracy... not to attack the Supreme Court or its representatives. On the contrary... we went there as to a Court of honor and of laws, because the Supreme Court and the Council of State have demonstrated conscience and dignity."

There was a lot more of the same. For "security reasons," said Pedro, he could not answer any of my questions at this time. What was important was that I should understand that all the things I had heard or read about the attack were lies; the M-19 never conceived of the seizure of the building as a hostage taking operation; all of their own people had died protecting the lives of the justices and other innocent civilians, all of whom were butchered deliberately by the army and the killers in Belisario Betancur's government.

"For truth and democracy..." Sitting in that dirty little room face to face with the fanaticism, the self-righteous myopia that had led to the tragedy in the Palace, I felt unutterably despondent. I thought about the horrible deaths the M-19 had brought to the men and women who represented the best of Colombia's legal system. I thought about the families of the innocent victims of the M-19's bid for power, whose lives and ambitions for happiness had been torn to bits in those terrible November days. I thought about the anguish of the families of the young employees of the court who had "disappeared" into the cells of army intelligence after escaping from the conflict. And I felt overwhelmed by the sordid reality that this pathetic meeting with the M-19's messenger was nothing but a contemptible attempt at public relations. I had nothing to say to Pedro. Not a single question occurred to me that I wanted to ask.

We left as quickly as we could. I liked Miguel, and felt embarassed and uncomfortable for his sake. Miguel too was a victim. He was very young, very serious, an art student whose own life had been irrevocably damaged by his father's participation in the Palace attack. He wanted desperately to believe that his father's death had not been criminal, or senseless. Miguel was intelligent. He had gone to great lengths to help me, and I knew he cherished the unspoken hope that somehow I would endorse his father's actions. The fact that this wish was never directly articulated somehow made me feel it all the more strongly.

BOGOTÁ, FRIDAY, APRIL 12. At last, I have tracked down Felipe. That is not his real name. I do not want to appear overly dramatic, but in Bogotá, people like Felipe lead unprotected, vulnerable existences. I do not want to expose him, or anyone like him, to any additional risk.

Felipe has a new job now. He works in the largest, most overcrowded hospital in Bogotá, the one in the southern part of the city, the one for poor people. No urban planning there. Just row after row of small, mean houses giving way at the fringe to precarious home made shacks, linked only by a network of sagging electric cables. The cables criss-cross this typical Third World slum, bringing stolen light to the dismal homes that stretch across a muddy wasteland to the horizon.

Felipe looked at me over his glasses (which are new) with the wry smile I remember so well. "So you're back," he said. Then: "You left Bogotá in a bit of a hurry last time." I felt the tensions of the last few days slip away. It's O.K. to be back. We can pick up our friendship again right where we left it on that May morning five years ago when he appeared out of nowhere in the departure lounge of Bogotá airport to see me off.

Felipe is absolutely central to this story. He is its conscience.

I will always see him as I did that first time, standing in the rain beneath an archway near a back entrance to the city morgue. The width of the pavement separated us as I stood waiting for a cab with my back to him; I don't know how long he stood there, watching me with that quizzical look I came to know so well, before he decided to call out to me. He was smoking a cigarette, and his hair, long by Bogotá standards, curled over the collar of his white medical smock, and what struck me immediately about him was a quality of concentrated stillness.

On that day in May 1986, when Felipe walked into the center of these investigations, he brought fresh urgency to the task of unravelling the mysteries hidden in the rubble of Colombia's Supreme Court. The date was six months after the last of the M-19's ammunition ran out, after the guns fell finally silent, after the tanks of the Army withdrew. Unlike most of the people who wanted to see the story told, and unlike all of those who did not, Felipe had no personal axe to grind. No close friend or member of his family had been incinerated or shot. He held no brief for the M-19 or for the government. But as a pathologist working in the City Morgue, he saw and studied the victims brought there by the army when it was all over. And what he learned from the human remains of the catastrophe contradicted key elements of the story that was broadcast around the country and the world. Felipe cared deeply about the buried history of his land and he was determined that at least once it should not be permanently distorted to serve the self-interest of the "men of always," as Colombians outside the system refer to those who run it. In the aftermath of the Palace tragedy, the official cant about "Democracy" and "the Defense of the Institutions" had sickened him. He brought a fierce commitment, fueled by the experience of a lifetime as an acute observer of the Colombian scene, to the task he now assigned himself. Just once, just this one time, he wanted to see the truth told. He wanted justice. For the victims. For the sake of their families. For his country.

The morgue is located seven blocks from the Palace of Justice. For two days and a night in November 1985, Felipe had listened to the murderous mayhem that was unleashed within its fortress interior. In the middle of the night of November 6 the army had launched a massive fresh assault on the besieged building that housed the Supreme Court and the offices of the Council of State, and at 2:30 a.m., on that morning of November 7, Felipe and a colleague had gone to the roof of the morgue and watched the glow lighting up the sky above the burning Palace. "It must be the end" they said to each other. But they were wrong.

The bodies began arriving at the morgue at around 7:00 p.m. on that November evening, and thereafter the morgue was militarized. The images are with Felipe still. I don't expect that they will ever fade. He saw the secret agents from the Department of Administrative Security (the DAS) spitting on the body of one of the women guerrillas as it was brought in and overheard them tell each other, "this is the bitch who was firing the sub-machine gun." Then, in the morgue courtyard, he watched a surreal spectacle unfold: "It was like a cocktail party" he says. The City Morgue was the place to be that night. Elegant couples, members of Bogotá society, government ministers and their wives, some of the women dressed in evening gowns and jewels, jostled each other between the rows of corpses laid out in rows in their desolate plastic bags, trying to identify the prominent victims, and "*echando gritos al cielo.*" (Literally translated: "Throwing shouts at the sky"). "What were they shouting," I asked. "Oh the usual: '*Que Horror!* What brutes! What fanaticism! What animals could do this?'" Meanwhile the families of the dead were kept outside and the morgue staff were unable to work, awaiting orders that the morgue director refused to issue.

Then the intelligence agents arrived. Staff from the XIIIth Brigade which had led the counter-attack, policemen and personnel from all the security services, the B-2, the F-2, the DIJIN, the DAS, and the specialists in counter-insurgency from the Charry Solano Brigade of the Intelligence and Counter-insurgency Battalion. The secret agents donned white smocks, and disguised as medical staff, finally allowed the relatives to search for their own among the mutilated bodies laid out in the courtyard. While the search progressed, the agents, seeking to identify relatives and sympathisers of the M-19, watched and took notes. Many of the mourners not related to one of the judges were subsequently taken away for questioning.

Later, when Felipe and the other pathologists began to perform autopsies on the bodies, they uncovered a number of crude irregularities in the procedures carried out by the military judges who had supervised the removal of the victims from the site where they had died.

On the afternoon that we first met I had come to the morgue to see his boss, the morgue director, searching for answers. Six months after the event now known in Bogotá as "The Holocaust at the Palace of Justice," everything that touched on the Palace story was still shrouded in mystery and lies. It was not even impossible to get the answer to a simple statistic: how many people died? But on that wet afternoon the morgue director, grave, charming, and evasive, had no explanations and no new information to give me that could illuminate any of the multiple contradictions in the reports from his institution. "We here know less than anyone," he assured me with just the requisite degree of chagrin. Adding, as he accompanied me courteously to the door, that he would be most interested in the results of my investigations and hoped he could have a copy of my conclusions when they were published.

On that afternoon I had been in Bogotá for nearly two weeks investigating the story on assignment for *The New York Times Sunday Magazine*. Time and money were both running out and I was getting nowhere. In the absence of proven facts the Bogotá rumor mill was running on overdrive. All over town there were people who swore they knew someone, who was a friend of someone, who had seen, heard, met, or could introduce me, to some impeccable source with first-hand information. There were even, it was claimed, some missing, "disappeared" people who were still alive.

The trouble was that the "impeccable sources" did not keep appointments. The promised phone calls never came, the introductions did not materialize; nor did access to the incriminating newsreels, nor to rumored, pirated audio tapes of army and police conversations during the attack itself. Since November, the outlines of a dirty war strategy, directed at all who questioned the official version of the Palace story, had emerged. Already by that May of 1986, two hundred activists of the Unión Patriótica Party had died since the Palace attack the previous November. Every one of the major survivors of the Palace attack, those justices of the Supreme Court and the Council of State who had talked so freely to the Bogotá press in the first few days after their escape, had so far refused to see me. By the time that Felipe appeared my frustration was reaching the point where patience comes to seem like cowardice and recklessness threatens.

At the heart of the investigative process there exist those heightened moments when suddenly, under pressure, one is confronted with the decision whether to trust some totally unknown person. The door that opens, the voice that beckons one to leap into unknown, dangerous territory in the company of a stranger, is like the call of a new love affair. Risk ceases to be a lonely abstraction, an idea to play with at the fringes of one's mind. Suddenly, risks shared acquire a wholly different dimension, vulnerable and human.

And so it was when Felipe beckoned to me to follow him into the cul-de-sac beside the morgue. I realized instantly that this curious figure in the white doctor's smock did not want to be observed talking to me from the windows of the morgue building, and I followed him. Almost immediately I discovered that we had a friend in common who had alerted him to my visit. "Is it true that *The New York Times* will publish what you find out?" he asked, and

I saw the glimmer of excitement in his careful eyes. "What is it you want to know?"

I listed some of my problems for him. I told him I had been given an official tour of the ruins of the Justice building and had been inside the devastated marble-lined bathroom that had served as the guerrillas' last hold out. I had seen the blood-spattered walls, the shattered basins, the multiple bullet holes in the toilet stalls, but I could make no sense of any of it. There were too many conflicting versions about who was responsible for the bloodbath in that bathroom, and I needed to understand what had happened there during the last few hours of the siege. Then I also told him, that according to many of the reports I had heard at the time, the husband of a friend of mine, a young lawyer for the Council of State named Carlos Urán, was still alive when the fighting inside the building ended. Carlos Urán had turned up dead, in strange circumstances, twenty four hours later. I had a hunch if I could find out what had happened to Carlos, a lot of other pieces in the puzzle would fall into place.

Felipe listened. The steadiness of his gaze did not falter. "I am working on something a bit difficult," he said casually when I finished talking. "A reconstruction of the last few hours inside the Palace for one of the judges working for the official Commission of Inquiry. Perhaps we can help each other." We made a date to meet later that evening in a small bar and coffee house much frequented by the actors of the Candelaria Theater, near the bullring. "This project is a team effort," he said. "I'll try to speak to the others and see if they will agree to work with you."

That evening he brought the other members of his team with him, and to them too I extend the protection of anonymity: they will be Juan and Mauricio. Juan, an experienced ballistics expert, was older, elegantly dressed, a quiet and careful man who listened silently as I made my case for sharing their knowledge with *The New York Times*, and Mauricio, an eager young topographer with a shock of unruly hair and shining, intense eyes, which darted frequently from face to face assessing the reaction of his seniors. I left them to make their decision. I returned to wait restlessly in the hotel lobby, aimlessly leafing through magazines to while away the time before I could make a pre-aranged phone call to Felipe's house from a public phone booth. "Don't use the telephone in your hotel room," he had said, "the army routinely checks the phones of visiting reporters." When I spoke to him he told me that if I could spend the weekend with him and his team they would show me everything they had.

This book could not have existed without their work. Without the days and nights that we spent together, the four of us locked away in a small house in the south of the city where they had assembled all of their accumulated information, I would never have been able to piece together those final, deadly hours inside the besieged Palace of Justice.

Felipe had explained that once we got to the house on Friday evening we should not leave again until rush hour on the following Monday morning. So we brought provisions, a bottle of whiskey, plenty of Coca Cola and Nescafe, bread, cheese, cold-cuts and chocolate, and for two days and three nights we went to ground. They had blacked out the windows so as not to draw attention to the lights that burned through the night as we screened hour upon hour of videos; studied and compared the results of the official postmortems with the ballistic evidence from the tests Juan had made on the guerrillas' weapons; pored over Mauricio's detailed drawings and three dimensional models; checked and re-checked their calculations against the slides and the videos that Felipe had taken inside the ruins and the oral testimonies of survivors; listened for hours to the audio tapes of the communications between the military and police commanders, recorded by an amateur radio buff during the battle.

By the time we left that house, to melt into the rush hour traffic on Monday morning, Felipe and his team had taken me through the horror of the last hours inside the stricken building. By the end of that weekend I knew at last how, and where, and when, and by whose hand, army or guerrilla, the last of the victims had died in the final spasm of irrational, unnecessary violence. I also knew what had happened to my friend's husband, Carlos Urán.

One week later, on the morning that I was leaving for New York, I could not find Felipe anywhere to say goodbye. On my way back to my own world, the rational world of laws and structures where a person can speak freely on the telephone to their friends, or wander out to buy a pack of cigarettes at the corner store at night without fear of being bundled into an unmarked car and 'disappeared,' the vulnerability of someone like Felipe worried me. It made me intensely uncomfortable. He and his friends faced a future without any certainties or protections, in a city where many people who thought like he did, and who had done far less than he had, had already died or been disappeared. So I left the hotel hoping that he was once again secluded in the little house on the south side of the city where I could not make contact since I had no address and the house had no phone.

Then he walked into the airport lounge and at a glance I saw that once again he had spent several days without sleep. "Watch the Colombian press over the next three weeks," he said; "we finished writing our report an hour ago. Juan is making the copies now and will be handing one over to the judge this morning." He was exhausted and elated. Nervous too, his eyes constantly roaming the departure lounge looking for something, I didn't know what. He had brought me a final cassette of the army's internal communications during the course of the battle and we were both a little afraid that at the last moment I still might not make it onto the plane with the evidence: the tapes, the sketches, the copies of the autopsy reports, and my own copious notes, all jammed into the bulging briefcase under my arm.

Back in New York, in the course of the next few weeks, I searched in vain for any reference to Felipe's report in the Colombian press. Then I saw a reference in *El Tiempo* to an article in the Spanish newspaper *El País* in the form of a short statement from the Minister of Defense: "Total fiction and lies," said General Vega Uribe; "the reporter must have been dreaming." I found the *El País* article: A front page report, featuring all the information that I knew could only have come from Felipe. But when the Commission of Inquiry's official report appeared, a month later than promised, it not only ignored the findings of Felipe's investigation, parts of it read as though drafted specifically to contradict them. But by that time I had troubles of my own: *The New York Times* was having second thoughts about publishing my controversial material to coincide, as had been planned, with the first anniversary of the Palace attack.

* * * * *

On this April evening, almost exactly five years later, Felipe and I leave his office at the hospital and go downtown together for a beer. He is changed after all. It's not just his new glasses, or the grey in his now short hair. It's certainly not just exhaustion, because I never knew him when he was not stretched to the limits of his strength. Something else has changed in these five years that I can't quite define. Something within, some inner spring seems to have snapped. He has lost his passion, his sense of mission. The belief that he could make a difference, which used to sustain his intensity and cast a glow of vitality around him, has been worn away. "All our work was for nothing" he says now, his voice flat; "I doubt that anyone even read it. I expect they threw it in the garbage."

After the main points in his report had been leaked in *El País*, he had tried to persuade one of the main Bogotá newspapers to publish his information in full. But the editors insisted that the team must go public with their names. "What were we supposed to do," says Felipe bitterly, "come right out and sign our own death warrants?"

We talk for a long time. "I gave up my work in the morgue," he says, "because I lost all hope of ever being able to achieve anything. Working for human rights in this country is an absurdity. What the investigators find out is so frightening that they give up. Where are the prisoners for all the murders of the Unión Patriótica? Is anyone ever going to be held accountable for their deaths? Who killed the three presidential candidates last year? And now they dare to talk to us about peace, when they've given away the country to the Mafia and filled the cemeteries with our dead?"

We walk down the street together looking for a taxi. The city is emptying out. Now the office workers, shop assistants and civil servants are rushing to board the over-loaded, dilapidated buses that sway and hobble through the potholes, taking them home to suburbs in the south and west with names like "Ciudad Kennedy" and "Libertador." Soon the city streets will be deserted and dark.

As we say goodbye, in that casual, throw-away style of his, Felipe says: "Be a little careful. Your subject is still very delicate for them. They were onto your tracks last time. I got word to warn you that you were asking too many questions." I don't need to ask who "they" are. I will not ask who got him word to warn me. I've always felt Felipe must have some "extra-official" contacts in the army or police, contacts too sensitive to expose to any visiting reporter. Yet while a tremor of the old fear flickers through me, I do not believe that after all that has happened anyone would bother to harass a foreign reporter writing about a story that is five years old.

BOGOTÁ, SUNDAY, APRIL 14. Sunday morning, in the duplex studio of Ramón Jimeno. All white. Peaceful. Lived in. Beside me, a delicious cup of strong *café con leche* and a fresh croissant. Sunlight streams through the skylight. It flows over piles of books and magazines, alights on children's toys, on the bright hues of Indian weavings, on clothing and bits of pottery and old photographs. The sound of a Mozart concerto, playing on a compact disc one floor below, reaches me up the connecting, spiral stairs that lead to this attic refuge. I have chosen this civilized, harmonious place to catch my breath and get a fresh perspective after the alarms of the last twenty four hours. With his customary generosity to all visiting reporters, Ramón, who has written the only substantial book on the Palace of Justice, has left me here alone at his desk with a bunch of his own research files.

This morning I am troubled because I'm behaving like a coward. I've cancelled a meeting for this evening. I've decided to take the day off to read and to rest, because I'm scared and I think I'm being followed. Those who appear to be watching my movements want me to know that they're there; it's just a warning. Yet

I've let it get to me. I'm half sure I'm being paranoid but I can't shake it off. Besides, as always, if there is a danger it is not directed at me but at the people that I meet. The ones who are helping me.

Last night, when I wanted to go home late from Felipe's flat, he and his wife insisted that I stay over and sleep on their sofa. Earlier, around ten o'clock, we'd gone out to buy cigarettes and beer and there had been a man, a leather-jacketed, snappily dressed, heavy set young man, just hanging out at the entrance to the apartment building. Felipe said it was better to wait until daylight. But at seven thirty this morning there was another man outside the building, similar in dress and build, talking to the hall porter. When I emerged onto the steps the porter looked distinctly embarassed, almost startled, to see me. He broke off his conversation and hurriedly re-entered the building. "Leather jacket" remained, alone. Leaning against the railing he stared at me, arrogantly, as I waited for my taxi, turning his car keys over and over in his hands. Most Bogotános are too polite to stare like that. I also had the unpleasant conviction that the reason the hall porter had broken of his conversation so hurriedly was to go and make a prearranged phone call of the "she's leaving the building now" variety.

When the cab came I sat in the back at the angle where you can watch what's happening on the street behind you in the driver's rear view mirror without turning your head. And as the cab drove off I saw "leather jacket" leave the steps and saunter off up the street. So he never did finish the conversation with the porter that was interrupted by my arrival. But he didn't follow my cab either. However, when we drove onto the quiet residential street where my cousin lives, seated on the low garden wall of the house opposite there were two young men; just regular guys in jeans and sneakers and clean Sunday shirts, who seemed to be watching his house. My cousin and his family are in the country so the house is empty. I watched the watchers—if that is what they are—from the window of my room. They were still there two hours later when I left to come and seek the comfort of Ramon's secluded studio. Just sitting, idly swinging their legs, smoking and laughing and watching the house. Watching me leave.

Last night, sitting around the table in Felipe's tiny apartment with Juan and Mauricio, and Felipe's wife, reviewing the slides that Felipe took inside the wrecked Palace of Justice, examining anew Mauricio's scale drawings recreating the path taken by the army's tanks and the angles of their fire, I was once again overwhelmed by their courage. They have not changed—Juan and Mauricio. Juan is as elegant and low-key as ever, Mauricio just as vital and eager. Only Juan's car shows the strain of these last five years. The fumes that penetrate to the interior have reached alarming new levels of toxicity, and the explosive noises that it makes on its erratic course promise imminent disintegration. Yet I would trust my life to Juan and his car.

Last night they brought fresh evidence, further detailed autopsy reports. We went over new materials and additional information that had become available in the last five years. All of it supports their original findings. The order from the judge to reconstruct the scene had come almost four months after the event. In the interim, the army had removed everything that was portable from the building. So when they visited the ruins, accompanied by three survivors of the siege and a photographer, when they penetrated to the bathroom where the guerrillas had held out to the bitter end, there was not much to go on. Just blood sprayed on the ceiling and the walls, and bullet holes, and fractured basins, and toilets.

The slides and the drawings we were looking at may be the only documents in existence capable of providing a coherent, visual analysis of the final hours of the attack. These bits of paper, this box of slides, may be the only proofs in existence that give the lie to the official version of events within the Palace walls. It is this realization that makes me nervous. At one point during the evening, as I looked around a room in which every inch of available space was covered with papers and scale drawings, Felipe's small apartment seemed absurdly vulnerable.

BOGOTÁ, MONDAY, APRIL 15. In the offices of the Attorney General, Jaime Córdoba—small, dark, intense, very "Bogotáno" with his old-fashioned courtesy and gentleness—provides me with a vivid description of the maps and three dimensional models constructed by Mauricio, the ballistics tests conducted by Juan, the slides taken by Felipe. Jaime, who heads up the Human Rights division, refers to these materials that I know so well as "The Morgue Report." Not only, I now discover, was the reconstruction done by Felipe and his team not rejected, it provided the basic evidence that was used by a former Attorney General to file charges, in 1989, against two of the senior army officers involved in the Palace siege.

However, after the Attorney General had brought his indictment against the General of the XIIIth Brigade who commanded the attack and against the Colonel of Army Intelligence who ran the security checks on the escaped hostages, many of the files belonging to the case, including Mauricio's only three dimensional model, and the originals of his scale drawings of the reconstruction of the final attack, were stolen from Jaime Córdoba's official car when he was taking them to a professional studio to have them photographed. "All I have left," he says sadly, "are the original slides of the interior. Here, let me show you." But when he goes to look for them, in the bookcase where he saw them "just a few days ago," they too have vanished. He sends for his secretary, who conducts a hectic, fruitless search. A "mole" has infiltrated the Attorney General's office.

So the State no longer holds some of the prime evidence against the two army officers. And the case has gone into limbo. Like hundreds of others involving the army in human rights abuses, it is not expected to be heard from again any time soon.

The staff of the Attorney General's office is understandably demoralized. Since the attack on the Palace of Justice, two Attorney Generals who tried to investigate what happened have been brought down by the fury of the politicians, whose determination to sustain the myth of official innocence has only hardened over time. "The evidence of the crimes that were committed was buried in the mass grave of the municipal cemetery," says a disillusioned former judge. "Legal impunity in Colombia has been institutionalized. Most of the time, those who are committing the worst crimes, officers in the secret agencies of the state, are the very ones who walk in here with 'the proof' that such and such a massacre or assassination has been committed by the drug mafia, or by the guerrillas, or by private paramilitary armies. And sometimes it's true. But in too many cases it is not. We know where the problems are, but honest investigators and judges are assassinated, or intimidated. What is a poor judge to do?"

Outside Jaime Córdoba's office, meanwhile, a crowd of sad and patient people wait in line. They are Colombia's equivalent of Argentina's Mothers of the Plaza de Mayo: they are the famililes— the fathers, mothers, brothers, sisters, wives and children of Colombia's "disappeared." In Bogotá these relatives don't march or carry banners. Who would they appeal to? *"Aquí no pasa nada."* Local opinion will not validate their stories. International opinion doesn't care. The Colombian story is too complex, too confused. Colombia has a democratic, popularly elected, civilian government. Colombia's government is a government under siege, fighting for its survival against the savagery and corruption of the drug mafias, and the ruthlessness of a communist insurgency—the guerrillas of the FARC—that can field 100 seperate fronts against the Colombian army at will.

One by one, Jaime, the deputy attorney for human rights, will see all of the unhappy people who wait with the resignation of the damned outside his door. He will give to each of their personal tragedies the dignity of his courteous, serious, and concentrated attention. He will open new files or dig into old ones as the case may be. He will tell them to stay in touch. He will initiate enquiries. Write letters. Make phone calls. It is all that he can do.

MONDAY, APRIL 15, EVENING. Tomorrow morning I meet former President Belisario Betancur. The man who presided over the tragedy at the Palace of Justice.

Five years ago, in 1986, former President Betancur's refusal to see me doomed the publication by *The New York Times* of my report on the Palace of Justice scheduled for the first anniversary of the attack. At the time the President had struck *The New York Times* off his list of friendly news publications because that paper's senior Latin American reporter, Alan Riding, had insistently included some reference to the seizure of the Palace of Justice in all his reports from Bogotá. Alan claimed that, "the military counter-attacked without waiting for civilian orders." The President said Alan was a liar and would have nothing more to do with his newspaper.

The questions I had wanted to ask Betancur in 1986 still go to the heart of the matter. But I won't get the chance to ask them tomorrow either. The former President has had our mutual contact inform me that he has said everything he has to say about the Palace of Justice and the subject is *prohibido*. I understand. From the first pronouncement that he ever made, on television, just seven hours after the tragic end of the crisis, Betancur has been locked into the consequences of his own statement:

> I, the President, for better or for worse, personally
> took all of the decisions, gave all of the respective
> orders...

At the time almost no one found his claims of personal responsibility for the army's counterattack credible. But in Bogotá a lot of people found it comforting that he assumed sole responsibility. "With much character and dignity," a group of senators described his statement, as they absolved him from the Attorney General's charge of violating the Geneva Conventions and the laws protecting civilians in time of war. Other *Bogotános* were dismayed, resenting the fact that through this one, gravely enunciated lie, Betancur had distorted the truth in order to protect himself, his government and the generals.

His version of the truth has been amply documented. In the only interview he ever gave on the subject, to the Spanish magazine *Cambio 16*, he said his decision not to call off the army and initiate a dialogue with the guerillas was easy since there was no alternative. He was feeling good on that day. The Congressional Justice Committee, set up to study the charges brought against him and the Minister of Defense by his own Attorney General, had just reported that:

> This Committee does not have the sufficient ele-
> ments under the law to question, from a legal point
> of view, the free and autonomous decision taken by
> the President of the Republic... since this consti-
> tuted a typical Act of Government, executed by the
> only persons authorized so to act, namely the
> President of the Republic and the Minister of
> Defense.

In the rush to restore the President's democratic credentials, the establishment was doing no more than recouping their own. The Emperor had temporarily lost his clothes. It would take all the ingenuity and creativity of his acolytes to get him dressed again. And it would take intimidation.

The world that Betancur comes from and the world he lives in are different. Although he shares the white skin and European features of the ruling class, Belisario Betancur was born poor. A vociferous promoter of the myth of Colombian democracy, Betancur has used his own experience to prove the all-embracing possibilities of his country's system. (In Mexico City one night Rafael described the first meeting between the M-19 leaders and Betancur, when the Colombian President and the M-19 Commander in Chief, Iván Marino, spent most of the evening determining which one of them could claim to have been born in greater poverty.)

The poor boy from a small town received help early in life from an important patron, a member of the local Conservative Party, who paid for his schooling and opened crucial doors for him. Betancur, ambitious, hard working, went on to achieve success in law, business, and local politics. In quick succession he became wealthy, ran a successful campaign for Congress with the backing of the Conservative Party, and by 1962 he entered the government as a Minister of Labor.

It was in this post that the future President revealed for the first time how far he would go when pushed to support the values and the attitudes of the dominant culture in which he was determined to play a decisive role. In February of the succeeding year,

CAMARA DE REPRESENTANTES
COMISION DE ACUSACION

Bogotá,

P R O P O N E M O S

DECLARESE QUE NO HAY LUGAR A INTENTAR
ACUSACION ANTE EL SENADO DE LA REPUBLICA CONTRA EL PRESIDENTE
DOCTOR BELISARIO BETANCUR CUARTAS Y SU MINISTRO DE DEFENSA –
GENERAL MIGUEL VEGA URIBE, POR RAZON DE LOS HECHOS OCURRIDOS
DURANTE LOS DIAS 6 Y 7 DE NOVIEMBRE DE 1985 EN RELACION CON
LA TOMA POR PARTE DEL M-19 DEL PALACIO DE JUSTICIA, Y EN CON
SECUENCIA A R C H I V E S E EL PRESENTE INFORMATIVO

CARLOS MAURO HOYOS JIMENEZ   HORACIO SERPA URIBE

DARIO ALBERTO ORDOÑEZ ORTEGA

CAMARA DE REPRESENTANTES COMISION DE ACUSACION- SECRETARIA GENERAL-
Bogotá octubre diez y siete (17) de mil novecientos ochenta y seis
(1.986.)

La anterior Fotocopia es fiel tomada de su original.

HERNANDO RAMIREZ LEYVA
Secretario General.
Comisión de Acusación.

A facsimile of the decision by the Justice Committee of the Colombian Congress absolving President Betancur and Minister of Defense General Vega of all wrongdoing.

faced with labor unrest, he presided over one of the worst massacres of striking workers and their wives and children since the 1928 attack on the Cienega banana workers. This time the business interest involved was a cement factory from his own state of Antioquia. When the government sent in the army to resolve the conflict, troops from a battalion of Lancers fired into an unarmed crowd of one hundred and fifty workers and their families. Twelve people were killed, fifty-two were wounded. The strike, a pathetic protest not three weeks old, was terminated.

Almost no one, in this country afflicted with national amnesia, even knows about that February massacre of 1963 anymore. Nineteen years later Betancur reached the presidency as an independent with the greatest majority of any Colombian presidential candidate in the past twenty years. "*Aquí no pasa nada...*" The M-19 leaders should have remembered. It might have given them pause for reflection before invading the Palace of Justice. But then again, perhaps not. Perhaps they believed the times were different. Perhaps they thought that Betancur in 1982 was a changed person from the Betancur of 1963. Or perhaps they thought the Colombian system had changed, and that somehow the civilian government they were out to destroy had magically acquired the autonomy and the authority over the military that the Constitution and the laws said they had.

BOGOTÁ, TUESDAY, APRIL 16. His house does tell me something I might have overlooked about the price of power in Colombia today. It is a lovely, modern, split-level chalet-style house, dominated by his security needs. Secluded, or rather suspended, on the side of the mountain midway between two major avenues in the most fashionable quarter of Bogotá's "el Norte," the front entrance can only be reached by way of a steep stone staircase. Climbing the front steps in the high altitude, I arrive out of breath to face the video cameras recording my approach. Within the thick walls of this three-storey chalet-style fortress, the ex-President and various members of his family and staff work in a warren of air-conditioned rooms behind permanently sealed, bullet proof windows.

Ever since his government signed the extradition treaty with the United States in the aftermath of the assassination of his first Minister of Justice in 1984, Betancur has needed all the security he can get. There was a period, after he left power, when he had no fewer than forty bodyguards providing twenty-four hour protection for himself and his family. And only days before this interview his daughter, with quite remarkable courage, had faced down and narrowly foiled a crude kidnap attempt as she arrived to pick up her young daughter from school. In just such every day nightmares must the price of power and wealth be calculated in today's Colombia.

The first object to catch my eye as I wait in the hallway of the ex-President's home is a framed copper-plate reproduction of a page from *The New York Times* above the central fireplace. The dateline is October 6, 1983 and the headline reads: "Lyrical Colombian brings the United Nations to its feet." A reminder of the former President's glory days: the days when he was going to heal all the ills of Latin America; when Sandinistas and Contras and Miskito Indians and Salvadoran FLMN rebel leaders all trooped through the Presidential Palace of Bogotá, and the "Betancur Peace Process" brought the local Colombian rebels of the FARC and the M-19 to sign historic, if largely hollow peace treaties with his government.

"Lyrical" strikes me as the right word to characterize the style of this ex-president, who came to power in 1982 on a wave of populist, nationalist exuberance. Betancur promised peace and social transformation to a country weary of the pain of decades of civil conflict and social misery. He turned the heads of the naive young revolutionaries of the M-19, who saw in his gestures of friendship only what they wanted to see. He was their kind of Colombian: a maverick from a humble background who had made it to the top, a man prepared to take on the oligarchy, the party leaders, the military and big business. His analysis of the causes of Colombian violence echoed their own rhetoric. His vision of a pluralist democracy promised an open door through which the power they had been unable to win by force of arms could become theirs, legally. It was heady stuff. "If you deliver thirty percent of what you promised during your campaign, just thirty percent, we will accompany you to the public squares of Colombia to defend your government," the self-deluding young leaders of the M-19 told him at their first face to face meeting with him in Madrid in 1983.

But the love affair between the President and the rebels was doomed from the start. It's failure, and the legacy of bitterness, the sense of betrayal it left behind on both sides, led directly to the horror of the Palace of Justice. The historic encounter in Madrid, and a later one in Mexico City, occurred behind the backs of Betancur's own military. Later, when Betancur and the guerrillas began serious negotiations, the courageous and committed men who made up the membership of the President's Peace Commission would be dispatched by him to meet the M-19 leaders in their clandestine hold-outs in the mountains in secrecy. A practice that on various occasions came perilously close to chalking up some dead Peace Commissioners, caught in a no-man's land between army and guerrilla bands with no safe-conduct passes.

The President relished toasting his peace initiatives with the revolutionary leaders, (whiskey in Madrid and champagne in the Presidential Palace in Bogotá). And he basked in the international recognition of his audacious, imaginative embrace of Colombia's rebels. But Betancur stopped short of confronting the opponents of his policies within Colombia. He did not take the time to build effective alliances with other political leaders. And he failed utterly to prepare any defense against the ferocious resistance to his promises of reforms, even though the opposition came from all of the predictable sources. As the polarization of Colombian society intensified, Betancur became increasingly isolated. Old friends and supporters, like nobel laureate Gabriel García Márquez, and a hard-core of Betancur loyalists in the peace commission, rallied to his cause. But they were outsiders, mavericks in a political culture dominated by traditional forces. They too had become a liability. When the M-19 guerrillas finally put down their guns and sought the great national dialogue they had been promised as a prelude to the reforms, they found no one in the government willing to talk to them. There was no reform program. And no commitment to implement one. In embittered response the M-19 took to the airwaves and the streets. And the polarization of Colombian society intensified.

Faced with increasing criticism the President faltered and sulkily withdrew. The dirty war of assassination against the newly amnestied guerrillas, conducted by elements within the army, the police, and their allies on the far right, flourished. And when, under pressure, the rebel leaders needed reassurance, Betancur and his closest, most trusted mediators had become unreachable. Amid charges and counter-charges of betrayal, the truce, only ten months old, disintegrated. The Peace Process and all discussion of economic and social reforms foundered in the belated and bitter realization, on both the left and the right, that the "Peace President" who had launched an innovative policy of enormous historic importance and potential was not going to be able to implement it. Long before its explosive end in the Palace of Justice, where the President, the M-19, and the Army, were all revealed with no clothes on, Betancur's presidency had become an empty shell.

"Belisario" is an unusual name in Colombia, and most of the time, when people mention the ex-president in ordinary conversation, that is how they refer to him. Sometimes they simply call him by his initials, as in "B.B.," though I doubt that he appreciates the nickname. He enjoyed the pomp and circumstance attached to being "*El Señor Presidente*" too much. He still does. To this day he expects to be addressed as such. As in, "*El Señor Presidente* will see you now," spoken by an elegant young male assistant who impresses me as succeeding quite magnificently in communicating both his own sense of self-importance as a member of the ruling elite, and, secondarily, the importance of his boss.

As I climb the stairs to his second floor office Betancur emerges to greet me with all the warmth and charm for which he is famous, and I am immediately reminded of how much I used to like him. I remember my first note after watching him on television on the night that the tragedy in the Palace of Justice ended. It read: "He is obviously a *decent* man, also very weak." At the time I was also convinced that he had effectively lost all his power to the generals and was trying his best to hold the line to prevent a military coup. At the time I had not yet understood that in Colombia nothing is ever quite what it seems.

Now, he sends for *tinto*, the little cups of strong black coffee that Bogotános drink in frightening quantities all day long, and sitting beside an original oil portrait of Simón Bolívar, "a present to me from my friend the great Colombian painter Obregon," the ex-president begins talking in clichés about the peace process that he initiated. He also identifies his enemies: "All those fundamentalists, all the Khomeinis of the world." And he quotes philosophy: "Descartes compares peace to a house, peace is a kind of house of the human spirit..." A house through whose doors the Colombian fundamentalists of the two dominant parties bar entry. "Alas," the ex-president sighs, "human nature is like that." The ex-President is also famed for his ability to find the apt philosophical or literary allusion for every occasion. Belisario Betancur inhabits a world of high culture. He takes art very seriously. He also writes poetry.

Gradually, from peace then, to peace now, we begin to talk about the M-19. "*Señor Presidente*," I ask, "many people say that the only difference between the M-19 and yourself is that they carried guns. It is said that their program was essentially no more than 'Belisarismo with guns.' Would you care to comment?" "Indeed," he replies, "there are no great differences separating me from them. Now everyone can see this. The "Emme" has produced a program for a new Constitution that in large part I can easily accept." So how does he feel about the fact that the same people who invaded the Palace of Justice are now sharing power with the traditional parties and helping to re-write the Constitution?

Betancur becomes animated. "When Carlos Pizzarro (the M-19's assassinated Presidential candidate) and Antonio Navarro came to see me, here in this very room, just a year ago—Pizzarro sat where you are sitting now—there were many scenes on television at that time of the three of us embracing. My daughters said to me: 'Father, isn't it excessive that you should embrace those people who took over the Palace of Justice?' And I said to them: 'Daughters, perhaps it is excessive for the people of my age, but I do this, I make this public act of reconciliation, thinking of you, and of your children. That is to say, thinking of the future. The future of our country can only be built on the basis of reconciliation.' And they asked: 'But father, it must be very difficult for you to do this, you must have to make a great effort?' And I replied: 'No. I don't have to make any effort. I have a large abundance in my heart for reconciliation.'" That is as close as we ever got to talking about the Palace of Justice.

THURSDAY, APRIL 18. A cold, drenching rain was falling in Bogotá on the afternoon of November 6, 1985, when the fate of the Palace of Justice and its inhabitants was sealed. The same rain is falling today, five and half years later. I had forgotten how miserable it becomes when winter closes in on this Andean capital, so isolated on its high mountain plateau from the luxuriant climactic variety of the tropical country which it attempts, so unsuccessfully, to dominate. Robbed of its proud, defiant escort of mountain peaks, submerged in mist and cloud, the city of Bogotá turns in on itself. It becomes sullen, diminished, and an ancient weariness, the persistent melancholy and pessimism of the high Savanna plains, flows in on the thin, high altitude air. On such a day depression seeps into the innermost fibres of the city where it lies, stretched, submissive, flattened under a lead-grey light. A city ravaged, laid waste by the elements. Mud the predominant color. Mud swirling through the streets and plazas, brought down in rivulets off the invisible mountainside; mud in the pot-holes; mud the color of the sky, the buildings; and mud-colored exhaustion too on the faces of Bogotá's teeming, increasingly desperate population. I had forgotten.

On that afternoon in 1985, people knew something catastrophic was going on downtown, but it was impossible to find out what. After the live radio broadcast of Chief Justice Reyes' telephone conversation with a reporter all further live coverage from the scene of the battle was broken off: "Attention Colombians! We have an announcement of extreme importance for the Whole Nation! The soccer games scheduled for tonight WILL take place as planned. Eight o'clock in the *Campín de Bogotá*! Be there! We repeat... Tonight's game between the Champion Teams of *Millionarios* and..." The crudeness of this bread and circuses appeal was not missed by the Bogotános. It spelled farewell to the life and death struggle on the Plaza Bolívar. It signalled the first notes of the cover-up to come. Later that night, a series of massive explosions rocked the center of the city and the great building began to burn. From my room on the eighteenth floor of the Hotel Tequendama, just fourteen blocks north of the Palace of Justice, I watched as a lurid orange and purple glow spread across the night sky above the stricken building. In the room behind me Colombian television alternated coverage of the soccer with scenes from that other national obsession, the Miss Colombia beauty contest.

These memories flood over me as I stand on this April afternoon five and a half years later, in the center of the Plaza Bolívar. For years the blackened hulk of the ruins of the Palace of Justice stood abandoned, a gaping wound on the north side of this splendid nineteenth century plaza dedicated to the greatest Colombian of them all. Of course Bolívar was a Venezuelan, not a Colombian, and he was chased from this City of Holy Faith of Bogotá, to his desolate and lonely death on the Colombian coast, by mobs of Bogotános screaming for his blood. Yet he is honored as this country's founding spirit, its finest self. And today, under his austere gaze, the Palace of Justice is finally under reconstruction. It is being rebuilt according to its original design.

After the Palace siege many people said that the country would never be the same. They were right. Everything that has happened since has served to confirm it. Throughout these long and bloody years since the tragedy, the Colombian government has succeeded in presenting an image of itself to the world as a helpless victim, trapped between guerrilla violence on the left, private paramilitaries on the right, and an all-powerful drug mafia, hell-bent on destroying the Colombian democratic system. In spite of the presence of the world press at the attack on the Palace, no lessons have been learned about the nature of the Colombian regime.

The real story of these last years, like the real story of the Palace of Justice attack, is complex. It involves a civilian government that has ruled under state of siege conditions for almost forty years. This government decided, in the early eighties, to try to end thirty years of guerrilla warfare by co-opting the guerrillas with promises of political participation and pluralism. It decided to try and do so without seeking the participation of the military or of the traditional sectors of power. The story involves a national army, whose reason for being is to repress the political opponents of the civilian government and so maintain this government in power. In the last forty years, this army was brainwashed by the national security doctrines of its North American trainers, brutalized by thirty years of a counter-insurgency war that it was unable to win and corrupted by its links with right wing terrorists. When this army found itself in ideological conflict with civilian leaders whom it had grown to despise, it turned to more effective allies among the newly rich and powerful drug barons for the prosecution of its generations long war against the communist threat. The mafia's virulent anti-communism, secretive, criminal networks, access to wealth in excess of the national budget and ruthlessness, offered the army an ideal partnership. Together they could pool the men, the weapons and the know-how for a dirty war against subversion—against those same guerrillas whom the civilians in the government were foolishly and traitorously wooing.

A number of courageous Colombian journalists who tried to investigate and expose the alliance between sections of the Colombian army and the drug mafia have died: Over forty journalists have been killed or disappeared since the Palace of Justice attack. So have staff investigators for the Attorney General, countless lawyers, judges, and human rights workers. So have secret agents belonging to the DAS, a Colombian version of the FBI, and the only civilian security agency that did not, at the time of the Palace attack, report directly to the Minister of Defense. In 1988 when General Maza, the tough, tenacious Indian from the coast who ran the DAS, brought the proofs of collusion between the army and the mafia to the President of the Republic, he got no response. General Maza was forced, several months later, to leak documents to the press to get any action. A few heads rolled. The army commander who was caught red-handed training paramilitary armies with the help of British and Israeli mercenaries was ousted. And then silence. There was no outrage. Nobody drew any conclusions. "Every barrel has a few rotten apples, every army a few corrupt men." Eventually the existence of the paramilitary armies was acknowledged. With great fanfare some of the most notorious were disbanded, to be quietly replaced by newer versions. The names changed. The killings continued. And the big lie, the one about official helplessness and a democratic system of government under siege, was perpetuated.

Inside the graveyard of forgotten massacres that this country has become, those few courageous people who insist on raising a memorial stone to the victims are isolated. Their voices of protest do not resonate in this fragmented, frightened society, where those who do not belong to the dominant culture of the elites must live in a kind of permanent seclusion. A little knowledge, a little awareness, can all too easily unleash violence upon their unprotected heads. In a country that has lost its way, so long as the price of survival remains that "tolerance of the intolerable," of which Juan Manuel speaks, the population of Bogotá will seek its survival by escaping into private worlds. Bogotános cannot afford to offer solidarity to those rare, exceptional individuals who are willing to risk everything for the common good.

I must be leaving Bogotá again soon. For the first time in my life I feel no ambivalence about going. I feel only relief. Will the friendships, the familial ties, the way of life with its warmth, its courtesy, its exuberance, pull me back again? Probably. There is much that I value deeply here. I have known extraordinary people and experienced many happy times in this strange city. But I do not belong here. Something more than a visitor, something less than a citizen, there is no place for me here anymore, not now.

PART I

CHAPTER 1

Antecedents

In which the seventh son of a landless banana worker from Colombia's Caribbean coast journeys to the nation's capital to the City of the Holy Faith of Bogotá, where he becomes a successful labor lawyer, a popular congressman, and, in his middle years, one of the founders of the M-19 Revolutionary Movement, and hence a guerrilla leader.

"To the Europeans, South America is a man with a moustache, a guitar, and a gun," the doctor said, laughing over his newspaper. "They don't understand the problem."—From *No One Writes to the Colonel*, by Gabriel García Márquez.

Shortly before seven o'clock on the evening of Tuesday, November 5, 1985, Andrés Almarales retired to the bathroom of the small apartment that he shared with his girlfriend María to shave off his moustache. His personal things were packed: two changes of underwear, socks and a couple of clean shirts. Clothes were important to Andrés and he intended to look good in front of the television cameras during the coming, historic days. María, and his son from his first marriage, Ivan, had already left to fetch Ivan's car from the parking lot and in half an hour he would join them at the corner of the street behind his building. Together they would drive to the appointed meeting place where the *compañeros* should be waiting for him. There he would switch cars and be driven to join the rest of the M-19 assault force in the safe house, in the south of the city, where they were to spend the night together prior to the invasion of The Palace of Justice on the following morning.

Barring some unforeseen eventuality the dye was cast. It was too late now for second thoughts, though he could still remember the stab of fear, the nauseous, hollow feeling that had risen from the pit of his stomach when Álvaro Fayad, the M-19 Supreme Commander, had first told him of his plan for holding hostage the members of the Supreme Court and the Council of State. Yet when Fayad had asked him to accompany the invasion force into the Palace of Justice Andrés had been unable to turn him down. The M-19 needed his presence inside the Palace of Justice, Fayad had explained. Andrés' national reputation, his unique role as the elder statesman of the organization, were crucial to the success of this, the most politically ambitious action that any Colombian revolutionary movement had ever embarked on. The operation at the Palace of Justice needed all the weight and the respectability of the M-19's best legal and political brains, Fayad had said, because once the guerrillas had seized and secured the building, the success of their enterprize would depend on the skill and sophistication of their lawyers and negotiators. Every one knew that Andrés Almarales was one of the best negotiators in the country. The M-19, and the country, needed him to lead the negotiations with the government and the judges once the Palace of Justice was in their hands.

So Andrés had said "yes," and ever since, every instinct in his body had been trying to tell him that Fayad's idea was doomed. But he refused to listen. He had ignored the quiet voice of caution inside his head. That voice, he told himself, was nothing but the unacceptable cowardice of a man growing old. And whatever else he was, Andrés Almarales was not a coward. He was a *"macho"* and a Colombian revolutionary. He was an M-19 *Commandante*. And even if, when surrounded by the young men and women whose enthusiasm for this high-noon encounter with the Colombian government shone in their eyes, he sometimes felt like their grandfather, he had a crucial role to play. The *compañeros* needed him.

Colombia needed him. The cause to which he had devoted his entire life needed him.

Besides, he had not argued, he had not even tried to play the devil's advocate, because he knew that Fayad and the others in the National Directorate of the M-19 Superior Command would not listen. When he had taken a stand against breaking the truce only five months earlier, and had pleaded with them to stay with the peace process and keep the dialogue with the government going, he had been overruled and outvoted. He had gone along now because he had no alternative to offer. The M-19 had its back to the wall, and for the first time in his life he had lost confidence in his own judgement. He had no answers. The truce had been a disaster. The dream of an all-encompassing national dialogue between the government and the amnestied M-19 rebels had never materialized. The promised reforms had been stillborn. The M-19 leaders had trusted the man in the Presidential Palace but they had been manipulated and betrayed. And in the process they had lost some of their most valuable people, killed in cold blood by anonymous death squads when they came out of hiding. They had also lost most of their constituency. For no matter how you dressed it up, the bitter truth was that even their own supporters laid the blame for the failure of the peace process at their door.

The M-19 had to fight for its political survival now, and no one had come up with a better idea. If things went according to plan, Álvaro Fayad had said, the M-19 would emerge from the seizure of the Palace of Justice leading a new and transformed country. Besides, Andrés loved Fayad. He loved his audacity, his courage, his inspired craziness. Andrés Almarales could not, he would not, let him down.

*   *   *   *   *

As he shaved the black, Zapata-style moustache that he had grown so many years ago in the banana fields of his native, Caribbean coast, the face that stared back at Andrés in the mirror, shorn of its most distinguishing feature, looked diminished. As if some inner connection between that aggressive, irrepressible growth and the flamboyance and vitality that were such marked characteristics of his personality had been severed. The reflection that now confronted him in the mirror was the face of an uprooted 53-year-old campesino who had long ago lost his way in the maelstrom of Colombian radical politics.

That at least was what many of his friends and admirers said about him later when they heard the news. "Andrés lost touch with the reality of this country," they would claim sorrowfully when confronted by the image of that naked face staring disconsolately from the front pages of the national newspapers. All those former colleagues of his, veterans of the campaigns to organize landless peasants and urban workers of the fifties and sixties, fellow parlamentarians who had sat beside him in the Congress in the seventies, listening patiently to his impassioned, rather old-fashioned rhetoric. They shook their heads in hurt bewilderment at his irrational behaviour, and then they went about their business. Faced with incontrovertible proof that this former parlamentarian and labor lawyer had helped lead one of the most lethal and ill-conceived acts of political terrorism in recent history, they told each other that he had lost his way, that he had become incoherent, crazed. It was an easy way to dismiss the reasons that had led him to participate in the fatal seizure of the last symbol of the Colombian state which he still respected: The Palace of Justice, home to the Colombian Supreme Court and the Council of State.

So there would be no painful post-mortems. In the silence that descended over the career of Andrés Almarales, many of those who had been with him in the days of the campesino and worker organizations, or the days of the abortive attempt to develop an alternative political party, understandably scurried for cover. So many of his and their own former colleagues were also dead, victims of an official repression that had functioned systematically for the last thirty years. Theirs were "anonymous deaths," caused by "anonymous killers." The deaths of these "humble laborers," whose bodies, when discovered at the side of the road, were only sporadically reported in the pages of the national press, under a "gentleman's agreement" with the authorities not to alarm the citizenry.

Anonymous murder, that deadly fact of daily life in Colombia, was an effective silencer of the living as well as the dead.

Only those who had been closest to Andrés Almarales, those who had loved him and known him intimately in his various earlier lives, would consider speaking out about the meaning of his life and death. People like his wife, Marina Goenaga. Beautiful still, a calm, reflective woman living modestly today on the outskirts of Bogotá, with a bureaucratic job in the Attorney General's office, she was not afraid to speak about the father of her two children. For their sake she had distanced herself from Andrés in the late sixties. But Andrés was not someone with whom you could sustain a relationship at a distance, and the marriage, put on hold, had died. Yet, five months after his death in the Palace of Justice, and almost sixteen years after they had parted, she recalled their first meeting with such depth of feeling that the years between, and the sorrow of his final foray into the wrong battlefield, for a doomed cause, faded. On the day that we met, in the spring of 1986, Marina Goenaga Almarales evoked the emotions of a time when the youthful illusions inspired by the ideal of making Colombia a happier, more just society for all of its citizens were still vibrantly alive.

She was an attractive radical young lawyer then, just out of law school, when the minuscule socialist party in Bogotá asked her to help a young man who was languishing in jail for organizing demonstrations of landless peasants agitating for agrarian reform in the banana territories of the coast. "It was," she recalled, almost thirty years later, "like a scene from a movie. There he was, sitting on his poncho on the floor of his cell, accompanied by an adoring young woman to whom he was making speeches about his social and political theories. That was Andrés. That was his scene. He announced that I had three days to get him out—if not he was going to escape."

Marina sprung him from jail and stayed on to help his campaign for land reform. "Andrés," she says by way of explanation, "had an extraordinary way with words. He was really an educator, and a brilliant negotiator. That was his greatest strength. He could persuade people of anything, even his enemies. If they allowed him to talk he could convince them to see things his way. And they knew that. That's why they always resorted to violence against him in the end. One day he made so many speeches to me that I finally said, 'all right, I'll stay and help you.' I stayed quite simply because I ran out of arguments!" The year was 1957. The place, Cienega, site of the 1928 massacre of striking banana workers, and Andrés Almarales' home town.

Andrés Almarales was the seventh son of a former United Fruit Company worker. His father had been forced to flee Cienega to escape the persecution of witnesses in the aftermath of the massacre. One year later, Andrés' father had participated in the wave of land invasions that had swept across the coastal region, as landless peasants and unemployed banana workers seized abandoned United Fruit Company holdings in the wake of the company's withdrawal to less disputed territories. Andrés was born on this illegally held farm in 1932, and had grown up in the shadow cast by that now forgotten tropical savagery, among people who did not forget, because their lives had been forever altered and scarred by it. From earliest childhood he was what Colombians call '*inquieto*' —he had an unquiet soul. As a small boy he rebelled against the drudgery of peasant life, and his fierce determination to get an education finally drove his father to hand over the farm to his elder sons and return with the younger children to Cienega. There Andrés went to school, in a town with unpaved streets, no public water supply, and a broken, trashed spirit.

The ghosts that haunt the wretched half century of Colombian history that spans the life and times of Andrés Almarales are not difficult to identify: Cienega in 1928; the assassination of a great radical leader, Jorge Eliecer Gaitán, in Bogotá, twenty years later, his death triggering civil war; in the sixties, the dream of an independent trade union powerful enough to provide the base of a third political force, mangled and destroyed by death squads; election day, April 19, 1970, when the presidential candidate of a populist opposition movement, two million votes ahead, was bought off, and the traditional Conservative Party candidate duly installed in the Presidential Palace by the outgoing Liberal President.

That day led directly to the formation of the M-19: M for Movement, 19 in commemoration of the date of the stolen election; the event which finally slammed shut the door on any further hope of achieving change through legal electoral politics.

Andrés was sixteen years old and still in high school when Gaitán was killed, and from that day he modelled himself on the slain hero and martyr. He was not alone in his devotion to the lost leader. In interviews with a Colombian journalist in the early eighties, each of the leaders of the M-19, most of whom were still children at the time of Gaitan's death in 1948, rooted the story of his or her personal political awakening with the words: "On the day that Gaitán died..." Like the massacre in Cienega, only more so, the death of Gaitán is a watershed in the history of twentieth century Colombia, and his unsolved murder haunts the country's political life to this day. For the promise represented by Gaitán was of a break, finally, with the country's feudal past, and his death robbed the country of a never to be repeated opportunity to introduce modern, pluralistic, issue-oriented politics to Colombia.

The assassination of this remarkable figure, shot down by two "anonymous gunmen" as he stepped out of his law office to go to lunch, on April 9, 1948, triggered violent riots in Bogotá. Known ever after as the *Bogotázo*, the city's enraged poor torched and sacked most of the beautiful, colonial heart of the old city, including the original, 19th century Palace of Justice. Within hours, the anarchy in the capital quickly escalated into the only spontaneous, national insurrection in Colombian history as the *Gaitanistas* seized and held every important state house and municipal building in the land. Yet without a leader, the rage and despair that had fueled the uprising was manipulated and redirected into a bloody civil war between the grassroots followers of the two ruling clans. For the next six years—a period known simply and graphically as *"La Violencia"*—some three hundred thousand poor rural Conservatives and poor rural Liberals slaughtered each other in the name of feudal, quasi-religious passions that had nothing to do with the wretched conditions of their own lives or the futures of their hungry, terrorized children.

In 1953, the dynamic of this indiscriminate bloodletting threatened to acquire an ideological character with the emergence of the first, organized, communist-inspired Liberal guerrillas, the forerunners of today's guerrilla forces. The traditional political leadership took fright. The political parties, the business leaders and the Catholic Church buried their differences and sent for the army to sort things out, and there followed Colombia's only period of military rule—the four year dictatorship of General Rojas Pinilla. Brought into power by the establishment to crush their opponents on the left, when the General's idiosyncratic mix of repression and economic populism ran foul of their interests, the elites joined forces once more and conspired to oust him.

The formula whereby the two traditional parties terminated their partisan, tribal conflict and retrieved power revealed the absence of any real ideological difference between them. Under the guise of fighting "tyranny," the Conservatives and the Liberals buried the hatchet and reasserted their control through a unique power-sharing arrangement: from 1958 to 1974 all other political forces were outlawed to permit each of the two traditional parties to rotate, once every four years, through the revolving door of the Presidential Palace. Colombian democracy had acquired a novel, a stifling stability. From now on commentators and critics referred with resignation to *"la democracia cerrada,"*—the "closed" democracy. Known as The National Front, this pact between the elites ended the partisan warfare of the previous decade; however, by criminalizing opposition activities, it drove all dissident politics underground and into the mountains. Sixteen years of "closed democracy" gave to Colombia a crop of violent guerrilla groups and rule by permanent State of Siege.

For Andrés Almarales, the National Front years were the most crucial of his life. He spent them, with Marina beside him, fighting the battles of the new urban workforce in the provincial capital of Cali. By 1961, a combination of increased repression and the passivity of the local peasants still traumatized by the legacy of 1928, had driven Andrés and Marina to abandon the struggle for land reform on the coast. "It was hopeless," says Marina. "The terror of the peasants had to be seen to be believed. They were quite inca-

pable of any confrontation." Marina describes the scene on a day
when she was sent for to help a group of peasants arrested for
attempting to demonstrate: "There were eighty people who had
been arrested and brought to town by two policemen. And it
turned out that these eighty people did not all fit in the jail so they
were left outside on the square. A delegation came to ask me to go
and see what could be done for these prisoners. So I went, and I
saw the situation and I told them to go home. But they said, 'we
can't go home, don't you see, we're prisoners.' They were just sitting there on the ground in front of the jail. So I said, 'What's the
matter with you? Go to your homes!' And they said 'But no, *señora
doctor*, how can we go home when the *señor* judge and the *señor*
mayor have told us to stay here?' There was nothing to be done.
Just sit down with them and laugh, or cry. And these were the
people we were going to make a revolution with?"

In the sixties, Colombia, as elsewhere, rode a roller coaster of
turmoil and hope. By 1962, Castro had repelled the American
invasion at the Bay of Pigs; John F. Kennedy had launched an
Alliance for Progress in the southern hemisphere; the Pentagon
was becoming increasingly involved with Latin American armies,
in pursuance of a new, continent-wide National Security Doctrine;
and North American multi-nationals were establishing subsidiaries
in Colombia in cities like Cali and Medellín, where a swollen population of peasant migrants, refugees from the rural violence of the
fifties, guaranteed an unlimited supply of cheap, non-union labor
to companies like Coca Cola and Goodyear. So when the call came
to help organize these uneducated, vulnerable workers, Andrés and
Marina packed their bags and left for Cali.

One of the paradoxes of the Colombian system is a raft of progressive labor laws dating from the thirties which no Colombian
government since then has ever tried to enforce. At the beginning
of their involvement in union politics Marina and Andrés quickly
discovered that the traditional trade union movement was part of
the problem. Corrupt, reactionary, and subservient to the Church,
the politicians and the employers, the old style union bosses were
incapable of providing the leadership that the times and their
members so urgently required. "We were talking a different lan-

guage," says Marina. So she and Andrés struck out on their own and started an independent union. Moving swiftly and effectively, with Marina in charge of legal documentation, and Andrés at his most impassioned and persuasive as organizer, educator, strike leader and negotiator, the fledgling union began to attract support across a spectrum of small, socially progressive groups. There were strikes and hunger strikes and the solidarity of the workers held. In plant after plant, contracts were signed guaranteeing job security, pensions, health care, cost of living increases and paid vacations— all 'innovations' actually mandated by the existing laws. The independent union movement grew in strength, education and numbers. It was becoming a catalyst for change.

And then the violence began. The traditional union leaders, seeing their power ebb, accused the new union of "communism;" Coca Cola and Goodyear mobilized their international legal departments to fight back and refused to negotiate; local companies, with the support of the Ministry of Labor, brought in expensive legal help from Bogotá to help them evade the law; strikes were banned; new laws were passed that gave targeted industries special protection as public enterprises. Then the physical repression began. The strikes—illegal now—became violent; the government called in the army to break strikes and enforce lock-outs; then the companies' death squads emerged and began picking off selected targets: labor activists, organizers, teachers. "We had made too much headway," says Marina, "and they were determined to break us... we should have needed to use weapons to defend ourselves, or industrial sabotage and terrorism. But we didn't have the people or the means." By the late sixties, the independent union movement had been crushed and many of Andrés' young colleagues had fled the menace of the death squads and gone to the mountains to join a rapidly growing guerrilla movement.

Andrés too was chased from Cali by death threats. With neither money nor prospects, he left alone. He and Marina had two small children now, and for their sake she withdrew from Andrés and the turbulence that she knew was destined to accompany him for the rest of his life. Marina foresaw Andrés' future involvement in revolutionary violence, and she determined to distance herself from him before it engulfed her and the children. "I knew it was inevitable he would end up with the guerrillas," she says, and her voice, almost eighteen years later, is coloured by sadness and the waste and the loneliness that her choice exacted from her in the prime of her life. "Already in Cali, in the sixties, I could see it coming. Because it was no longer possible to fight legally. If you want to pursue the fight, here in Colombia, there is no other way than violence. Oh! You can always keep up a sterile opposition in some small group or other and sit around endlessly talking in circles. But if you want to take any action that could have repercussions and some larger resonance, there is no other way."

The day that Andrés bid his family farewell was the blackest of his life. He carried with him the image of Marina and the children waving goodbye to him from the water's edge, when the barge on which he travelled downriver and back to the coast, drew away on the current. It was an image he often referred to later, always with renewed pain. Although their separation was not legalized until a few months before the attack on The Palace of Justice, their life together was over. The Cali experience had demoralized him. He was burnt out. He would not act on what he had learned at the hands of the Cali industrialists and their accomplices in government and the police for several more years. But after Cali whatever tenuous faith he had ever had in the rule of law deserted him. Marina was right. Cali changed Andrés. It started him down the path that ended in The Palace of Justice.

It would take one more national trauma, one last incontrovertible proof that no legal alternative to Colombia's minority rule masquerading as democracy would ever be permitted, before Andrés was ready to cross the line and take up arms. After Cali he had held back. He had not gone to the mountains and joined the insurgents then, as so many of his colleagues did. When Andrés left Cali the National Front was entering its final, dreary years, and under the banner of a new opposition force, the populist National Popular Alliance, or *Anapo*, Andrés embraced electoral politics. *Anapo* had attracted an interesting group from the professional class—doctors and lawyers, journalists and academics. They were the bright, the ambitious, the discontented and the idealistic. New to politics, the *Anapistas* represented a generation who had no stomach for entering politics through the old parties. They believed the moment was ripe for a breakthrough, and they foresaw a landslide of popular support from the hitherto unrepresented "majorities." They felt they were riding a wave of radical, populist activism that would sweep away the narrow "government of the minorities"—historic bastion of those "men of always." But in their haste and enthusiasm they failed to identify a fatal flaw at the heart of their movement. For the founder of this populist alliance, and its candidate to the presidency, was none other than the discredited former military dictator, General Rojas Pinilla.

At best the *Anapo* represented a confusion of competing ideologies and personal interests, at worst an unscrupulous conglomeration of conflicting interests, each using the other to gain their own ends. The General provided the movement with a nationally recognizable figurehead. His victimization in the fifties inspired sympathy, and his second-rate demagoguery filled the town squares with that majority of alienated voters who, confronted by a constitutionally mandated, preordained result, had long ceased going to the polls. Then too, the General had a daughter who delighted in posing in the mystifying role of a Colombian Eva Perón.

In 1970, Andrés and eight other *Anapista* candidates ran successfully for Congress in a campaign that resounded with the themes first articulated by Andrés' life-long hero, Jorge Eliecer Gaitán. But in the presidential stakes, when the Alliance led the poll count by a million votes, and the *Anapistas* were prematurely dancing in the streets celebrating their triumph, the radio reports fell suddenly silent. The vote count was abruptly interrupted. The establishment had moved to protect the status quo. No one ever discovered the details of the deal the General cut that night with the outgoing Liberal President, Carlos Restrepo, but when the count resumed *Anapo* had lost the election by a narrow margin and General Rojas withdrew from the contest. Sending word to his supporters to maintain calm, he returned to the comfort of his Spanish estate, leaving his embittered and divided colleagues to pick up the pieces. There would be no uprising. No mobilization of the cheated, leaderless voters. There was massive, unfocused, destructive anger in the streets, repression under the State of Siege, and everything went on as before.

It was after the fiasco of this April 19 election that the legendary figure of Jaime Bateman came looking for Andrés Almarales to help him found yet another revolutionary political movement. By now Andrés was ready. Jaime Bateman was a former guerrilla in the ranks of the communist Armed Revolutionary Forces of Colombia (the FARC) who had defected over differences of ideology, strategy and style. He had watched the *Anapo's* successful mobilization of a mass opposition movement with fascination, and he interpreted the lesson of the stolen election as proof of the urgent need for the integration of an armed vanguard within such a mass movement. Such a vanguard would support the movement of the masses through the strength of its weapons, while in turn, the armed struggle would gain support and backing from the masses in the streets. That was the theory.

According to Bateman's analysis, a lack of popular support for the guerrilla struggle was the logical result of the sectarianism, ideological extremism and divisiveness within the existing communist leadership. The time, Jaime thought, was ripe for unity. The history of Colombia proved conclusively that nothing could be accomplished without firepower. Or, as another of Andrés' *Anapista* colleagues in the Congress expressed it, "the masses are strong in numbers, but weak and unarmed and their dead are falling in the public squares; while the armed movement has the strength of its weapons but no numbers, no support among the people to give resonance to their actions."

A new movement, said Jaime Bateman, on the day in 1972 when he and Andrés met to discuss the situation in the old Cafe Metropole in downtown Bogotá, would have to be unlike anything that had ever existed before in Colombian politics. It must be truly representative of *"the mayorías"*—that great company of their disenfranchised compatriots from every walk of life. It should use imagination and humour to light sparks of hope and warmth in men's minds and hearts. It should have nothing to do with foreign ideologies. Rather it must revive, and if necessary reinvent, the national cultural identity that had been stolen and devalued by the oligarchs and the Americans. It must recover the long lost cultural and political ideals of the great Simón Bolívar and the men of Colombia's glorious eighteenth and nineteenth century struggles for independence. Besides, they would have fun and good times, as only Colombians know how. *"La Revolucíon es una Fiesta..."* The revolution is a party. Jaime Bateman was Andrés' kind of Colombian. An impulsive, warmhearted, broad-minded leader of men: articulate, irreverent and generous. And like himself, Jaime Bateman was *"costeno,"* a man of the tropical Caribbean coast, a true *"compadre."* Andrés would have followed Jaime's lead any-where.

"Commandante Almarales!"* The sound of Jaime's laughter had echoed through the crowded cafe as they drank to Andrés' new identity. Farewell to the formal *"Honorable Doctor Representante."* Hail to the revolutionary *"Commandante!"* The word had a good, clear sound to it. A macho sound. When he left the cafe that evening Andrés felt at peace with himself for the first time since he had been forced out of Cali.

The M-19 would have a military wing and a political wing. It would build on the political base that had already been developed by *Anapo.* Three other *Anapista* congressmen followed Almarales into the core group of twenty-two people who joined Jaime Bateman to launch the M-19 in January 1974. Andrés was not being asked to go to the mountains and take up a gun. His new identity would remain secret for as long as possible while he stayed in the city and continued doing political work inside *Anapo.* He would concentrate on what he did best: grass roots organizing, running workshops, infiltrating community groups, preparing the ground for the coming transformation of Colombia among associ-ations of prostitutes, shoe-shine boys, students, clerical workers, bus drivers...

People had a tendency to smile whenever they talked about Andrés Almarales, and the stories that they told about him, blazing his way into the public conciousness with the help of a generation of young, disaffected journalists who were charmed by his bravado and seduced by his lack of sectarianism, reflected an image of a man who was perceived by friends and enemies alike to be a little larger than life. The man they described had a big ego and energy to burn. He had needed it to make the journey from poverty to national prominence on his own terms. He developed a reputation as a man of the Left whose undogmatic approach kept open the door to a broad spectrum of his fellow Colombians. He was gregarious, a "life-and soul-of-the-party man." A man who loved fiestas, where he would dance through the night, and who enjoyed eating well and drinking long and deeply with his friends. He was vain of his virile good looks, took pains to dress smartly, and his native machismo was tempered by a sensual tenderness which made him extremely attractive to women.

But something seemed to happen to Andrés when he joined the M-19. He was not used to the discipline and as the M-19 became increasingly militarized he was never comfortable with the expectations of a quasi-totalitarian, unquestioning obedience to the hierarchy of a national command structure, with its military jargon, its "superior officers" and "superior orders." Then too, Andrés was not suited to conditions of underground life. Nor to the increasing reliance on guns and terrorism. He was hopeless with firearms, and no matter how patiently the *compañeros* tried to teach him, he had never really learnt how to handle a gun. "He just about learned enough to be able to load and fire one," says his girl friend María, "but as far as military strategy goes he knew precisely zero." María, herself a disillusioned veteran of a particularly disastrous guerrilla campaign by the Army of National Liberation in the early seventies, recalls that when Andrés and two of his fellow congressmen were ordered to go into hiding in the mountains in 1980 she had vehemently opposed it. "I told Jaime Bateman I thought it was absurd. There was no justification for taking these people away from their political work in the city to go to the mountains. They were the only major, public figures the movement had. But Jaime said no; he said that they had to go, even if only for a time. So what did they do? They went off to the mountains like a couple of little bourgeois and rented a house. If you're going to hide in the mountains you take a hammock and a tent. Or you rent a house in a strategic position. But no. They rented a peasant's shack in an unpopulated clearing on the top of a hill, and when the army arrived they surrounded the house from all sides. A sergeant who was involved in the operation told me the soldiers had been in the area for two days and the *compañeros* hadn't even noticed."

By 1980 most of the top echelon of the political wing of the M-19, and many of the military leaders too, were in jail, captured by the army in the immediate aftermath of the M-19's first urban 'spectacular'—the theft of hundreds of tons of weapons from the barracks of the Bogotá Brigade's Headquarters on New Year's Eve, 1979. The M-19 were proud as fighting cocks of the success of this, their first frontal attack on the military. They acted as if they had finally broken into the big-time, had become stars in their own revolutionary script. But what they actually achieved by this public humiliation of the Colombian Army, inflicted on the most important military installation in the country, was more dubious. Within weeks the army had recovered all of the arms and captured most of the M-19 leadership, who went to jail and stayed there for the next two years. The action brought terror to their civilian friends and supporters, hundreds of whom were caught up and tortured in the repression and mass arrests that followed. But the most destructive legacy of the arms theft was the unrelenting bitterness that would characterize all future aspects of the M-19's relations with the Colombian Army. Experienced by the top army commanders as a mortal wound to their institutional honor, the arms theft poisoned the peace process five years later, and undoubtedly fueled the final savagery of the conflict inside the Palace of Justice.

1980 was also the year when the M-19 made their mark internationally with the seizure of the Dominican Embassy in Bogotá during a diplomatic reception in honor of Dominican Independence Day. The attack on the Embassy, in which almost half the Bogotá diplomatic corps—including the Ambassador of the United States—were trapped and held hostage for over a month by sixteen lightly armed guerrillas, was conceived and planned by one Luis Otero. Luis, Lucho to his friends, was an anthropoligist who had fought in the sixties with the communist guerrillas and had defected with Jaime Bateman to become a founder member of the M-19. The seizure of the Embassy made history for the M-19. When it ended, after over a month of daily, cliff-hanging headlines, the hostages walked out unhurt, the M-19 was one million dollars richer and they had won an undreamed of public relations triumph. The implications of that success, like the arms seizure, also resonated down the years, all the way to the doors of the Palace of Justice.

In late 1982, when a new President came to power promising peace, reforms, and a national dialogue with Colombia's armed insurgents, Andrés Almarales and the rest of the M-19 prisoners were amnestied. Then, in August 1984, after protracted and contentious negotiations, the truce between the M-19 and President Betancur was finally signed. Andrés had a role to play again. The early days of the truce were intoxicating: days and nights of mass rallies in the squares and streets. Talk shows and interviews with the former guerrillas on television. Meetings and negotiations with congressional leaders and government officials. But these were also days of extraordinary confusion. The crowds went on massing in the squares. The speeches became more radical, more shrill. But nothing new was added to a political process that had stalled before it began. And there was no end to the violence.

In 1984 there was a vacuum in the M-19 leadership. Jaime Bateman, who had originated the concept of a national dialogue between the insurgency and the government, was dead. His plane had disappeared over Panama in 1983 while carrying him to secret peace talks with the President's envoy. The M-19 had no one as gifted to replace Bateman. President Betancur, beset with economic problems and under assault from his critics in the establishment and the army, was in retreat from his own program. A dirty war had picked up where the official war had ended, and M-19 militants and supporters were still dying in the streets and in their homes. Seen from the perspective of the anxious young revolutionaries, they had been duped. The signing of the accords, which should have been the start of a profound political renewal aimed at radical social, political and economic reforms, had brought neither peace nor reforms. From the point of view of the M-19 it was business as usual in Colombia.

In December 1984, just four months after the signing of the peace accords, the twelve-man National Directive of the M-19 held their Congress in Havana. The internal debate was about peace and war, about whether to hold the truce or break it. It raged long and inconclusively. At the time the national issue was further clouded by pressure from the Cubans and the Sandinistas to keep the M-19 military fronts in the field to help ward off a feared invasion of Central America by the United States. In Havana, the M-19 leadership split down the middle. The political wing, which included Andrés, Antonio Navarro and three former Congressmen from the founding group, voted to give the peace process more time. The militarists, led by Bateman's successor, the new Supreme Commander, Iván Marino Ospina, with Álvaro Fayad, Carlos Pizzarro and Luis Otero, all sought an immediate return to war.

In effect, although the M-19 held the truce for six more months, the future of the peace process was already visible that December in Cuba. Just when the paralysis of will in the Presidential Palace was deepening, the division between the militarists and the politicians in the M-19 leadership sapped the will and creativity of their commitment to the pursuit of their goals by peaceful means. Throughout that spring of 1985 the situation in the country deteriorated and polarized. The dirty war escalated, claiming new victims in the ranks of the M-19 political leadership. The militarists on both sides, in the army and in the M-19, pursued their sterile vendetta amid charges and counter charges of betrayals of the letter and the spirit of the peace accords. By June of that year, the M-19 leaders made the decision to return to the mountains and wage "total war." But by then the majority of their countrymen were so confused and disillusioned, hardly anyone cared enough any more to disentangle fact from fiction, lies from truth, good guys from bad guys. Across the depressed nation, among ordinary people struggling to survive in a sinking economy with 82 percent inflation and 30 percent unemployment, the majority view held it that the "*muchachos*" of the M-19, who had enjoyed an *eighty-five percent* approval rating when President Betancur came to power three years earlier, had had their chance and blown it. Weary of being harangued on all sides, and sickened by the daily body count, Colombians had withdrawn into apathy and cynicism.

The M-19 were desperate to dispel this public perception of their responsibility for the collapse of the peace. Yet shut out from access to the media now that they were underground again, their marginalization only increased. Overnight they had become an unimportant, fringe element, minor players in the Colombian power game. Now, as never before, they needed a "spectacular," a "*Golpe Revolucionario Publicitario*" to set the record straight and propel them back to the center of the political scene. In August 1985, the newest Supreme Commander of the M-19, Alvaro Fayad, conceived the idea of seizing the Palace of Justice.

It was Fayad's idea to present 'An Armed Petition' to the highest court in the land. The violent history of Colombia's nineteenth century civil wars in the post-independence era offered a historic precedent for such an attack, which Fayad used to good effect to sell his idea to the other members of the M-19 National Directive. Once in control of the court, Fayad said, the revolutionaries would demand the presence of President Betancur, or his delegate, to face charges of betrayal of the publicly expressed will of the Colombian people for peace, and for breaching the provisions of the truce accords signed by his government with the M-19. Such a public rendering of acccountability for the collapse of the truce would vindicate the M-19 and would prove conclusively, to the country and the world, the criminality of the Colombian government and its murderous agents in the Security Forces. This historic trial, prosecuted by M-19 lawyers and supervised and adjudicated by the Chief Justice and his Supreme Court colleagues, would bring this government of the minorities tumbling down and create an irresistible dynamic for a new, majority government led by the M-19.

Before presenting his plan to the National Directive, Fayad consulted with Luis (Lucho) Otero, the architect of the seizure of the Dominican Embassy. Luis was excited. Not least because, at the time of the attack on the Embassy, although he had masterminded every strategic detail of the operation, at the last moment Jaime Bateman had given his blueprint to one of the other senior commanders to execute. Jaime had refused Otero any role in the actual attack on the grounds that he did not have the temperament to stay cool enough under fire when so much was at stake, and Luis had never got over it. Now, when Fayad asked him to study the military feasibility of invading and holding the Palace of Justice, Luis Otero saw his chance to prove that the late, great Jaime Bateman had been wrong. How long, Fayad wanted to know, would it take Luis to draw up the military plan of attack and to select and train the assault unit? Eight, ten weeks at most, Luis said.

With Luis Otero's enthusiastic commitment, Fayad then presented and sold his plan to the other members of the National Directive, all of whom embraced it with fervor. No one thought to question the wisdom of the choice of Otero to lead such a venture. The Dominican Embassy attack was five years ago and Lucho had matured. He was a brilliant strategist, and as the senior military commander in the Superior Command, the role of *Commandante Uno* was his by right. No one could expect him to sit out on the sidelines twice.

No one pointed out that there was a fundamental difference between the international protection that the ambassadors of seventeen sovereign nations had enjoyed at the time of the attack on the Dominican Embassy and the vulnerability of Colombian justices, some of whose recent judgements had placed them in direct, critical confrontation with the military command. Nuance was never a strong point with the M-19. Evoking the romantic memory of one of Colombia's most popular eighteenth century rebels, Antonio Narino, an early precursor of the struggle for Independence jailed by the Spanish Viceroy of his day for publishing the text of the "Rights of Man," Fayad entitled the coming assault: "Operation Antonio Narino For The Rights of Man." In memory of their most recently slain commander in chief, the assault group took the name "*Compañia Iván Marino Ospina*." The planning for the attack went into high gear.

With Otero in command of the military aspects of the operation, Fayad delegated responsibility for the political and legal aspects of his plan to Andrés Almarales and Alfonso Jaquín. Both men were senior members of the National Directive, both had legal experience, both were known and respected nationally. Jaquín was a slim, dark, good looking man in his early forties, with prematurely grey, curly hair. Like Almarales he was a lawyer from the coast, and another of the original group of disillusioned Congressmen of the National Popular Alliance who had joined Jaime Bateman in 1972 to found the M-19 Revolutionary Movement. Arrested with Andrés in the aftermath of the weapons theft from the Bogotá Brigade in 1980, Jackin had spent the intervening years until the recent amnesty in jail. Like Andrés, he had minimal experience of armed conflict, but during the truce, his nervous, intense, bespectacled presence had become well known to television viewers in Colombia. During the months of national debate surrounding the peace process he had emerged as one of the most articulate spokesmen for the programs and objectives of the M-19. Now, Fayad explained, it would be the responsibility of these two senior figures to prepare the legal case against the government.

In the weeks that followed, while the younger men and women competed for the honor of participating in the assault, Andrés Almarales, Alfonso Jaquín and Álvaro Fayad spent long hours studying the documents of the peace accords with the help of civilian lawyers, who, suspecting nothing of their plans, helped analyse their content to bolster the legal case against the government. The M-19 invaders would bring with them to the court, for presentation to the justices, the documents of the Peace Accords and the accompanying texts relating to the National Dialogue. They would demand the publication of the results of the investigations of the official Commission of Verification of the President's own Peace Commission, which had made an exhaustive study of each major outbreak of violence during the truce. The government had repeatedly refused to publish these findings. Well, they would be published now. The M-19 were confident that the Verification reports must support their case, and their public transmission would be the first order of business once the M-19 was in control of the Justice Building.

Once the trial began, it would fall to Jaquín and Almarales to prosecute the M-19's case against the President, or his delegate. The entire country, participating through the media at this bizarre event, would comprise the 'jury.' "Gentlemen of the Court," the M-19's Proclamation read in part, "in your condition as the last reserve of morality in Colombia, you have the great opportunity, before the country, to preside over a memorable trial: From the stage of the Honorable Supreme Court, transformed by the force of history into the setting for an exceptional trial, The M-19 calls upon all Colombians... to participate.... Let this trial have the force and the greatness to call into being a New Act of Government." The booklet, containing the text of the M-19 Proclamation to the Country, came printed on bright yellow paper with a mimeo-graphed reproduction of a photograph of the Palace of Justice on the cover. It contained thirty pages of radical political analysis of the contemporary Colombian scene and was to be released to the press once the attack had been launched. "Let the journalists help us to spread the word of our accusations" the M-19 proclamation read, "so that the truth can be transformed into a fundamental pillar of peace. Conquering the lies is basic to ending the war." So, they might have added, was propaganda. *"El Golpe Revolucíonario Publicitario,"* as the M-19 conceived of the seizure of the Palace of Justice, was about winning maximum publicity for the M-19's cause.

One day in early October, Colombians listening to one of the main Bogotá radio stations heard, among the advertisements for the coming attractions, the following brief announcement: "In the coming days" a pre-recorded voice announced, "the M-19 is going to pull off something so sensational, the WHOLE WORLD will be talking about us!" The M-19 was constantly blasting off. Bogotános weary of their bombastic threats merely shrugged their shoulders. Initially the attack on the Palace of Justice was planned to coincide with the forthcoming State visit of Francois Mitterand, in mid-October, since the presence of the French President in the Andean capital guaranteed a large contingent of foreign journalists. The M-19 loved the idea of playing out their sensational scenario to a captive audience from the international media. The French press had always been friendly to Latin American guerrillas and now that the glitter had worn off on the local media scene, their enthusiasm was precisely what was needed. The M-19 leaders saw themselves expounding their views in the pages of *Le Monde*, anticipated double-spread color photos in the *Nouvel Observateur* and *Paris Match*. But on October 16, just twenty-four hours before the arrival of the French delegation, in a routine raid on the house of some M-19 supporters in Bogotá, the army found M-19 documents outlining Luis Otero's plan of attack on the Justice building. President Mitterand was due to begin his three day state visit on the following day. The M-19 had planned their attack to coincide with the final day of his visit.

They would have to wait. The assault would be postponed.

There was a big holiday weekend coming up in Bogotá on the first weekend in November, the traditional celebration of the Day of the Dead. No one would be at work on Monday and Tuesday too would be a slow day. Luis Otero chose the following morning, Wednesday, November 6, to launch the attack.

*   *   *   *   *

At exactly 7:30 p.m., on the evening of Tuesday, November 5, Andrés Almarales left his apartment. He walked around the block to where his son and María were waiting for him in Iván's pale blue Volkswagon beetle, climbed into the front seat, and set out on the first leg of his journey to the Palace of Justice. It was a dreary, dark evening. The drizzling rain and his own gloomy premonitions were hard to dismiss. By this time tomorrow, if all went according to plan, the whole world would know of their case against the murderous servants of this treacherous government. By this time tomorrow the future of Colombia would be irrevocably changed. He believed that. He believed this was the last, best chance. If the M-19 won this time, won big like they had at the Dominican Embassy five years ago, they would break the government and come out of the Palace leading a transformed country. It was the dream he had clung to, the one that had nourished all of his struggles throughout his life. He could not fail that dream now. What was death, for a macho, for a fighter, compared to what was at stake in the next twenty-four hours?

But death was on his mind. "Tell me, María," he said, "if I should catch a bullet on my way in tomorrow, if things should go wrong, you'll manage to get my body out of their clutches, won't you? You'll know who you can count on for help." It was the one thing he dreaded. To be dumped by his enemies, like the carcass of a dead animal, into the municipal mass grave. When the time came, a decent funeral with his friends was very important to Andrés.

The traffic in Bogotá was light and they reached their destination, at the corner where the Calle 19 intersected the Carrera 14, five minutes too early. Iván suggested they should drive around the block, but Almarales said no. They waited. At ten minutes past the appointed hour the *compañeros* had still not arrived. "Let's go home," said María. "Something must have gone wrong." "Not yet," Andrés replied. "We'll give them another five minutes." It was silent in the car. Each of the three people were locked into their private thoughts. Then, just as Ivan was about to turn the key in the ignition, the second car arrived, and almost before his family knew it Andrés Almarales was gone. He had always, ever since that terrible parting from Marina and the children in Cali, hated having to say goodbye.

CHAPTER 2
The Court Under Siege

In which, twenty-four hours after the mysterious disappearance of the armed police guards at the Palace of Justice, in the heart of downtown Bogotá, Capital city of Colombia, an M-19 Commandante, one Luis Otero, assaults the building that houses Colombia's Supreme Court and Council of State.

It was raining in Bogotá on the morning of Wednesday, November 6. Mean, bitter showers in gusty squalls, driven before the wind coming off the surrounding mountains, down the narrow streets of the old part of the city known as the *Candelaria*. Only artists, poor people, and a few adventurous foreigners live in these dilapidated streets that climb east from the center of town up the steep slope towards the shrine of the city's patron, the virgin who takes her name from the mountain, Our Lady of Montserate. On good days, the Lady looks down benevolently on the inhabitants of this sprawling urban landscape from her lofty vantage point where the mountain's peak meets the blue horizon. But on this wet November morning the mountain is concealed by clouds. Downtown, right at the point where the sloping, ill-kept streets with their battered vestiges of colonial grace emerge finally onto level ground, at the junction where the Carrera 7, meets the Calle 12, on the northeastern corner of the Plaza Bolívar, the buildings housing the legal, religious and administrative hierarchies of Colombia face each other across the open spaces of the square. On this grey November morning, the Plaza Bolívar has been swept clear by wind and rain of the usual mid-morning loiterers.

To the judges and staff of the Supreme Court and the Council of State arriving at their offices in the Palace of Justice on foot on that Wednesday morning, the deserted square was an unaccustomed sight. Ever since the army raided a guerrilla "safe house" and found, according to press reports in all of the major newspapers at the time, plans for an assault on the Justice building by guerrillas of the M-19, a squad of twenty policemen, armed with automatic, military issue Galil submachine guns, have been guarding the threatened building. During these last three weeks, the members and employees of the highest court in the land have grown used to their presence, patrolling outside the sole street level entrance to the Palace from the square, checking the identity of all who enter. But since the day before, the police have withdrawn. Things have returned to normal. As they climb the stone steps to the entrance one of the judges turns to a colleague and remarks, "well, I see they've decided to give the guerrillas a free pass." The two men laugh, and pass swiftly through the great bronze doors, pausing to flash their identity cards to the single private security man sitting at a desk inside the lobby.

Lonely in the center of the square that bears his name, isolated at the top of the circular stone steps of his memorial, which on most days provides seating for Bogotá lovers and office workers sharing their traditional mid-morning coffee break with a flock of pigeons, the figure of Simón Bolívar dominates the empty square. Bolívar, like everything else of worth in this city, gazes northwards, his raised right hand pointing imperiously at the facade of the Palace of Justice, over whose huge portals is engraved the stern warning of his lifelong rival, first President of Colombia and founder of the Conservative Party, General Francisco Santander: "*Colombianos: Las Armas Os Han Dado la Independencia. Las Leyes Os Darán la Libertad.*" [Colombians: Arms have given you Independence. The Law will give you Liberty.]

Ever since its original 19th century structure was burnt to the ground during the "*Bogotázo*" riots in 1948, the rebuilt Justice Palace is the only building on the square that conflicts with the

graceful, early nineteenth century architectural harmony of its surroundings. Occupying the length and breadth of a city block, from
the Carrera 7 in the east, to the Carrera 8 in the west, and from
Calle 11 in the north to the Calle 12 in the south, the modern
headquarters of the Colombian judicial system is an imposing, aes-
thetically alienating structure, flanked on all sides by Colombia's
Colonial heritage: to the east by the National Cathedral, to the
west by the complex of buildings housing the Bogotá City Hall and
the administrative offices of the City Council, while southward, at
the opposite extreme of the square, it faces the massive *Capitolio*,
Colombia's Senate and Congressional building.

After the riots of 1948 there was never any possibility that the
administration of the day would restore the burnt out shell of the
Palace of Justice to its original elegant design. Now, with security
the primary concern, the rebuilt Palace of Justice would resemble a
medieval fortress. The entire complex—including a magnificent
law library containing the nation's most important legal archives,
inumerable law offices, conference rooms, courtrooms, and a cafeteria where the staff served daily lunch to almost four hundred
court employees—was encased in a solid, exterior granite wall.
This ramparts-like structure masked a twelve-foot moat-like space
separating the building from the outside world. Within this protective shield, the four-story offices bordered a spacious, ground
floor courtyard open to the sky. All the rooms and offices of the
upper floors led onto terrace-like passageways along the circumfer-
ence of each floor, overlooking the courtyard and parts the ground
floor. With only two access points from the street—the main
entrance leading from the square and a second entrance through
an underground garage—the reconstructed Palace of Justice was
universally believed to be impregnable.

By the autumn of 1985 the Justices of the Colombian Supreme
Court and the Council of State needed all the protection they
could get. After the June breakdown of President Betancur's peace
policy, the threat of violence menaced the Court and its most
respected members from a number of quarters. Among them, iron-
ically, the guerrillas were the least feared. To be a judge, a good
judge, in Colombia, is a thankless and frequently dangerous occu-

pation. Traditionally, members of the judiciary come from the despised middle class. Consequently they play little or no role within the social structures of the elite. Intellectuals in a philistine and aggressive society, they are shamefully undervalued and wretchedly paid. To survive in the Colombian judiciary requires special qualities: integrity, idealism, and, in a violent land, unremiting courage. The same dedication to the rule of law that drives them to the top of their profession necessarily exposes them to the most danger.

By 1985 the judges of the highest court in the nation were on a collision course with two of the most powerful sectors in the country. For reasons deeply rooted in the politics of the counter insurgency war that President Betancur had tried and failed to terminate, certain high-ranking military officers and police commanders had forged links with members of the drug mafia. This lethal collaboration had first been exposed in 1983, in the course of a judicial investigation headed by Betancur's Attorney General into murders, disappearances, torture and kidnappings in the city of Medellín. In the early 1980s few Colombians were prepared to believe the existence of an unholy mafia-military alliance and the overt accusations of the Attorney General were discredited. Certain myths have, it seems, eternal life, and the myth of the honor and virtue of the Colombian Armed Forces was one such. Everyone, on the other hand, understood and accepted the obvious and well-reported threat to Colombia's honest judges from mafia boss Pablo Escobar and his Medellín cartel. In the spring of the previous year, Betancur's first Minister of Justice, Rodrigo Lara Bonilla, had been assassinated, allegedly by members of the drug mafia. His death marked the beginning of a vicious campaign of intimidation of the judiciary by members of the Medellín cartel. Allegedly, Rodrigo Lara had been murdered for publicly exerting pressure on President Betancur's government to enact an Extradition Treaty with the United States for drug-related crimes. After his minister's death Betancur had immediately enacted the controversial treaty, and ever since the cartel had openly declared war on the courts. By the late summer and autumn of 1985 a series of mafia inspired challenges to the constitutionality of the new

Extradition Treaty had finally reached the Supreme Court. As the justices studied their decision, on which the future of this controversial treaty now depended, no one doubted that the lives of these individual members of the Constitutional Court and the Council of State were highly vulnerable.

In recent months, five of the justices of the Constitutional Court, including the President of the Supreme Court, Alfonso Reyes, had received repeated, graphic, death threats. These arrived in multiple copies, by mail and by phone, at their homes and at their offices. Sometimes they were accompanied by recordings of the private telephone conversations of members of the judges' families. Proof that the hit men of the drug cartel were able to tap the justices' home telephones with impunity. Most, though by no means all, such missives originated in Medellín, provincial headquarters of the most powerful of the cartel bosses, Pablo Escobar, and were frequently signed "The Extraditables." All threatened the lives not only of the justices themselves but of their wives and children. "We have not written to you before," read a typical note received by Judge Carlos Medellín, member of the Council of State, "because we made the mistake of thinking that you would act sensibly, with nationalism, in an impartial and just manner regarding the appeals to the Extradition Treaty... we thought that our telephone calls would be sufficient. But no. You have earned membership among those who head the list of future candidates to the ownership of a trench in the Gardens of Peace. If the Extradition Treaty does not fall, we will bring down the justice system of the nation, we will execute magistrates and the members of their families. We are ready to die, for we prefer a grave in Colombia to a jail cell in the United States. If you act intelligently, silently, nothing will happen. You alone are responsible for your own future and the future of your family.... Not all of our enemies can enjoy the privilege of prior notification and warning. We act suddenly...."

The justices' problems with the military stemmed from a series of judicial investigations of brutality following the M-19's theft of army weapons on New Years Eve, 1979. More recent cases related to dirty war activities in the military's conduct of the war on subversion. The court had also consistently opposed legislation transferring many categories of criminal offenses from the jurisdiction of civilian courts to the military courts. Under the leadership of the current Chief Justice, Alfonso Reyes Echandia, the Supreme Court had proved to be the only branch of government with the will to challenge, on constitutional grounds, the increasing militarization of Colombian life. In consequence the court had few friends among the hardline generals and colonels, many of whom regarded the nation's top judges as meddlesome opponents of a necessary war aimed at all those whose alienation from Colombia's restricted democracy they viewed as potentially treasonous.

Under Betancur, as the army criminalized the counter-insurgency campaign, relations between the judges and the military deteriorated dramatically. By early 1983 the government had proof that in its war against the opposition in Medellín the army had formed an alliance with the most notorious of the mafia trained and financed death squads, Muerte a Secuestradores (Death to Kidnappers). Betancur's Attorney General, Carlos Jiménez Gómez, took the precaution of sending his family out of the country before publicly releasing the names of sixty officers and soldiers charged with taking part in death squad murders, torture, disappearances and kidnappings. While publicly supporting his Attorney General, President Betancur moved to calm his high command with several billion additional dollars to the defense budget. For their part, the army chiefs instructed all officers to contribute one day's pay to a defense fund for the accused "members of the institution," and promptly decorated the highest ranking defendant, a colonel who was attending a special course for high level Latin American officers in Washington.

But the case that most clearly dramatized the conflict between the judges and the generals was more recent. In June 1985, an unprecedented ruling by the Council of State had convicted the current Minister of Defense, General Miguel Vega Uribe, the previous President, Turbay Ayala, together with his Minister of Defense and the Attorney General of the day, for the torture of a young woman doctor who had been swept up in the arrests following the M-19's arms theft. In 1979 General, at the time

Colonel, Vega Uribe, was commander of the Bogotá XIIIth Brigade from whose barracks the arms were stolen. It was within the Brigade's precincts that the alleged torture took place. Faced with evidence of systematic torture by the nation's armed forces, the justices had not minced their words. They went beyond the individual case of the young woman doctor involved, extending their writ to:

> the tortures suffered by all those persons, in the majority professionals and students, who fell into the net of the military intelligence of the time, and which were not prevented either by the President of the Republic in his capacity as Commander in Chief of the Armed Forces, nor by the Attorney General, the chief lawyer of the Nation... It is inadmissible, contrary to all law, that in order to maintain the rule of law, the executive should resort to irrational, inhumane methods, condemned by the law, rejected by the justice system, condemned worldwide by all human rights conventions, and that no civilized conception of the uses of power could either authorize or legitimize.

Only the M-19 cheered this landmark decision of the court. In Bogotá establishment circles it was much criticised for its "destabilizing" effects. And there was scant solidarity for the besieged judges of the Supreme Court. In an October communication addressed to the judge of the criminal division who was leading the investigation of anonymous death threats to the judges from the "Extraditables," the President of the Supreme Court, Reyes Echandia, included for good measure the most recent such anonymous threat. Entitled "Requiem for the Council of State," it read in part:

"After the decision of the Council of State in the much lied about torture case of Olga López and her daughter, we return to reality to see things from a different perspective. We remain convinced of our original view that the Council of State is made up of foreign puppets, most of whom do not deserve any serious consideration. Yet if we are supposed not to believe that the Colombian judiciary is undergoing a moment of crisis and decadence, then we must ask ourselves the question: has not this catastrophic result," [the indictment of the Minister of Defense for torture] "originated in the communist intervention and manipulation to which this particular case has been subjected?"

Against this background, the discovery by the military in mid-October of the M-19's plans to seize the building and hold the membership of the court hostage during the impending visit of the French President, came at a moment when high government officials were already devising special protection for those judges who were about to announce their decision on the Extradition Treaty. On October 16, when the Minister of Defense was handed a note about the M-19's plans, he ordered the Director General of the Police to place an armed police guard on the building "immediately and until further order." He also ordered his own military intelligence to infiltrate informers inside the justice building. And finally the army placed a number of military units based in the city, including the tank division of the Thirteenth Brigade, on permanent alert. Should any attack on the Palace of Justice materialize, "on this or any other date," the army would not be caught napping.

All these decisions to take special measures to protect the justices from the menace of the mafia had involved a series of high level meetings and consultations between members of the government, the military, the judiciary and the police. Yet when the justices returned to their offices after the long holiday week-end on the morning of Tuesday November 5, the police guard on the building had vanished. No one knew who had given the order for their removal. No one knew why the decision to remove the judges' protection had been taken. No one in the Ministry of Justice had been informed or consulted.

Later, those with a taste for conspiracy theories suspected that the removal of police protection from the building during the long holiday weekend that preceded the guerrilla attack was a deliberate maneuver by someone in the Ministry of Defense to lure the M-19 leaders into a trap. In the aftermath of the tragedy such theories were encouraged by the results of an official internal investigation. Within days of the attack, the army produced two colonels who claimed, in writing, that the order to remove the security from the building had been given to them by the late Chief Justice at a meeting in his office in the Palace of Justice on the previous Friday afternoon. But this attempt to lay the responsibility at the door of the deceased judge had to be abandoned when it was revealed that Judge Reyes was out of town, giving a lecture in the provinces, on the day that the colonels claimed to have received their instructions from him. According to M-19 spokesmen the guerrillas saw the removal of the police guard as purely coincidental; the M-19 has always maintained that their decision to move on November 6, three weeks later than originally planned, was unaffected by this major alteration in the security measures in and around the Palace building on the eve of their attack. Given the way in which the vanguard of the invasion force managed to infiltrate the building the next morning, this claim is not very convincing. But then considering the irrationality which characterized the M-19's entire operation it could just as well be true. Given the incompetence that marked all aspects of the military response to the crisis, it is equally possible that the removal of police protection from the Palace building on Tuesday, November 5, was simply the result of a bureaucratic foul-up, not some Machiavellian plot to lure the guerrillas to the building and get the M-19 once and for all time.

Whatever the reason, on Tuesday, November 5, the twenty-two armed policemen assigned to guard the approaches to the Palace of Justice from the Plaza Bolívar returned to barracks; the military intelligence agents, appointed to maintain surveillance within the building, remained at their posts inside the Palace complex; the tanks and other army units around the city remained on the alert. Twenty-four hours later, the M-19 assault force attacked the Palace of Justice. The building and its occupants were totally unprotected. The army was poised and ready to strike back.

* * * * *

Shortly before eleven o'clock on the morning of Wednesday November 6, a group of seven neatly dressed professional people, four young women and three men, equipped with smart, business-like briefcases, emerge onto the Plaza Bolívar from the south. They walk briskly across the square towards the main entrance of the Palace of Justice, and mingling easily with the other visitors coming and going up the stone steps, they step through the bronze doors into the lobby. One by one they present identity cards to the private security guard seated at a table inside the lobby. They then disperse inside the crowded interior of the building. One has an appointment in a law office on an upper floor; another needs to consult a brief in the ground floor library; a couple are lawyers who have come to do research on a particular case; a couple more are meeting a friend for a mid-morning cup of coffee in the ground floor cafeteria. All seven of these latest, mid-morning visitors to the Palace of Justice on this wet Wednesday have one thing in common: they all carry false identity papers, and somewhere on their persons, some, at least, conceal revolvers. Within ten minutes of their arrival, the vanguard of the M-19 force has successfully infiltrated the Palace of Justice and taken up strategic positions within its vast complex. This vanguard is commanded by the lawyer and former *Anapista* congressman Alfonso Jaquín, who is impeccably dressed for the occasion in a tan business suit, and a matching dark shirt and tie.

Alfonso Jaquín, proceding briskly across the interior courtyard to a bank of elevators located against the opposite, northernmost wall of the Palace, takes an elevator to the fourth floor. Exiting onto the passageway, he makes a complete tour of the floor, passing the outer offices of the Constitutional Court, several of the offices of the Councilors of State, and the office of the Supreme Court Justice. He ends up back at the head of a stairway, situated beside the elevators, which he now descends to the floor below, where he conducts a similar reconnaissance, continuing on down through the rest of the building, floor by floor. Satisfied that there is nothing suspicious, nothing unusual going on inside the building, he arrives once more on the ground floor. There is no overt police presence; no armed guards lurk in the ante-chambers of the justices or on the public passages and stairways. Secretaries and clerks, visitors and staff are pursuing the normal business routines of a busy day. Between 11:10 and 11:15 a.m. Jaquín enters a public phone booth adjacent to the ground floor cafeteria and makes a phone call.

The phone rings in a safe house situated nineteen blocks to the south of the Plaza Bolívar, on the Calle 6 South at Carrera 8, where Luis Otero, Andrés Almarales and the main unit of the M-19 assault force are standing by. Luis Otero takes the call. "Everything is clean," Jaquín reports.

The safe house on the Calle 6 South where most of the guerrillas have spent the night, was too small to accommodate the entire invasion force. Hence the rear guard, consisting of five guerrillas led by a young *Commandante* code-named "Lázaro," spent the night in a second house located three blocks away. Luis Otero's strategy for the seizure of the building called for an attack on both street level entrances simultaneously. It was a strategy requiring split-second timing and coordination. The main force of twenty eight guerrillas, travelling in a convoy of three stolen vehicles, would drive into the street that flanked the western boundary of the Palace leading to the Plaza Bolívar, [the Carrera 8] and head for the underground entrance, accessible only through the building's basement garage, located halfway up the block. As they did so, six members of a lightly armed rearguard, wearing flak jackets beneath their street clothes, and carrying 9mm revolvers, would be waiting at the corner of the Plaza Bolívar, poised to approach the main entrance on foot, and so seize and secure its great bronze doors.

But on the night before the attack Luis Otero changed his mind. He suddenly decided it was too dangerous to leave the rearguard at the corner of the square, waiting alone for the vehicles to arrive. Fearful that they might be spotted by police agents who habitually patrolled that precise location, at the last minute Otero made a significant, and as it turned out, fatal change of strategy. He decided that instead of going ahead to the Plaza Bolívar on foot and waiting there for the convoy to arrive at the entrance to the Palace garage, the rearguard should accompany the main force to the Palace. Driving their own vehicle, they were to lead the convoy as far as the Carrera 8, then accelerate up the street, past the entrance to the garage, straight into the square. There, abandoning the vehicle, they were to attack and seize the great entrance doors just as the main assault force was advancing on the underground garage.

On the morning of the attack, "Lázaro," the commander of the rearguard unit, was busy. At 7:00 a.m., accompanied by the members of his unit, he set out to steal the required transport. By nine o'clock they had acquired three, previously selected vehicles: a Ford pick-up, a Chevrolet pick-up amd a large, covered Ford truck. These he delivered to Otero's safe house on the Calle 6 South and remained to help load the truck with the M-19's supplies until it was time to drive Alfonso Jaquín and the members of the vanguard to the Palace of Justice. When he had dropped them off safely near the Plaza Bolívar, he drove back to his own safe house, to check that the rearguard was standing by, ready to join up with the main convoy as it drove past en route to the Palace of Justice. Then he returned to join Otero and wait for the telephone call from Alfonso Jaquín.

Otero was tense, nervous. "Are your guys ready?" he asked Lázaro. "You're sure? They must be in position, they must be waiting to pick up the lead when we drive down your street." Lázaro, reassured him.

For Luis Otero that morning had seemed endless. The final orders for the assault had all been communicated to the individual squad commanders on the previous evening. For weeks, each waking hour had been absorbed in the organization of every last detail of the operation. Now there was nothing left for him to do. The stress of waiting had started getting to him. Organizing a secret operation of this scale had had special problems. The biggest headache had been the acquisition of sufficient arms. Getting the money [several bank robberies had been necessary], finding the right weapons, purchasing them, transporting them, hiding them. From the start Luis Otero had identified the two elements essential to the success of the operation: sufficient firepower to hold the army at bay for several hours, and a sophisticated system of communications. It was, he deemed, crucial to have secure communications both within the Palace of Justice building and without, so as to keep open the lines of communication between his own commanders on the scene and with Álvaro Fayad and other members of the M-19 Supreme Command in hiding in Bogotá. Luis had given responsibility for organizing a system of high-powered radios and walkie-talkies to two young women, one a former journalist. But at the last moment he found himself a man short and so he had to switch the other woman, who was a crack shot, into his first line of defense. Otero had calculated that his forces had enough ammunition to hold out against the army for five days if need be. The assault force would be accompanied by an experienced nurse, who had left her job in a city hospital on the day before the attack in order to participate in the operation. They had plenty of medical supplies and high protein foods. They even brought two video cameras to record this epic.

On the night before the attack they held a party in the safe house. It had been a good evening. All dressed up in their combat gear the members of the assault force had posed for candid snapshots—dancing, drinking, embracing—several of the young lovers among the force had kissed for the camera. Pictures for posterity of Colombia's revolutionary heroes and heroines celebrating on the eve of making history. Luis Otero brought the roll of exposed negative to the Palace with him in his briefcase. When they walked out of the Palace victorious he intended that these pictures would circulate in glossy magazines around the globe, so that people everywhere would understand that in Colombia the M-19 stood for something more important even than courage and militancy; that to be "Emme" signified to share an ethos, a way of being and thinking, a love of life, of music and laughter and each other. To be "Emme" meant belonging to a revolution that celebrated human rights, human values and the good life.

When Otero hung up the phone after talking to Jaquín, he and Lázaro, the two commanders of the assault, who between them shared the responsibility of seizing and securing the two street entrances of the Palace complex, embraced briefly and wished each other luck. Lázaro jumped in his car and drove off to pick up the four waiting members of his rearguard unit. Otero ordered the twenty-eight members of the main force to take their assigned places in the three vehicles.

The convoy was led by four guerrillas armed with two subma-chine guns and two rifles in the Chevy pick-up; next came the Ford truck, with the bulk of the invading forces, fourteen guerrillas in all including Andrés Almarales and Luis Otero and all of the ammunition—the explosives, the cables, the machine guns, the grenades, the sacks of bullets, and all of their provisions and med-ical supplies. The second Ford pick-up, with ten armed guerrillas on board, brought up the rear. When they were all aboard, Otero climbed last into the back of the truck. The driver secured the canvas covering, concealing them all from view, and within moments of Jaquín's phone call the three-vehicle convoy set out for the Palace of Justice.

The street corner where the convoy was supposed to pick up Lázaro and his unit was at the junction of the Carrera 9 and the Calle 8 South, outside a friendly bakery which had been storing arms for the guerrillas for several weeks. The main safe house, Otero's headquarters, was located one block further east, and two blocks north.

Lázaro waited with his unit outside the bakery for the convoy to appear. After five minutes he began to get anxious. At this point he discovered that no one in his unit had a walkie talkie. There was no way of communicating with the safe house to find out what had caused the delay. After four or five more minutes Lázaro decided to return to the safe house on foot, figuring that if he met the convoy on the way they could give him a lift back to the bakery. But he saw no sign of the convoy. And when he reached the safe house it was empty, abandoned. No people, no vehicles, nothing to show that just ten minutes earlier the house and the yard had been teeming with people and vehicles.

Much later, the single survivor of the attack—a young woman who, coincidentally, happened to be in charge of the guerrillas' communications system—suggested that Luis Otero must have forgotten to pass along his change of plan to the drivers. Closeted in the dark, in the back of the covered truck, Otero himself could not have realized that when the convoy emerged from the safe house the lead driver turned immediately not south, toward the bakery, but north, so proceding by the shortest, most logical route, directly to the M-19's objective.

Twenty minutes later the main convoy arrives on the Carrera 8 outside the western exterior of the Palace of Justice building. Halfway up the block the lead pick-up suddenly accelerates, swings violently to the left, and closely followed by the truck and the second pick-up, all three vehicles plunge out of sight down a steep ramp leading to the underground garage of the Palace of Justice. At the bottom of the ramp two private security guards, standing, a little bored, beside the automatic barrier across the entrance to the garage, have no time to jump clear as the first vehicle crashes the barrier. One of the two men is run over; the second man is mown down in a volley of gunshots before he can draw his weapon. As the three M-19 vehicles penetrate to the interior of the garage, the occupants of the last vehicle leap out and slam shut the steel partition sealing off the garage from the street. In less than a minute, the M-19 attack has achieved its first objective and claimed its first two casualties.

Out on the street, the sound of gunfire from the basement garage continues to reverberate as a number of chauffeurs and individual bodyguards for some of the justices, surprised as they while away the morning gossiping and playing cards, leap for cover behind their parked vehicles and return the invaders' fire in a vain attempt to block access to the interior staircase and elevators that lead from the garage onto the first floor of the building. Lázaro's unit meanwhile is still four blocks from the Palace stuck in the traffic, when they hear the first burst of gunfire. Abandoning the car they race on foot to the Plaza Bolívar only to find that, alerted by the sounds of the battle in the building's basement, the two security guards on duty at the main entrance have long since slammed shut and secured the great bronze doors.

The time is 11:40 a.m. on this cold and rainy morning in Bogotá. Almost unopposed, the main body of the M-19's attack force, twenty-eight heavily armed men and women with all of their weapons and a truck full of ammunition and supplies, has successfully penetrated the underground entrance of a fortress that was believed to be impregnable. Yet with one key unit of his forces shut out on the square, Otero's entire strategy for securing the building from a military counterattack is already in disarray.

CHAPTER 3
The Search for Hostages

*In which the M-19 invaders follow
their leader's plan of attack for securing
the vast complex of the Palace of Justice
as best they can, and begin to fan out
through the building's offices, searching
for hostages among the most illustrious
inhabitants of the Court.*

"Not even the guerrillas ever thought it would turn out the way it did. They expected they'd have to hold out for six or eight hours, at the very most, and then they'd sit down with the judges and work things out. They wanted to negotiate. They thought it was going to be like the seizure of the Embassy. They said they knew the President wouldn't allow anything to happen to us. Since the judges represented the third branch of the government, they said that was enough of a guarantee that there would have to be negotiations. And we also believed that..."

I will call him "Gabriel." The anonymous public servant. The only hostage I ever managed to meet who had survived the entire 27 hours of the siege and who had the courage to talk about it to a foreign reporter. He pauses for a moment. His dark eyes hold a look of profound bewilderment as he stares in silence at me across the table and I sense his despair that he will never be able to communicate, to anyone, what he has been through. "There was a moment right after the gunfire started," he continues softly, "when we thought the army or the police were going to come and get them out of there. We thought we'd be holed up for an hour or two and then it would all be over..."

He had been sitting across from me at a table in the back of the nearly deserted Café Roma on the Avenida Jiménez for over an hour, talking incessantly in a quiet, flat monotone, pausing only to allow me time to take notes. There was no emotion in his voice, nor in his expression, and the only worry I could detect, lurking in his soft dark eyes when they probed mine, was a deep concern for the credibility of what he was telling me; the only fear, that his story might sound too far-fetched, and that I, a visitor from New York, from another planet, a journalist who read the press accounts and talked to important people, might not believe him. Because the truth about what had happened, his truth as he had experienced it, was fantastically important to Gabriel. It was the sole reason why he had taken the risk of talking to me.

Gabriel had selected the Roma, a large, impersonal, fast-food cafe in the commercial center of Bogotá, just two blocks from my hotel. "At eight o'clock, tomorrow morning. I'll meet you there before I go to the office," he had said the day before. When I told the friend who had found him for me, he shook his head. "You've made a mistake," he said gloomily. "When he agreed to talk to you, you should have insisted on going somewhere then and there. You shouldn't have let him go home tonight to talk to his family, his girlfriend. They'll get to him. You'll never see him again." It was early May, 1986, just six months after what had become known in the interim as "The Holocaust at the Palace of Justice." During those months, between November and May, a lot of people had disappeared, many Colombians had been killed, many more had been on the receiving end of anonymous, threatening, phone calls. There was a dirty war raging in Colombia and people were very afraid. I had been in Bogotá for over two weeks, and had so far failed to find a single witness to the carnage who would talk to me. Then a friend who knew that I was getting desperate had come to my hotel to tell me that his aunt, an employee of the court, knew a young clerk in her office who had been held hostage throughout the entire 27 hours of the siege. Perhaps, just possibly, he might be prepared to tell me his story if I would agree not to use his name.

So I had gone with my friend to meet his aunt, in the fancy new skyscraper guarded by soldiers in the north of Bogotá, where the offices of the court had been temporarily relocated from the ravaged ruin on the Plaza Bolívar, and "Gabriel" had come into her office from the photocopying room, and he had said yes, just like that. No hesitation, no need on my part for persuasion. He was short, and a little plump, quiet-spoken and tidy. His short brown hair was brushed flat above his dark, oval face with the smooth, almost hairless facial skin that denotes Indian blood. Gabriel was just twenty-one years old, and he had only begun to work at the court a few weeks before the attack. Not today, he said, he had too much work to do for the judges, but tomorrow, if my friend's aunt would give him leave to come to work late.

Gabriel remains the only hostage-survivor I ever met who had no ulterior motives, no hidden agendas, no political connections or ideology, no children, and no wife, to protect. The witness. The only one I ever met, in that spring of 1986, who was not paralysed by fear.

He arrived half an hour late that morning for our eight o'clock appointment in the Café Roma. Gloomily ready to submit to my friend's pessimism, I had already asked for my check and was about to leave when I saw him walk through the doors from the street, wearing a perfectly pressed dark blue suit that bore all the marks of being his "Sunday best." He was shy and nervous at first. We both were. But it quickly became clear to me that nothing was as important to him as this chance opportunity to document what he had seen and heard during the 27 hours that he had spent in the company of seventy other people, many of whom were dead now, inside a darkened bathroom in the Palace of Justice. As I listened to his story I became acutely aware how the falseness of the official version of the events he had lived through had hurt him. No one and nothing was going to deflect his determination to get the truth told, as he had lived it.

"It was about 11:45 in the morning. I was at a meeting in an office on the fourth floor when we heard gunfire coming from the first floor," he began. "We rushed out onto the corridor but we couldn't see anything. We just heard a lot of shouting: *"Viva*

Colombia!" and "*Viva la Paz!*" The voices all sounded very young and there were a lot of women's voices. Then Judge Medina said it must be the guerrillas and we'd better get back inside our offices. So everyone locked themselves in and turned out the lights. Some of the judges started calling their families on the phone. In the office where I was, Judge Gaona hung out a white handkerchief on the door."

When the M-19 invaded the Justice building on that grey November morning, there were over three hundred civilians in the building. Luis Otero's original strategy had depended on the availability of forty armed men and women deployed in different areas of the building in four separate units. The guerrillas were meant to be accompanied by a nurse, and by a woman video journalist; these two women were to be responsible for establishing a functioning medical and communications center in a secure, central location. Andrés Almarales, while also armed and in battledress, was nevertheless not expected to participate in the fighting. His role was essentially the delicate one of taking charge of the chief hostages. Above all, he was there to lead the negotiations with the government.

In his plan for the occupation of the building, Otero had subdivided each of the four combat units into two squads, each with a specific area of responsibility. Unit 1, led by Lázaro and staffed by the M-19's top explosives experts, had responsibility for the seizure and occupation of the first floor. Their first task was to instantly secure the main doors with explosives and land mines, thus defending the building from any attempt by the army to penetrate the interior of the Palace through the entrance from the square.

Unit 2, having secured the garage and the basement, and taken control of the elevators and the stairs that led to the ground floor through the cafeteria, would proceed to occupy the interior staircases leading from the courtyard to the fourth floor in the north, or rear wing of the building. There they would immediately set up their main defensive positions on the second and third floor landings of the northwest staircase; this would give them control over most of the open spaces of the ground-floor courtyard. The unit was also responsible for transporting all the supplies—the arms and ammunition, the explosives, the cables, the medical and communications equipment—from the garage to pre-selected distribution points in key locations around the Palace.

Meanwhile, units 3 and 4, led by two of the younger *commandantes*, would seize the staircases in the building's south wing, facing onto the square. Luis Otero himself would then link up with Alfonso Jaquín, who supposedly knew the office locations of the most important justices, and begin to move through the building's third and fourth floors. Eliminating any resistance as they did so, from the handful of armed bodyguards assigned to some individual judges, they would identify the leading figures of the court and take them hostage. Assembling them, in so far as possible, in a couple of key locations on the upper floors.

"Squad 1 will enter through the main staircase of the south wing and Squad 2 by the principal staircase of the northern wing. Squad 1 will go to the fourth floor and 2 will go to the third floor. Each squad will leave one man on the second floor." So read Otero's plan for the invasion and occupation of the heart of the building.

But squad 1 is Lázaro's rearguard unit, and it is standing, helpless, outside on the square. Their absence, and the loss of their specialist knowledge for laying plastic explosives inside the main entrance can never be recouped. Within the first ten minutes of the invasion Otero's entire strategy for the occupation of the immense complex has been thrown into chaos. As the unsuspecting guerrillas of his own unit storm the narrow staircase from the garage, expecting to meet up with Lázaro, they run headlong into gunfire from the alerted bodyguards and building security men who are still in control of the first floor.

In the opening attack on the basement, casualties among the Palace staff, in addition to the two security guards, include two of the judges' chauffeurs. Next to fall, as the attackers advance on the first floor, are the elevator operator and the administrator of the building. In those first few moments, the M-19's nurse and one of the guerrillas are also killed in the opening salvo in the garage, and three others are fatally wounded in the fighting on the basement stairs. Within the first ten minutes, the M-19's original force of forty-one guerrillas has been reduced to thirty. To compound their problems, within less than ten minutes the building comes under attack from a detachment of the Bogotá police who begin firing indiscriminately up at the windows from the square. In the chaos and confusion of the first fifteen minutes of the occupation, as the guerrillas struggle wildly to fill in for the missing unit, large amounts of M-19 supplies, including all of the communications equipment, get left behind in the basement garage. They will not subsequently be recuperated.

Nevertheless, during the first forty-five minutes, the guerrillas do manage to secure the basement and seize the first floor. They place a couple of homemade claymore mines inside the great bronze doors, and scramble to set up their headquarters in the northwest corner of the building around a stairway leading from the basement to the roof. On these stairs they place their two most powerful weapons—a 50mm and a 30mm machine gun. With these two guns strategically placed on the second and third floor landings, they are now able to control movement across much of the courtyard and are well positioned to guard the approaches to the upper floors in the north and west wings. They also control access to the all important third, and final entrance to the building from the roof. Led by Alfonso Jaquín, one of the units now begins moving through the upper floors searching for hostages among the senior figures of the court. Forty-five minutes after crashing the barrier into the garage they reach the office on the fourth floor where Gabriel is closeted with the judges of the Constitutional Court. "Suddenly we heard shouts just outside the door: 'They're in here! Come out with your hands up! We will respect your lives!'

Gabriel remembers that the tension inside the room was almost immediately diffused by a man whose humanity and courage he would grow to respect and admire during the next 27 hours. Judge Manuel Gaona had always defined himself as *gente del pueblo* (a man of the people). The son of lower middle-class parents, a scholarship student, he had paid his expenses during his years at law school by selling shirts in the Calle 19, the open-air market where the poor of Bogotá shop for their clothes. Gaona was one of the youngest judges of the court. He was also of those whose stance on constitutional cases had made him a marked man in the courts' conflicts with the drug cartel. At the time of the attack on the Palace, Manuel Gaona had received several assassination threats from the anonymous hit men of the "Extraditables" (drug cartel bosses like Pablo Escobar), but, a fervent anti-militarist, he had refused on principle to accept protection from the state. On the morning of November 6, Manuel Gaona has no bodyguards. Now, when the guerrillas reach his office, he gets up from his chair, turns to the others in the room, and says: "Well, we're the ones they've come for. We'd better go." "He blessed himself with the sign of the cross," says Gabriel, "and walked out onto the passageway." Gabriel and the others follow him out of the office.

"I walked out looking straight ahead. There was a guerrilla lying on his stomach on the floor pointing his gun at me and giving instructions: 'Move slowly. Not too fast. Keep your hands on top of your head.' Two other guerrillas appeared. They asked me my name, my position. They searched me and made me sit down on the floor beside the elevator with my back against the wall. From where I sat I could see a wounded guerrilla lying inside the elevator. We stayed there for about an hour."

The time was 12:30 p.m. Five minutes earlier, outside on the Plaza Bolívar, the first of ten armored cars and tanks of the Artillery Division of the XIII Bogotá Brigade had begun arriving in the square.

CHAPTER 4

The Counterattack

*In which tank commander Colonel
Alfonso Plazas Vega drives his tank
through the bronze doors of the Palace
of Justice; Commandante Andrés
Almarales teaches the hostages how
to survive the blast of a mine;
Commandante Luis Otero has a
change of heart; and the Chief Justice
makes a telephone call to the Palace of
the President, just up the street.*

The telephone call was received in the office of the Minister of
Defense, General Miguel Vega Uribe, just after 11:40 a.m. The
caller, who has never been identified, was speaking from a telephone within the Palace of Justice. He wished to inform the
Minister that the M-19 had just assaulted the building.

Present in the reception room of the Minister's office at the
time, waiting for an appointment, was his son-in-law, Lt. Colonel
Alfonso Plazas Vega. Colonel Plazas Vega was currently
Commander of the Cavalry School—now the tank division of the
Bogotá XIIIth Artillery Brigade. When the receptionist told
Colonel Plazas the news from the Justice Building he immediately
telephoned his superior, General Jesús Armando Arias Cabrales,
the Commander of the XIIIth Brigade. General Arias ordered the
Colonel to return immediately to his base at the Cavalry School,
nine kilometers North of the city, and stand by. Forty minutes

later, Lt. Colonel Plazas arrived in the Plaza Bolívar at the head of a battalion of ten tanks and armored cars. The time was 12:25 p.m.

In the other Palace, the Presidential one, the President of the Republic and his Minister of Foreign Affairs, Augusto Ramírez Campo, were receiving the credentials of several new Ambassadors to Colombia when the sound of the first volley of gunshots, coming from the direction of the Plaza Bolívar just three blocks away, intruded on the diplomatic ceremony. The troops of the Presidential Guard raced to secure all of the entrances and took up positions to defend the Palace from an attack. The President's aides rushed off to investigate the cause of the gunfire. The President and his Foreign Minister proceeded with the diplomatic ceremony. Fifteen minutes later the Chief of Protocol reappeared, and drawing the President aside quietly informed him that a guerrilla commando unit of the M-19 had invaded the Supreme Court. The President remained calm. He gave instructions for the General Secretary of the Presidency to stay on top of all the available information; he ordered his Military Attaché to contact the members of the cabinet, the military commanders, the police chiefs, and the heads of all the security agencies, to inform them of what had happened; he gave the order that all necessary actions be taken "to restore order and above all to avoid bloodshed;" finally, he dispatched a unit of the Presidential Guard to the Plaza Bolívar to support a detachment of the Bogotá police which had already arrived on the scene from the local police station. The President and his Foreign Secretary then continued to receive the diplomatic credentials of the new Ambassador from Uruguay.

The order to despatch the troops of the Presidential Guard to the scene was the first and only direct military order given by the President during the course of the next twenty seven hours. The first direct communication between the President and his Minister of Defense, General Miguel Vega Uribe, took place at 12:30 p.m., when the President requested his Defense Minister's attendance at an urgent session of the full Cabinet. By then Colonel Plazas' tanks were already circulating in the Plaza Bolívar, and a military action was already underway. It had been launched forty five minutes earlier by the XIIIth Brigade Commander, General Arias Cabrales, and involved the participation of over 2,000 troops, from eleven different army battalions, two military police units, and forces from all of the military and police intelligence and counter-intelligence forces. Pleading the urgent need to consult with his commanders, General Vega Uribe did not arrive at the Presidential Palace to participate in the Cabinet's discussions until three o'clock that afternoon.

It took General Arias less than an hour to get his troops to their battle stations. By 12:30 p.m. he had installed his own operational headquarters in the Museum of the Casa Florero, a two-story colonial building situated on the corner of the Plaza Bolívar, directly across the street from the Justice Building. For the next two days, the Museum, which held the relics of Colombia's heroes of the War of Independence, would function as the nerve center of the military counterattack. Here the head of Army Intelligence and Counter Intelligence, the F-2, Colonel Edilberto Sánchez, was stationed for the duration of the conflict, as was the Commander of the Bogotá Police Forces, General Vargas Villegas. Throughout the two day conflict, every hostage who escaped from the Palace of Justice was brought directly to this building by the soldiers to be screened and identified by army and police intelligence agents before they were permitted to go home.

General Arias and his staff, with the overall coordination and supervision of the Chief of Staff of the Armed Forces, General Rafael Samudio, and the direct participation of the Minister of Defense, devised the military plan designed to take back the building from the M-19. Their strategy consisted essentially in the massive and indiscriminate use of fire power, directed against the building from all sides, and the mobilization of tanks to penetrate to the interior. Between 12:30 and 1:30 p.m. the army surrounded the building and the square. Soldiers occupied the Clock Tower of the National Cathedral, overlooking the Palace from the eastern end of the Plaza Bolívar and took over all of the buildings on the streets running parrallel to the Palace, in the east, north and west. By 1:30 p.m. police helicopters, bearing troops of the only unit trained in urban anti-terrorist techniques, arrived and attempted to drop a squad of Special Forces on the roof. But the crossfire from army marksmen, shooting incessantly into the Justice Palace from the roofs and windows of these adjacent buildings, was so intense that the pilot refused to land and returned to base.

Within the Justice building the guerrillas continue their search through the offices of the third and fourth floors for the three members of the Court whom they consider their most important hostages—the President of the Supreme Court, Alfonso Reyes Echandia, the brother of President Betancur, Jaime Betancur Cuartas and the wife of the Minister of the Interior, Clara Forrero de Castro. As they do so, the greatest danger to the lives of the four hundred people trapped within the Court complex comes from the incessant, random firing into the building by the army.

Gabriel, who was seated under the guns of the guerrillas on the fourth floor passage beside the elevator, remembers that first hour of the siege vividly: "The gunfire was coming from across the street and we could hear the engines of the helicopters hovering above the roof. Then, suddenly, a hail of bullets struck the wall just above our heads. So we asked the guerrillas to move us to a safer place, and one of them went off to reconnoiter. He came back to say that the commander wanted us all to go down to the bath-rooms, one floor below. When we got there, Judge Gaona recognized the chief guerrilla. He went straight up to him, and he asked: 'Is this gentleman the *Commandante*? Is he in charge here?' and then he introduced himself and they shook hands. The leader was Andrés Almarales. He told us to keep calm and assured us that they had not come with the intention of harming anyone."

Even without his moustache Manuel Gaona knew Andrés Almarales. Political circles in Bogotá are small and inbred. Though the judge was eight years younger, he and Andrés had been students at the same school, had attended the lectures of the same professors, and belonged to the same professional associations. Then, for a while during the early seventies when Almarales had been a congressman, and again during the recent short-lived period of the peace process, they had moved in the same social circles, attended the same official receptions, and shared many mutual acquaintances. Consequently, the bizarre circumstances of their present meeting were offset for Gaona by a consoling sense of familiarity.

By November of 1985 the reputation of the M-19, once considered by many Colombians as a positive force on the political scene, had deteriorated to the point where few people took them seriously. Yet if they were now regarded by the majority of their countrymen as little more than a fringe element, by the same token the M-19 leaders had not developed a reputation for ruthlessness or brutality. The *muchachos* of the "Emme" were too closely associated to the mainstream of their generation and of their middle class origins. Unless you had been brainwashed by the editorials and reporting of *El Tiempo*, it was difficult to think of them as potentially cold-blooded assassins. Andrés Almarales in particular, with his warmth and the infectious charm and openness of his rough-hewn personality, was an unlikely murderer.

In fact, the hostage judge and the ex-congressman guerrilla leader were quite pleased and relieved to see each other. Almarales assured Gaona that the hostages would be perfectly safe if they would just step into the seclusion of the bathroom where he had established his headquarters. "This will all be over soon," he kept saying, gesturing vaguely in the direction of the fighting, as if the incessant gunfire ricocheting around the immense building were nothing more than a temporary inconvenience.

All of the bathrooms and toilets in the Palace of Justice were located on a series of mezzanines adjacent to the main stairway in the northwest wing of the building. The bathroom which the hostages, led by Gaona, now entered, was located on the mezzanine between the third and fourth floors. It was here that approximately one third of the M-19's forces, now, in the absence of Lázaro, under the reluctant command of Andrés Almarales, had set up their headquarters. The bathroom was tucked away behind the elevator shaft. The only approach to it was along a narrow passageway, running between the exterior of the elevator shaft and a floor to ceiling concrete wall that blocked the view of the toilets and urinals from the stairs. Guarded by the the guerrillas' largest gun, set up on the third floor landing directly below the mezzanine, the windowless, marble-lined room appeared virtually impregnable from attack.

The bathroom was a small, rectangular space, ten feet across by twenty feet long. To the right of the entrance, lining the wall, there were four metal toilet stalls; opposite the stalls, a line of basins; left of the entrance, at right angles to the basins and visible only after passing beyond the masking wall, were two urinals. When the hostages walked into this familiar room they found it had been transformed into an arsenal. Within its restricted space the guerrillas had stored all of their ammunition. Boxes of hand grenades and some Claymore mines ("shaped like an American football," said Gabriel) were piled on top of the basins and the urinals; bullets for the belts of their two 50mm and 30mm Mack machine guns, for the 7.62mm Galil rifles, the 7.36mm G-3 guns, the 5.56mm AR 15s, the Uzi 9mm sub-machine guns, the M-16s, the 9mm Browning revolvers—all were piled up in sacks on the floor. Three young women, two of them still dressed in their street clothes and one in army fatigues, were running a relay system to recoup the spent guns, load them, and pass them back to the guerrillas on the stairway who were engaged in a constant exchange of fire with army sharpshooters, firing into the building from the street. The guerrillas had come prepared for war; a long war, if need be.

"The guerrillas told us not to worry, that it would soon all be over, so we sat where we could," says Gabriel, "on the floor, under the basins, and waited. Then, suddenly, a guerrilla rushed into the room shouting: *Commandante! Commandante!* We're fucked! The army has broken in with tanks! There are tanks on the ground floor."

The clock in the bell tower of the National Cathedral on the Plaza Bolívar has just struck two o'clock in the afternoon when the first of Colonel Plazas Vega's tanks penetrates to the interior of the building. It is followed closely by two others. Firing its 90mm shells at close range it has taken less than five minutes for the leading tank to burst through the massive bronze doors. The mines, laid hurriedly by the guerrillas inside the entrance, fail to explode. Within a few short minutes the entire situation of the M-

19 and their hostages is radically altered. Now, army troops, under cover of the tanks, invade the courtyard, severing all access to the invaders' basement stores and cutting off any possibility of future communication between the two main units of the M-19 forces deployed in diametrically opposite ends of the vast building. The smaller of these two units—approximately ten or twelve men and women under arms, commanded by the militarily inexperienced Almarales—was well entrenched on the stairway in the northwest of the building. The larger force, under the command of Luis Otero, had their base in the southeast corner of the building, where Otero, Jaquín, and some seventeen or so heavily armed guerrillas were holding the most numerous, and strategically the most important of the hostages in unprotected offices on the fourth floor.

Inside the bathroom Almarales attempts to take the offensive: "We have to make a show of military strength," he announces. "We have to use the mines." The fuses have got damp in the bathroom, so in order to explode the mines they have to improvise by attaching hand grenades to them. However a grenade takes five seconds to explode after the pin is pulled out, and none of the guerrillas could figure out how long it would take for the mines to hit the ground once they had been dropped from the top floor. "Almarales asked us how long we thought it would take for a mine to travel from the fourth floor to the bottom. Gaona said two seconds. Andrés Almarales then instructed the guerrillas to take one of the mines to the fourth floor and count to three after pulling the pin on the grenade before dropping it. Then he showed us how to protect ourselves from the blast. He told us to lie down on our stomachs, and breathe deeply, deep down into our stomachs through an open mouth, and then hold our breath with our mouths open. 'When I shout, open your mouths wide and breathe,' he said. Then he told the guerrilla that before he dropped the mine he must shout: 'Mine away!'"

So the guerrilla goes to the fourth floor to drop the Claymore mine, and the hostages lie flat on their stomachs and follow Almarales' instructions to the letter: they hear the guerrilla's warning shout; they breath deeply into the bottom of their stomachs and hold their mouths open for dear life. There is a tremendous explosion, followed immediately by fierce and sustained gunfire. The bathroom shakes, but none of the hostages suffer any physical harm. "We felt protected," says Gabriel. "But later Almarales came to tell us that the mines were useless, good for nothing."

Soon after 2:00 p.m. the army is in control of the garage, the basement entrance, the main entrance, and the entire first floor. Now, in their haste to dislodge the guerrillas, the troops turn their guns and begin firing, indiscriminately, upwards from the central courtyard into the surrounding offices on the upper floors. At this point, soldiers who are doing battle with the guerrillas within the interior of the Palace of Justice also come under fire from their colleagues, who continue to press their attack into the building from the street and the surrounding buildings. There is no coordination between the military commands. Between 2:00 and 3:00 p.m. a number of civilian radio buffs around the city, tuned-in to the internal communications between the army and police commanders, overhear the following exchange:

> ARCANO 5: [Code for Colonel Bernardo Ramírez, deputy commander XIIIth Brigade, speaking from outside the Palace to Colonel Edilberto Sánchez, Head of Intelligence Operations in the Army Command Center in the Museum.] Look, Arcano 2, [Colonel Sánchez], they are firing into the basement and there are police personnel down there. Over.

> ARCANO 3: [Chief of Staff of the XIIIth Brigade in the Command Center]. The troops in the basement are from the tank division. They're on top of the situation.

> ARCANO 5: Yes, but there are also police personnel down there and the police are informing us that they are being fired on. Over.

ARCANO 3: Negative. There shouldn't be any police in the basement because it's under the control of the tanks. Over.

ARCANO 5: What I'm telling you is that the police are telling us that they are in the basement.

ACERO: [Police commander interrupting]. Yes. Repeat. There is exchange of fire in the basement. That is correct.

ACORAZADO 6: [Col. Plazas Vega, Commander of the tanks, speaking from inside the Palace building.] Arcano 5! They have just wounded one of the personnel of our own units firing from Carrera 7 into the sector. Over.

ARCANO 5: rpt. [repeat]

ACORAZADO 6: The Major is located on the second floor north. He says there are units on the Carrera 7 firing at him and they have just wounded one of his soldiers. Over.

ARCANO 5: Wrong. Wrong. I don't think they're firing on him from that side. Over.

ACORAZADO 6: Yes. They are firing. The Major is confirming what I'm telling you. He has no radio communication, only a telephone which he's using to speak to us. Over.

ARCANO 5: We'll check it out. I'll need the Major to give us his exact location. Over.

Meanwhile, all of the chief hostages being held prisoner by Luis Otero and his unit, which include the President of the Supreme Court, Chief Justice Alfonso Reyes Echandia, and eight of the justices of the Council of State and the Criminal Court, are trapped in offices on the fourth floor, overlooking the military mayhem in the central courtyard. Inside one of these offices, for the past twenty minutes, Luis Otero and Alfonso Jaquín have been closeted with the Chief Justice, Judge Alfonso Reyes Echandia, explaining to him the reasons for the M-19's invasion of his Court and presenting their case for the historic trial of President Belisario Betancur. The news that the army has penetrated to the interior of the building shatters the peculiar calm of this surrealistic conference between the President of the Supreme Court and his captors. When Luis Otero, the only man with military command experience in the room, realizes that the army have made bits of the M-19's defenses, he understands at once that the M-19's bid to achieve a historic political publicity coup has failed.

As the military brain behind the invasion, Otero also knows several other disquieting things. He knows that almost fifty percent of the guerrillas' ammunition stayed behind in the garage and is now lost. He knows that the army has split his inadequate force in two. Without the radios and walkie talkies, which are still in the garage, he and Jaquín have also lost contact with Almarales. Furthermore, Luis Otero knows that all the special conditions of the design of the Justice building—the fortress-like construction, the moat, the lack of more than two ground-level entrances—the very characteristics which would help it withstand a lengthy siege, have now converted the great building into a prison. His forces are now helplessly trapped, without any possibility of escape.

Luis Otero does a rapid about-face. He explains the military realities of the situation to the Chief Justice and proposes that in his capacity as President of the Supreme Court—a position which is constitutionally the equal in authority and power to that of the President of the Executive Branch—the Chief Justice should now telephone President Betancur to request him to order an immediate army cease-fire, so that the M-19 and the Chief Justice can sit down together and negotiate the immediate withdrawal of the guerrillas from the Palace of Justice.

Shortly after the incursion of the tanks, at a little after two o'clock that afternoon, Chief Justice Reyes, with Luis Otero sitting beside him, dials the number of the Presidential Palace and asks to speak to the President. The male voice who answers the telephone identifies himself as a secretary. He asks the judge to please wait for a moment and leaves to find the President. There is silence on the line. For the two men who sit facing each other across the Chief Justice's desk in the Palace of Justice, almost deafened by the incessant explosions of the guns reverberating upwards from the courtyard four floors below, the silence lasts altogether too long to bode any good.

Finally, the same voice in the Presidential Palace just up the street returns to the telephone and tells the Chief Justice that *El Señor Presidente* regrets that he cannot speak to him just now. *El Señor Presidente* is currently attending an urgent session of the cabinet. He asks that *El Señor Doctor* should kindly leave a phone number where he can be reached, and promises to call him back. The Chief Justice insists, courteously but with authority, that his call is urgent too. But the President's disappointing refusal to take his call does not overly surprise Justice Reyes. As though, yes, this too was to be expected on this day when everything else he feared, everything he said would and must occur, is indeed happening, right here inside his own courtroom, his own office. He was not surprised to hear the gunfire and the "*Vivas!*" of the guerrillas inside the Palace of Justice this morning, and he is not surprised now that the President will not take his call. Colombia's leading judge and Colombia's leading politician have known each other for most of their lives. Though both come from similar social backgrounds in the provincial middle classes there has always been a coolness between them. They are very different men: the warm, gregarious, ambitious politician and the austere, intellectual jurist. Shortly after two o'clock, on that afternoon of Wednesday, November 6, the President's secretary takes the Chief Justice's telephone number and promises that President Betancur will call him back. The Chief Justice tries a more direct approach: he hangs up the phone, goes to the door of his office, and begins shouting to be heard above the din of the gunfire raging below. "Please stop firing!" he yells. "This is the President of the Supreme Court speaking to you! Hold your fire! We are hostages! We have wounded people! We need the Red Cross! This is the President of the Supreme Court, Alfonso Reyes Echandia speaking to you! Please! Stop Firing!"

CHAPTER 5

No One Calls the Chief Justice

In which the President and his cabinet, assembled in the Presidential Palace two blocks away, decide to leave the solution to the problem posed by the guerrilla invasion of the Palace of Justice to the military; and Luis Otero, the Commandante Uno *of this ill-fated invasion, tries another approach to reach the President; while the Generals continue to deploy tanks and armored cars through the interior spaces of the great building, shooting at everything that moves.*

Inside the Presidential Palace, beyond the far end of the Plaza Bolívar, the President can hear the battle raging just two city blocks away. When the telephone call is received from the Chief Justice, President Betancur is still waiting for his Minister of Defense, General Vega Uribe. He has been waiting for Vega for ninety minutes. True, the general called him a short while ago to inform him that the tanks were about to enter the building. "It is the only way to save the lives of the hostages," Vega had said. "The Army must penetrate to the interior of the building." Betancur had gone along. It was too late now for the President to have second thoughts.

Belisario Betancur had no military expertise. He had never tried to understand the mentality of the men who commanded

Colombia's Armed Forces. In the beginning of his presidency he had largely ignored them; by the time he realised what a mistake that was he had lost a lot of ground. When his peace process was being drowned in chaos, and his own presidency foundering, he had been forced to confront the reality. He had come late to an understanding that the reality of Colombia did not go away just because so many people—the guerrillas, the voters—had agreed with him that it should. His predecessor, the last President, Liberal Party leader Turbay Ayala had said it best: "In Colombia," Turbay had said, "you either govern with the military or you don't govern at all." It was Turbay who, in the wake of the M-19 attack on the Dominican Embassy five years ago, had given the military extra powers with his Security Statute. Betancur had revoked the laws enshrined in the Statute but the military had not relinquished their power. Thinking of Turbay, Betancur makes a mental note to call him. Turbay and all the other ex-presidents who have been criticizing him all these years must be contacted at once. He will need their support if he is to survive now.

With the President in the private residential quarters of the Presidential Palace are the First Lady, the Ministers of Justice, of the Interior, of Communications, Foreign Affairs, Health, Labor and Education. The President has requested other members of the cabinet to remain in their offices for the time being so that he can have the benefit of any information they might obtain from independent sources around the town.

The assembled ministers have spent most of the previous sixty minutes listening to the radio to find out what was going on at the Palace of Justice. In this fashion, they have just learned that the tanks have broken through the main entrance into the building, buckling the priceless antique bronze doors in the process. The Ministers have refused a request from the Director General of the National Institute of Television and Radio to broadcast live from cameras already set up on the Plaza Bolívar. They have listened over the President's sound system, in ever deepening gloom, to an audiotape recording of the M-19 Proclamation, transmitted directly into the Presidential office by one of the many radio stations which received hand-delivered copies within moments of the attack.

For Belisario Betancur, this aggression by the M-19 constitutes an insane, perverse act of betrayal by the very people whom he and his administration have befriended. Even after the collapse of the truce the previous June, contacts between the guerrillas and his administration continued. That very morning a member of his Peace Commission took the early plane to the provincial town of Cali, with his personal authorization to resume secret negotiations with the M-19 leadership and give the peace process a second chance. Betancur knew, no one knew better, what his peace policies had cost him in loss of support and esteem among Colombia's traditional establishment. He could imagine the headlines, the commentators' columns in tomorrow's newspapers. He knew too the low opinion, bordering on contempt, in which the High Command of the Army held him and his policies.

Seated in his office, listening to the rhetoric of the M-19 Proclamation, Betancur felt bitterly betrayed. He sat passively, as if all of his energy and his willpower had seeped from him. As the M-19 recording reached its conclusion with the hackneyed guerrilla rallying call: "Colombians! With our weapons! With the People! To Power!" he turned to his colleagues, his voice dull with resignation and disillusionment, and said simply: "There is nothing to accept. Nothing to negotiate."

This decision of Betancur's, made spontaneously and without hesitation, without discussion, would define the government's actions for the duration of the crisis. As a result of what some of his colleagues later qualified uneasily as the physical and moral collapse of their chief, there was never, among the assembled ministers, any analysis, any debate. Throughout the duration of the crisis there was no discussion of the circumstances under which negotiations or dialogue with the aggressors, might be productive. According to the official record of the cabinet meetings held on that day, shortly after two o'clock that afternoon it was decided that, "There exists no reason to establish, directly or through intermediaries, any kind of negotiation with the attackers, because the sole fact of holding such negotiations would seriously compromise the independence and the normal functioning of the public authorities—at least those of the Judicial and Executive branches of the government; that is to say, the autonomy and survival of these authorities."

And that was it. With the exception of one brief initiative urged during the night by Betancur's friend Gabriel García Márquez, the President will cling to his decision to the bitter end. The military had chosen their solution to the crisis unilaterally and the President and his government were committed to backing them. There would not be any attempt to consider any alternative approach. How was "the autonomy and survival" of the Judicial branch of the government supposed to sustain its "independence and normal functioning" uncompromised, in the midst of the raging battle? No one who signed the text of this official communique has ever seen fit to explain. The decision had been taken to leave the fate of the Court and everyone else inside the Palace of Justice in the hands of the military. The President would focus all his energies on reducing the threat to the survival of his government.

Inside the Presidential quarters during these early hours of the crisis, the cabinet, alert to the M-19's ability to use the media for its own political purposes, discuss at length the desirability of establishing some form of censorship over radio and television broadcasts. As a consequence of this discussion, the Minister of Communications dictates the following text, sent by telex to all directors of radio and television stations:

> The National Government is grateful to the communications media for their collaboration in regard to the events that we all know [sic] and requests them to abstain from broadcasting, by radio or television, any information regarding the operations of the military, directly or through interviews or communicados, since such [interviews and communicados] increase the difficulties of any operation directed at saving the lives of those persons occupying the Palace of Justice and neighboring areas.

Cordially,
Noemi Sanín Posada
Minister of Communications.

The rules for the confrontation have been set. They are the rules of wartime. In this, the greatest threat to a Colombian government since the *"Bogotázo"* in 1948, the military will operate free of governmental interference and free from criticism by the media.

Sometime before three o'clock, the President withdraws to his private study to place a number of long distance telephone calls to the men whose political support will be crucial in the coming days if he and his government are to survive. Most of those he now seeks have been foes of his policies. He places calls to the two leaders of the traditional parties—both former Presidents of Colombia—and to each of the three other surviving former Presidents, all of whom are Liberals. Then he calls all of the candidates in the coming presidential elections in 1986. The calls take some time because two of the men he is most anxious to contact are vacationing with their wives in Europe. When the Minister of Defense, General Vega, accompanied by his Chief of Staff and by the Commander of the Bogotá Police, General Delgado Mallarino, arrive at the Presidential Palace shortly before three thirty in the afternoon to brief the President and cabinet on the status of the battle to retake the Palace of Justice, Betancur has finally reached the leader of his own party, former Conservative President Miguel Pastrana Borrero, in his hotel suite in Monte Carlo. By the time that Betancur hangs up the phone it is 3:45 p.m. A whole slew of callers meanwhile have been trying to reach the President on behalf of his captive Chief Justice. The General Secretary of the Presidency has taken all of the messages and promised to pass them along to his boss.

*   *   *   *   *

Inside the Palace of Justice, the battle continues to rage. Between two and three o'clock the army regroups. General Arias now divides his forces within the building. He assigns the troops of the

Presidential Guard, who occupy the lower levels of the building's west wing (the garage, basement and first floor) the responsibility for retaking the western and northern wings. The task of dislodging the guerrillas from the southern and eastern wings falls to the Artillery units under the tank commander, Colonel Plazas.

A short while earlier, at a little after 2:00 p.m., a third force has entered the fray. Some two dozen men of the Police Special Forces, the *GOES*, have already failed once to land on the roof of the Palace. Now they make a second attempt. Once again the helicopters are prevented from landing by soldiers in the adjacent buildings, who, according to a *GOES* squad survivor, are "firing left and right without rhyme or reason." But this time the helicopters succeed in releasing their load of Special Forces, by hovering at a height some fifteen to eighteen feet above the roof while the soldiers jump. One lieutenant who lands awkwardly, breaks a knee. Painful though his injury is he turns out to be one of the luckier members of the Special Forces team.

The *GOES* troops are the only ones deployed in the military counterattack who have trained in urban anti-terrorist combat. Thrown into the battle one and a half hours late, by commanding officers who are engaged in their own inter-force rivalry with the Army, everything about their mission is improvised. They land on the Palace roof without radio communications, without explosives for breaking through the locked roof entrance, without additional ammunition for their army-issue weapons, and without floor plans of the building. In the drenching rain that has begun to fall, the Special Forces will spend the next three hours on the exposed roof of the Palace, dodging the friendly fire of their trigger-happy comrades. Finally they will succeed in breaking down a door, only to find that it leads, not to the interior of the Palace, but to a sealed room containing the building's heating system.

The guerrillas, meanwhile, due largely to the strategic placement of their big machine guns, continue to control crucial access to the main stairways in the north and west. The hostages being held by guerrillas under the command of Almarales remain protected within the seclusion of the mezzanine bathroom. In the north and west of the building the guerrillas continue to hold all of the second and third floors. The stairways in the south wing, giving onto the square, are also controlled, though to a lesser degree, by the M-19 machine guns firing across the open space of the courtyard.

At around 2:30 p.m., artillery troops fighting their way up the main stairway to the right of the front entrance reach the second floor, where they rescue some one hundred and forty terrified people who had locked themselves in their offices when the M-19 invasion began and thus avoided being taken hostage. For the most part they are low-level employees of the court, secretaries, clerks, assistants to the judges, visitors to the court, members of the building staff, elevator operators, guards, chauffeurs, and the young employees of the building's cafeteria.

But not all of those rescued will be allowed to go home to their anguished families. In the interior of the Museum of the Casa Florero on the corner of the Plaza Bolívar where General Arias has established his headquarters, army intelligence, under the command of Colonel Edilberto Sánchez, is looking for two kinds of people: guerrillas who might try to escape dressed in civilian clothes carrying identity cards stolen from the hostages, and members of the staff of the building or the court who might have collaborated with the M-19. High on the army's list of suspected guerrilla collaborators are the workers in the cafeteria. When the manager of the cafeteria, Carlos Rodríguez Vera, and the eight young members of his staff, are brought by the soldiers to the Museum, Colonel Sánchez orders one of his agents to take them away for questioning. According to the later testimony of a defector, the colonel's instructions to his agents from the Charry Solano Counter Intelligence Battalion regarding Carlos Rodríguez Vera are precise: "Take him away; work on him for me; give me a report every two hours." Carlos Rodríguez is handcuffed and taken to the barracks of the Cavalry School to be tortured.

*   *   *   *   *

Inside his fourth floor office, where the Chief Justice, Luis Otero, Alfonso Jaquín, and eight other justices of the Supreme Court and the Council of State wait for the promised callback from President Betancur, Luis Otero decides they have kept the phone line open long enough. Smoke, from the incessant firing of the machine guns, tanks and hand grenades, rises through the building and has begun to seep into the crowded office. The noise and the smoke make it impossible to think and increasingly difficult to breathe or even to see through stinging eyes. It is time, Otero decides, for a fresh initiative.

It is 2:30 p.m. when the telephone rings in the downtown office of Juan Guillermo Ríos, an influential journalist, a man well-known to all of the M-19 leaders. "This is *Commandante Uno*" the voice says, "speaking from the Palace of Justice. Please call the President and tell him that if he orders a cease-fire, we will be able to settle this problem."

Also present in the Juan Guillermo's office when he receives the call from Luis Otero, is the only son of the Chief Justice, Yezid Reyes, for whom this attack on the Palace of Justice is the realization of a long dreaded nightmare. Yezid, who is himself a lawyer, has taken the continuous threats to his father's life very seriously. Only yesterday he met with the man directly responsible for the judge's safety, Chief of the Bogotá police General Víctor Delgado Mallarino, to complain that the protection being provided for his father was insufficient. The Police General, an old personal friend of the Reyes family, had assured Yezid that his fears were exaggerated, that the bodyguards assigned to his father were among the most experienced men in the Bogotá police force.

But Yezid was not convinced. Yezid has clients in the Bogotá jails, small-time criminals with contacts. Recently, the son of the Chief Justice heard from his clients of the rumors circulating through the underworld where politics and crime and drugs intersect: rumors that spoke of an imminent attack on the Palace of Justice by the M-19. Ever since the death of his mother a few years earlier, Yezid, who is unmarried, has been living with his father, and yesterday evening, at dinner, he determined to persuade him to accept a recent invitation to go to Europe to lecture. On that evening of November 5, Judge Reyes had accepted his son's advice. Father and son agreed that it would be prudent for the Chief

Justice to leave Colombia for a few weeks right after the Court announced its decision on the constitutionality of the Extradition Treaty. That night, last night, Yezid went to sleep relieved, calmed by the thought that within a week or so his father would be safely out of Colombia.

Now Yezid realizes that his efforts came too late. He has come to see Juan Guillermo Ríos, in whose office he now sits, believing him to be the man best situated to give him an accurate reading of the nature of this insane confrontation that has broken over his father's head. So when a flustered secretary bursts into her boss's office to announce the call from the Palace of Justice, from *"Commandante Uno,"* Yezid is able to speak directly with his father. When Judge Reyes takes the phone from Luis Otero to speak to his son, the first thing Yezid hears is the barrage of gunfire. It sounds as though the guns are firing right inside his father's office. "Don't worry," his father assures him. "Things in my office are calm. No one here with me is firing." And then comes the bad news: "I have tried to speak to the President," he says, "but he wouldn't take my call. Do whatever you can to get word to him that it is urgent to call an immediate cease-fire or there will be a massacre here. We must have a cease-fire in order to be able to talk."

There were two telephones on Judge Reyes' desk. Throughout the afternoon he uses one to make calls to the outside world and keeps the other free for the hoped-for return call from President Betancur. He reaches an old friend, the Chief of the Bogotá Police, General Delgado Mallarino. He reaches the director of the Secret Police, the DAS, Colonel Maza. Both men assure him they will pass along his request for a cease-fire. When Yezid calls back a few moments later his father is calm. "It must be that the order has not yet reached the troops fighting inside the Palace," his father says. "You keep up the pressure from your end and I'll keep trying to reach members of the government from here." Then, every five minutes or so he goes to the door of his office and repeats his litany of pleas to the Army. Hostages trapped in offices on the floor below will later testify to having heard his voice above the din of the battle as he called on the soldiers to hold their fire, to send in the Red Cross to evacuate the wounded, to rescue two pregnant women workers who have joined the group within his crowded office.

Yet as the afternoon wears on there will be no letup by the Army in their incessant onslaught and no return phone-call from President Betancur. By mid-afternoon the Army begins using gas in the building.

CHAPTER 6

The Radio

In which the Chief Justice, Judge Reyes Echandia, enlists the help of the President of the Senate, who talks to the President of Colombia, Belisario Betancur, who does not talk to the Chief Justice; the Judge talks to a radio reporter; and the citizens of Bogotá find out some facts about what is going on inside the Palace of Justice.

"The army was firing gas; the gases were coming up through the waste pipes into the bathroom. It was a blue-white color, very thick, and people were getting sick, some of the women began to faint, and it also burned—eyes, mouth, nose, ears..."

Gabriel's voice doesn't vary in pitch. It is very quiet in the *Café Roma*, the large room is almost empty, for it is the dead hour between breakfast and "onces,"—the traditional Bogotá eleven o'clock coffee break—and Gabriel has been talking, in his gentle, quiet monotone, for almost two hours. For almost two hours I have been scribbling, too busy and involved to notice that right behind him there sits a solitary man in front of an empty cup of coffee pretending to read the morning newspaper. Bogotá paranoia? I don't know, but fear concentrates the mind fast and I start to scrutinize him over Gabriel's shoulder. He holds the newspaper very still. He is not reading. "The guerrillas took off their jackets and soaked them with water and put them over the sink holes..."

135

Gabriel is back inside that claustrophobic bathroom with over forty people and the guerrillas and the ammunition and people vomiting and women fainting and people trying to help each other and the deafening, incessant roar of the guns. It all happened six months ago, but in his troubled eyes I see that it was last night, and every night, and that he cannot forget and has not yet escaped from that room. He cannot stop talking, and yet I must stop him. I don't want to alarm him, but I must, for his own sake, interrupt his story, because this idiot who is listening may be an informer working for the F-2 or B-2 or S-2 or the DAS or the DIJIN or the BINCI or who knows what other alphabet soup of intelligence, counterintelligence, secret police and army security agencies who populate Bogotá. Equally, he may be just a curious onlooker, or a journalist from the *El Tiempo* newspaper offices down the street, or a man waiting for his girlfriend who is late, and there is no possible way of knowinge. Please Gabriel, I say, forgive me for interrupting you, but would you mind if we went to my hotel? It's quieter there.

*   *   *   *   *

Three o'clock, on that afternoon of November 6, and raining. Across the Plaza Bolívar, from the windows of his office in the Congress building that look out directly onto the facade of the Palace of Justice, the President of the Senate, Senator Álvaro Villegas Moreno, has a ringside view of the battle. At three o'clock, a secretary comes into this office and hands the Senator a message with the phone number where the Chief Justice can be reached. He dials the number and to his intense relief the call is immediately answered by Judge Reyes in person. The two men converse briefly, succinctly, and within moments the President of the Senate calls the Presidential Palace, where the secretary who is monitoring all the calls immediately transfers the call to President Betancur. The Senator repeats to the President, word for word what he has just been told by the Chief Justice: The situation for the hostages is extremely dangerous, but the M-19 commanders are with him in his office waiting to commence talks aimed at their complete withdrawal from the building. As a first and indispensable step however, there must be a cease-fire. The Chief Justice is asking for the President to please order the Army to halt their attack. It is urgent. The lives of the hostage Supreme Court Justices and Councilors of State and scores of other innocent people depend on the army holding its fire. Senator Villegas gives the President the telephone number where the Judge can be reached. Betancur takes down the number, thanks the President of the Senate for his help, hangs up the phone, and continues his interrupted calls to the ex-Presidents, the party leaders and the presidential candidates.

*   *   *   *   *

Inside the Chief Justice's office on the fourth floor of the Palace of Justice, the hopes of the occupants, which had surged briefly during the course of the telephone call from the President of the Senate, fade. As the Army continues to pursue its relentless attack from below, the vanguard of the artillery troops, advancing up the stairs, threatens to overrun the guerrillas' defensive positions on the third floor. Luis Otero looks around the room at the judges. He sees the faces of nine men who, in any normal circumstance, in any country in the world, would command respect. "Don't any of you know anyone who has the power to stop them?" he asks. "Don't you understand that you're all going to die?" It is a foolish question, deserving of the contemptuous silence with which it is greeted.

The idea that he himself holds in his own hands the power to save the lives of the hostages by ordering the M-19 to lay down their guns unilaterally does not enter into Luis Otero's calculations. Guerrillas, Colombian guerrillas, live by a golden rule: they never submit. They may face defeat, failure and death, but they will die fighting. The alternative, to surrender, to give up their arms and hand themselves over to the enemy, is not an option. Too often it has resulted in extrajudicial execution, or death by torture. So the idea of taking upon themselves the ultimate consequences of their actions is not available. Luis Otero and Alfonso Jaquín would like to live, but if they have to, they will be ready to die for

"Freedom," for "The People," ready to go down fighting for "History." They are not ready to deal with the reality that faces them in the all too concrete and vulnerable human shape of the men and women who are trapped between their guns and the guns of their mortal enemy, the Colombian Army.

A hard and obvious moral choice, an eminently political choice, faced Luis Otero and his companions on that Wednesday afternoon. It shared the room with them in the individual figures of their hostages. But there is no evidence that any of them paused to give it a moment's thought. Or that they were even aware of it. Like the army officers commanding the counterattack, like the members of President Betancur's civilian government, the M-19 leaders had long ago locked their minds shut to any issue larger than the pursuit of their own agenda. Luis Otero, *Commandante Uno*, will tough it out. When the time comes, he will go to his own death, dragging the justices with him. By that time, he and the rest of the guerrillas will probably have convinced themselves that they are fighting to defend the lives of the hostages from a common enemy.

But first, there will be a change of tactics. Otero and Alfonso Jaquín begin calling the press, the radio and the television stations: "If the government doesn't call off the army, we will slaughter the judges one by one and throw their bodies out of the windows into the square..." they announce. "Let the President and the army take responsibility for the deaths of the hostages... "

Sometime before four o'clock, after two hours of incessant fighting on the stairs, the army reaches the third floor and the guerrillas retreat onto the passageway right outside the Chief Justice's office. In despair, Judge Reyes telephones the President of the Senate. Villegas Moreno is on the Senate floor having called a special session to draft a public resolution supporting the government in this hour of grave, national crisis. However, he has left instructions to be called out if word should come from the Chief Justice or from the President, and within five minutes he returns the Judge's call.

This time, when Judge Reyes picks up the phone, the Senator can hear the volleys of the guns exploding right beside the telephone. This time, there is a note of anguished incomprehension mingled with the urgency in the Judge's voice: "No," he says, "President Betancur has not called. We are on the fourth floor and the soldiers are on the third floor. We are surrounded. We are under the guns of the invaders and they have announced that if the troops reach the fourth floor they will kill all of us. They are going to kill us all, Villegas. For God's sake do something!" And then the phone is snatched from the Judge's hand and Alfonso Jaquín shouts hysterically down the line: "Tell the President that if they keep on firing we will blow up the Palace of Justice! We have enough dynamite in the basement to do the job. So what if we all die; but tell him! Urgently!"

Across the square, two blocks away, in his study in the Presidential Palace, President Betancur has just finished speaking to the leader of the Conservative Party, Miguel Pastrana Borrero, in Monte Carlo, and has begun receiving the first briefing from the Minister of Defense and the Chief of the Bogotá Police on the progress of the battle. He accepts the call from Villegas Moreno.

The Chief Justice? No, says Betancur, he hasn't talked to him yet. As a matter of fact he did try to reach him but that telephone number the Senator left must have been disconnected, there was no reply. On the contrary, Villegas replies. I've just hung up the phone, I've just been speaking with him at that number and he's waiting for your call now. And the Senator gives the President, word for word, the Chief Justice's eyewitness report of the situation on the fourth floor of the Justice Palace.

Betancur listens calmly, then, to the Senator's surprise he takes him into his confidence and informs him of his decision not to negotiate: "This is for your ears only," says Betancur, "I have consulted with all of *los Señores ex-Presidentes*,—with former President López in Paris and former President Pastrana in Monte Carlo— with the former Presidents Alberto Lleras and Carlos Lleras and Turbay Ayala, as also with all of the Presidential candidates. My decision is final. I will not intervene."

"Throughout my long life I have made it a constant to seek consultation and advice. Before any decision of transcendental importance I always try to listen...." So did the President later explain to the Special Commission of Inquiry investigating the events at the Palace of Justice the motive and the significance of the calls that he made to political leaders on that afternoon of November 6, while the battle between the Army and the guerrillas raged. "The gift of advice," he said, "for those who have the faith, is, additionally, a gift of the Holy Ghost; and I am a man of faith. Unhappily, this gift for advice is quite rare, but it does exist, and the gentlemen who are our ex-Presidents have it."

There was, nevertheless, as would be pointed out by various commentators later, something not entirely accurate about this description by the President. First, his decision not to negotiate and to give the army a free hand in the conduct of the operation had already been made long before seeking anybody's advice. Secondly, according to reports by some of the very people he contacted, the advice they gave him was actually quite varied and conflicting.

If anyone in Colombia was qualified to give advice, it is the former Liberal President, Julio César Turbay Ayala. It was Turbay's government that had successfully weathered the previous M-19 hostage-taking safari at the Embassy of the Dominican Republic, in 1980, without a single casualty. Turbay would later testify that when the President called he told him that, "it was my impression that if [the guerrillas] were allowed a little time to reflect, they would not act in the criminal manner that had characterized thus far their attack on the Palace." And he added his personal view, that "people who are given time to think will usually hesitate before putting their lives at risk, and the whole thing can then be concluded satisfactorily, as it was in the Embassy, when they gave themselves up simply in exchange for their lives and their freedom." And, the ex-President neglected to add, for one million dollars in cash.

Another Liberal leader, Luis Carlos Galán, the presidential candidate of the dissident "New Liberalism" wing of the party, advised that: "above all, the Government should not precipitate any action that might put at risk the lives of the hostages."

The advice that President Betancur evidently considered more congenial came from his own party's leader, former Conservative

President Miguel Pastrana, who told him: "For my part, what is at stake here is not simply a government, or a system, nor even the future of our society, but the entire system of values that form an intrinsic part of all our traditions and of the Christian civilization of which we form part; that is what is at risk here."

President Betancur is on the phone speaking with ex-President Pastrana when the Minister of Defense walks into his office. "One moment please Miguel," he says to the former President and leader of the Conservative Party. "If I put General Vega on the line, would you be so good to repeat to him what you have just said? I should like him to hear in your own words what you have just told me." And just in case the newly arrived Minister of Defense should have any lingering doubts about where the President stood in this gravest of national crises, Belisario Betancur passes the phone to General Vega Uribe.

*　*　*　*　*

The next caller to the Chief Justice was his son Yezid. Working out of the office of journalist Juan Guillermo Ríos, he has been trying for the past two hours to make contact with the President or indeed with anyone else in a position of authority. He has also been listening continuously to the radio reports and he has an idea: "Ask the *Commandante*," he suggests to his father, "if he thinks it might help if I arrange for you to talk to the radio?" And the answer that came back from the *Commandante* was a resounding "Yes." So at four thirty that afternoon, Yezid calls the news director at Radio Station Caracol, and gives the radio station the telephone number where his father can be reached.

In Latin America the radio is the cheapest and least censored medium of communication, and in consequence it is the most popular and the most influential. In Bogotá, throughout that long Wednesday afternoon, it was as if the entire population of the city had attached themselves to a radio set as to a lifeline. That the attack on the Palace of Justice would eventually find its place in the history books was never in doubt. So from the first salvo echoing across the open spaces of the Plaza Bolívar, the citizens of Bogotá had put the normal rhythms of their lives and their work on hold, and had come together in the bars and cafes, in shops and offices, even on buses and in the street, where pedestrians clung to their walkmans, or congregated in the cold November drizzle at street corners around anyone with a transistor. The magic of radio was that it alone could bring them information they had learnt to trust: the unguarded statement, the overheard exchange, the nitty- gritty details, which later, in the privacy of their own minds, they would recall and savor, as they fought to hold onto the scraps of recognizable truth. These would be their only defence against the miasma of lies.

And so it transpired that at 4:30 p.m. that afternoon, this rapt, skeptical audience, united in a common commitment to search for clues, read the signs, remain alert to catch the fleeting moment that might illuminate some aspect of a national catastrophe whose full significance could only dimly be intuited—found itself listening to the calm, compelling voice of the most respected jurist of his generation. His words punctuated by fusillades of machine gun fire and the deeper, more resonant explosions of the 90mm cannons of the army's tanks, his voice at times drowned out by other, desperate voices, screaming orders and obscenities in his immediate vicinity, the Chief Justice now tells his fellow citizens that from where he sits, at the very center of the battle raging between the army and the guerrillas, something is horrendously out of control.

Unless the President of the Republic takes immediate action to halt the fighting, the Chief Justice says, there is going to be a massacre in the Palace. Audibly shaken, the radio reporter on the other end of the telephone pulls himself together sufficiently to stammer out a question: "But Judge, Chief Justice Reyes, what should we do? What can we do?" And the answer comes back clearly, rising above the mayhem raging around him: "The details are not important. What is important is that the order finally be given, here within the building, for a cease-fire. Help us, please. The situation is dramatic. There must be an immediate cease-fire. Here within the Palace."

The reporter, doing what reporters are trained to do, tries to ask further questions: Is anybody wounded? How many of the judges are with the Chief Justice in his office? What are the demands of the guerrillas? Has any government official paid a visit to the Palace? What are the names of the justices imprisoned with him? Judge Reyes, his customary courtesy conflicting with his sense of urgency, tries a number of times to deflect the questions with a "Please, not at this moment," or "Please, later," or "No, not now, please," until finally the situation overcomes him and he cuts the reporter off: "No. Help us. It is a matter of life or death. Help us to get a cease-fire and we can talk later. Thank you." And the judge hangs up the phone.

In the Presidential Palace where this interview with Judge Reyes has played live to the stunned members of the cabinet gathered around their radio in the Presidential quarters, the reaction is immediate. The Minister of Communications rushes to the phone and moments later all live reporting from the Palace is broken off to bring an announcement of transcendental proportions: "Attention Colombians! We have news of the utmost importance for the entire nation! The football matches scheduled for tonight between *Millionarios* and *Unión Magdalena* here in the nation's capital, and between *America* and *Nacional* in Medellín, WILL take place as planned. Kick-off in the *Campín de Bogotá* at 8:00 p.m.. Be There! We repeat: The football matches planned for tonight..."

Among the millions of radio listeners across the country, the message is clear: from now on the radio coverage will be controlled. Not shut down, because, after all, this is Colombia, Oldest Constitutional Democracy in the Latin American Hemisphere. But every listener that afternoon understands. From now on, in accordance with local mores, the owners of Bogotá's radio stations, if they wish to continue their coverage from the scene, will follow certain "guidelines." "In the interests of the safety of the hostages" is how the Minister of Communications explains it to Yezid, when she orders his father's voice taken off the air. There will be no further live interviews transmitted from inside the besieged building. The tape of the conversation with the Chief Justice will not be replayed. Yet the sound of Judge Reyes' voice will continue to sear the memory of all who heard him. And the implications of his brief broadcast will continue to resonate from the grave, challenging and giving the lie to the official version of the events of this day, long after the battle's end.

The Plaza Bolívar, and the Palace of Justice, before the siege. *Courtesy of Ivan Rada.*

Wednesday, November 6, 2:00 p.m. The first tank approaches the Palace entrance. *Courtesy of El Espectador*.

Two other tanks follow closely behind. *Courtesy of El Espectador.*

Firing 90mm shells at close range, the leading tank bursts through the massive bronze doors. *Photograph by Daniel Jimenez, courtesy of Cromos.*

Led by Captain Talero, the "Hawk," the GOES troops land on the Palace roof a little after 2:00 p.m. *Courtesy of El Espectador.*

Wednesday, November 6, 10:30 p.m. Flames light the sky above the roof of the burning Palace. *Courtesy of El Espectador.*

Thursday, November 7, 2:00 a.m. A shell fired from the opposite end of the square blasts a jagged hole in the granite facade of the Palace, through which a thick column of black smoke escapes into the night air. *Photograph by Daniel Jimenez, courtesy of Cromos.*

Interior wall of one of the toilet stalls with the exit points of several bullet holes marked and counted by the morgue investigators. *Unpublished photograph, courtesy of the morgue investigators.*

The Palace bathroom after the battle. *Courtesy of El Espectador.*

The inner wall of the bathroom exposed after explosives have ripped away the outer wall protecting the air duct. *Unpublished photograph, courtesy of the morgue investigators.*

The openings caused in the bathroom wall by the penetration of the first rocket. *Unpublished photograph, courtesy of the morgue investigators.*

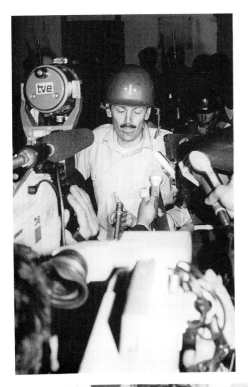

Wednesday night, November 6.
Colonel Alfonso Plazas Vega exits
from the Palace. *Photograph by Daniel
Jimenez, courtesy of Cromos.*

General Vega Uribe (center), Minister
of Defense, and General Mallarino
(behind Vega), Commander of the
Police, arrive on the scene after the
battle is over. *Photograph by Daniel
Jimenez, courtesy of Cromos.*

Thursday afternoon, November 7.
Doctor Martínez Saenz talking to the
press outside the Museum command
center. *Photograph by Daniel Jimenez,
courtesy of Cromos.*

"Operacíon Limpieza." Army intelligence agents at work. *Photograph by Daniel Jimenez, courtesy of Cromos.*

"Operacíon Limpieza." Survivors leaving the building under arrest. *Photograph by Daniel Jimenez, courtesy of Cromos.*

The interior of the Palace, with people under arrest. *Courtesy of Sygma.*

A wounded survivor leaves the Palace under arrest. *Photograph by Daniel Jimenez, courtesy of Cromos.*

The "rescued" hostages leave the Palace of Justice under escort. In the background, the museum command center—their immediate destination. *Courtesy of Sygma.*

The President, Belisario Betancur Cuartas. *Courtesy of El Espectador*.

The Minister of Justice, Enrique Parejo. *Courtesy of El Espectador*.

▲ Chief Justice of the Supreme Court, Alfonso Reyes Echandia. *Courtesy of Ivan Rada.*

Supreme Court Justice Manuel Gaona Cruz. *Courtesy of El Espectador.* ➤

Commandante Uno, Luis Otero, founding member of the M-19 Revolutionary Movement.
Courtesy of El Espectador.

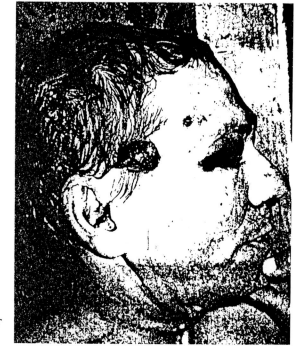

The corpse of Andres Almarales, photographed in the morgue, showing the bullet wound that killed him.
Unpublished photograph, courtesy of the morgue investigators.

CHAPTER 7

The Other Palace

In which the Commander of the National Police, General Mallarino, telephones Chief Justice Reyes in his besieged office on the fourth floor of the Palace of Justice; and the Minister of Justice tries to call Judge Reyes back, and fails, and has an argument with the Police Commander; while the Generals send a calming message to the Cabinet Room as they close in on their enemy on the fourth floor of the Palace of Justice; and when a true account of these events in the besieged Supreme Court does finally reach the Presidential Palace, it is not heeded.

The radio interview with the Chief Justice affected the dynamic within the Presidential Palace. Those among the President's ministers who are uneasy about their chief's passivity now feel emboldened to push for some involvement in the crisis. There is a discussion.

According to the report furnished to the cabinet by General Vega and General Delgado Mallarino, the army is now closing in on the last of the guerrillas, the remnants of whose forces are barricaded on the fourth floor. The generals claim the M-19 will not be able to hold out much longer because their ammunition must soon run out. This, the Generals explain, is the reason for the continuous barrage of gunfire that the ministers can hear from where they sit, gloomily waiting for some ray of hope from the military men who stalk in and out, pacing the corridors, sending and receiving strange, coded messages to each other, over the crackle of their walkie-talkies.

The guerrillas will soon be forced to exhaust their stores of ammunition, the Generals insist, because the troops arrived in the building in time to prevent the M-19 from unloading most of their supplies. Any talk of a cease-fire, just when the Army is on the point of a breakthrough in their efforts to free the hostages on the fourth floor, could be fatal. Nothing that might permit them to regroup and improve their position militarily or strategically can be considered.

There is also, the Generals add, some danger of an uprising in the streets of Bogotá—it is possible that something similar to the "*Bogotázo*" of 1948 could happen, manipulated by those criminal elements who support the M-19's political positions. Naturally Army Intelligence is on top of this subversive activity and will contain any outbreaks that occur, but certain streets and stores in the center of town have already been attacked and looted, and in such circumstances a cease-fire could demonstrate a lack of will. It would be interpreted as an indication of official weakness.

The President and his cabinet have no independent intelligence to counter these reports from the Generals. Cut off from any objective, independent analysis of the crisis, their isolation renders them particularly vulnerable to the psychological intimidation of these military experts. The very idea of the conflict in the Palace of Justice spilling out into the streets of Bogotá and other cities across this disorderly, anarchic country is naturally a terrifying one to the politicians. The ghost of the assassinated Gaitán haunts the cabinet room.

Into the middle of this discussion comes yet another desperate telephone call from Judge Reyes. As he talks to the Secretary of the Presidency, the assembled ministers listen to the conversation on the President's conference phone. The Secretary takes the Judge's number, makes yet another promise that someone will call him back, very soon. The ministers discuss whether indeed the voice they have heard really belongs to the Chief Justice. Some think it does, others are not so sure. The President makes a decision: The person who should talk to the Chief Justice, he decides, is Judge Reyes' close, personal friend, General Delgado Mallarino, Chief of the National Police. So General Delgado is instructed to call the Judge back to explain to him the point of view of the military and the government's decision not to negotiate with the M-19 leaders. He is further authorized to send a message to the M-19 from the President: If they surrender to the Army now they will receive all the protection of the law and a trial in the civilian courts.

It is close to five o'clock when General Mallarino speaks to his old friend of many years, Judge Alfonso Reyes Echandia. The President and the cabinet listen in on their conversation. The guerrillas by this time are firing at the advancing soldiers from inside his office as the Chief Justice vehemently insists that only a cease-fire will save the lives of the hostages. General Mallarino replies that the army and the government are doing their utmost to save the lives of the hostages but that "the institutions of Colombia are at risk and the government is under the constitutional obligation to defend them." The General then asks to speak to the guerrilla leader.

Commandante Uno, Luis Otero, comes to the phone. "You are surrounded" Mallarino tells him. "If you surrender now you can save a great many lives, including your own. The government is prepared to guarantee that your lives will be respected and that you will receive an impartial trial in a civilian court."

There is a brief moment of silence on the line. A moment during which Luis Otero recalls only the broken promises, the many incidents in the recent past when amnestied, unarmed guerrillas had surrendered to police or army units and been shot down in cold blood. Luis Otero misjudges the situation; he makes the dreadful mistake of thinking that now, finally, negotiations will begin; he thinks that this is only the first offer from a government in distress. "There is no way that we can accept that kind of an offer from you," he replies. "We know how your police respect our lives. The M-19 came to the Palace to carry out a military-political operation of vital significance to the country, which must proceed at whatever cost, and the lives of our hostages are precisely the guarantee that we will prevail."

General Mallarino counsels Otero to reflect on his offer and when he has thought it over to call him back. Otero replies that if that is all the General has to say to him he needn't bother to call again. Then, one last time, Judge Reyes seizes the phone: "They are going to kill us Víctor Alberto," he says; "how can you people allow them to kill us?" But Víctor Alberto has no answer for his good, life-long friend Alfonso. He promises to call again and hangs up the phone.

Inside the Judge's office the guns are blazing away, laying down a stream of bullets along the passageway leading to the access point onto the fourth floor, at the top of the stairs. Otero, with the frantic Jaquín beside him, is still bluffing. But after his conversation with his old friend, the Director of the National Police, Judge Reyes must have understood that the unthinkable is going to happen: he and all of his colleagues have been abandoned by a government too weak, and too compromised in the eyes of the military, to attempt now to extricate them from the insanity of this war that is breaking over their heads. Never mind that it is his life, and the lives of the men and women sharing the room with him, whose combined intellect and character constitute the soul and fiber of the 'institution' in whose name, and over whose 'autonomous' existence, this fight will be permitted to continue. They, and everything he cares about, every value to which he has committed his life, are worthless now. They are only the battlefield on which others will settle old scores. Those with the guns will have the last word. So has it ever been in Colombia.

Judge Reyes will not give in to despair. For the next two hours he continues to make calls, to receive calls. He will go on striving to get his message across to the soldiers as they advance. But he must have known it was useless.

*　　*　　*　　*　　*

It is past five o'clock. The Army has cut the electricity and it is dark already inside the Palace of Justice. Outside, the Plaza

Bolívar, lit by the lamps of the television cameras, resembles some Hollywood war movie. Crews from CBS and NBC have joined the Colombian journalists milling around the square. Soon, the pictures they are taping will be beamed by satellite into millions of homes in Miami, New York and Los Angeles in time for the seven o'clock news. The pictures will horrify and also confirm the viewers' preconceptions of Latin America as a place of incomprehensible violence and bad government. Nothing in the presentation of the news will help shed any light on the central questions raised by these pictures on their television screens, namely: to what purpose is a national army using tanks to attack the building that houses the country's Supreme Court? What possible relevance can 90mm shells, fired into such a building at close range, have to any operation whose stated objective is to save the lives of hostages? Who is in charge of this carnage?

Inside the Cabinet room in the Presidential Palace, no one raises these questions either. No one feels equipped to do so. The questions themselves are off limits. It is "a military matter." It is not for civilian politicians who have, in any case, brought this disaster upon themselves and their countrymen by encouraging the guerrillas in the first place.

Still, the original consensus of the government to do nothing, born of the initial shock of the M-19 attack, is growing shaky. Nerves are fraying. Something of the desperation they have heard in the words and the voice of the Chief Justice, lingers stubbornly in the claustrophobic air of this protective enclave where the ministers feel themselves trapped ever deeper in their helplessness. And the tension, that the optimism of the Generals does nothing to allay, intensifies. The Generals sense it. President Betancur, too, sensitive in the extreme to how his role will be perceived by that larger audience of his peers in the *clase dirigente*, he also feels it.

Some among the cabinet discuss the difference between holding the line on "no negotiations," and opening a space "for a dialogue," with the M-19 leaders. The Minister of Justice, Enrique Parejo, is particularly distressed by the tone of the conversation between the Chief of Police and Luis Otero. Parejo, like most Colombian intellectuals of his generation, has had frequent contact with people from the M-19 and he knows that the Chief of Police was the last person who should have been delegated at this moment to speak to Luis Otero. Parejo knew Jaime Bateman, and he is a friend of Andrés Almarales. The two men are *paisanos*, they come from the same small coastal town of Cienega and as children they sat together in the same tropical classroom. Later, in the Colombian way in which local antecedents and loyalties survive everything except personal betrayal or dishonor, they remained friends. During the peace process, through all their disagreements, they continued to see much of each other.

Now Parejo, supported by the two women in the cabinet, the Minister of Communications, and the Minister of Education, leads the challenge against the military. Later, the military will not forgive this bid for independence, nor his refusal to be intimidated, his courageous public recounting to the Commission of Inquiry of the facts as he lived and experienced them inside the cabinet room on that Wednesday afternoon. If, he says now, he can just reach Andrés Almarales by phone, then maybe he can talk some sense into him. Almarales is a reasonable man. He will listen. What is more, he will trust Parejo's word that the government will honor the deal being offered to the guerrillas by the President.

After about thirty minutes of discussion, Enrique Parejo persuades some members of the cabinet to go along with him and Betancur gives him authority to proceed. Between 5:30 and 6:00 p.m., the Minister of Justice tries feverishly to locate Andrés Almarales. He starts by dialing the telephone number in Judge Reyes' office on which General Mallarino had spoken to Luis Otero just thirty minutes earlier. The line is occupied. He waits a few minutes and dials a second time. The number is still busy. Grabbing the telephone book, Enrique Parejo and his two allies start methodically going through all of the phone numbers listed in the fourth floor offices of the Palace of Justice. The phones ring in abandoned, empty rooms.

Just then the door opens, and General Mallarino, who had left the cabinet room during the previous discussion, returns, complete with walkie-talkie, to give the ministers the very latest briefing from the Justice Palace. He has good news, he says. The troops of the Special Forces (GOES) have just located an iron door on the roof of the building and are within moments of breaking through it. As soon as the army drops them the dynamite they need to blow the door open, the combined forces of the Army and the Police will be in position to retake the fourth floor.

Appalled, Enrique Parejo stops dialing long enough to insist that it has been agreed by the Cabinet that he should try to reach Almarales and attempt to settle things peacefully. The least the military can do is to give the government enough time to make the contact. He says they must have an agreement that the Special Forces delay their attack on the fourth floor until he has had the chance to find and speak to Almarales.

According to the Justice Minister's later testimony to the Commission of Inquiry, both his colleagues in the Cabinet and President Betancur concur, and General Mallarino, the Chief of Police, leaves the room with instructions to pass along the government's order to the Army commanders to delay the attack by the GOES troops until further notice. Later, both the President and his cabinet colleagues will deny that any such agreement ever existed, or that any such "interference" with the military operation underway to rescue the hostages was ever attempted. However, on that afternoon, as the minutes run by and their level of anxiety surges, Parejo and the others continue to pursue their search for Almarales. Now, when the Justice Minister tries once again to call Judge Reyes' office, there is no reply. The phone rings again in another empty room.

Enrique Parejo is a highly strung, hot-tempered man. He is also intelligent, sensitive, and courageous. He cares a great deal about the lives of his many friends, trapped in the battle between the Army and the M-19. So when, at about ten minutes to six, General Mallarino re-enters the cabinet room, still carrying his walkie-talkie, to announce that the army commanders on the scene have just communicated to him that the GOES troops have successfully blown open the door on the Palace of Justice roof, and are even now retaking possession of the entire fourth floor, Parejo explodes. Before the horrified gaze of his colleagues he turns all of his frustration and fury on Mallarino and denounces the military.

He accuses them "of contemptuous disregard for an agreement worked out with the cabinet with the acquiescence of the President." He says the army have made fools of the government. He says now he understands why there is no reply to any of the phones on the fourth floor. The army's tempestuous entry onto the fourth floor, he says, in the very area where the justices were being held hostage, has probably cost the lives of all of the hostages.

President Betancur did not witness Parejo's outburst. He had left the room sometime earlier to try once more to reach the only ex-President with whom he has not yet made contact—Alfonso López Michelsen. López, on vacation in Paris, is dining out that night with a mutual friend of his and the President's, Gabriel García Márquez. It is midnight in Paris, and Betancur, knowing full well that García Márquez' many friends in Colombian political and press circles will certainly be calling him from Bogotá, is extremely anxious to be the first person to reach López Michelsen with the news from the Palace of Justice.

So now General Mallarino, embarrassed, retreats before the onslaught of Parejo, to find out from the army what they know about the hostages. In five minutes he returns. There is no need to worry, he says. The Minister's fears are groundless. The army has just reported that when the troops broke in on the fourth floor they found no one dead or alive. It appears that the guerrillas have moved everyone to a bathroom somewhere, on a lower floor. Immensely relieved, Enrique Parejo is temporarily mollified. The atmosphere in the Cabinet room cools down.

It will take some time for the government to find out that the army is lying, that the battle for the fourth floor is just beginning, that the Army Commander, General Arias, and the Police Commander, General Vargas Villegas are at that very moment throwing artillery troops—advancing up the stairs from the south west— and Police, the GOES Special Forces,—entering through the roof from the southeast—into a desperate effort to dislodge the guerrillas. The M-19, far from retreating to a bathroom on a lower floor, have abandoned the Chief Justice's office to consolidate their position in a conference room in the north eastern corner of the fourth floor. From this room, where some thirty to forty hostages are trapped, barricaded behind office furniture and filing cabinets, Luis Otero and fifteen or so guerrillas prepare to make their last stand. From this room, over an hour later, Judge Reyes will make his final phone calls before all of the telephones in the building go dead.

The Chief Justice talks for the last time to Senator Villegas Moreno at seven-fifteen that evening. Senator Villegas was precise about the timing of Judge Reyes' last call, because it came after the Senator had left his office to preside over the Congressional vote on a resolution of support for President Betancur's handling of the crisis. The full session of the Congress began at 7:00 p.m., and shortly after that an aide arrived in the Senate chamber to tell the Senator that the Chief Justice needed to talk to him, urgently. In his letter to the presiding judges of the Commission of Inquiry, the President of the Senate wrote: "I left the Vice-President of the Senate presiding over the session and went to the second floor office; I rang the number that the Chief Justice had given me earlier. His secretary answered the phone, [then] I spoke with him; he was not the same man; he had been affected; he told me that it had still not been possible for him to speak to the President, in spite of the fact that he had called [President Betancur] repeatedly; he said they were all going to be killed, and asked me to please obtain a cease-fire, to please take action on the hostages' behalf. I told him I would do so immediately. I rang the [Presidential] Palace, and it was not possible to talk to the President. He was in a session of the cabinet."

The President of the Senate did not hang up, however, and he did manage to talk to the Minister of Foreign Affairs. Minister Augusto Ramírez Ocampo came to the phone and Senator Villegas gave him a blow by blow account of his conversation with the Chief Justice. "I informed him of the drama of this situation; I asked him to do something, to communicate what was happening to the President; I answered all kinds of questions that he put to me about the different phone calls; he asked me to repeat word for word what Judge Reyes had said, and he hung up, promising to transmit to *el señor Presidente* the pleas for help that Judge Alfonso Reyes Echandia was making on behalf of the justices."

This conversation with Senator Villegas, occurs about one hour after the arrival of the GOES Special Forces on the fourth floor of the Palace of Justice. It is the first piece of evidence that anyone within the Presidential Palace has received to alert them to the fact that the information they were given by General Mallarino was untrue.

Yet here the narrative breaks down. To this day no one knows what the Minister of Foreign Affairs did when he hung up the phone. At the same time that this conversation betwen him and Senator Villegas is taking place, in another room of the Palace, President Betancur is giving a very different picture of the situation in the Palace of Justice to ex-President Alfonso López, whom he has finally reached in Paris. As the evening progresses there will be no change in President Betancur's determination to do nothing to interfere with, or to question, any aspect of the "military operation underway to rescue the hostages."

Meanwhile, alerted by the Minister of Defense—after the agitation created by Parejo's row with General Mallarino—that the civilians are getting restless, General Rafael Samudio, Army Chief of Staff, passes along a warning to the Chief of Staff of the XIIIth Brigade, Colonel Ramírez Lozano, who in turn relays it to the Commander on the scene in charge of the operation, General Jesus Arias Cabrales. The recording of their internal communications sets the scene for the army's stepped-up attack on the fourth floor of the Palace of Justice moments before the final onslaught:

> *Paladín* 6 [General Samudio] says that the situation here has caught cold. There must be noise! There must be action! If you need more ammunition, make use of everything you need, but don't let up on them! He says the situation has caught cold, that it is getting cold. Over.

To which his interlocutor within the building, General Arias, replies:

> Well that may be what it looks like from there, but here we're still trying to knock out the groups on

the second, third and fourth floors, trying to drive them into a corner, with the objective of wiping them out then, within one sector, and so avoiding major destruction. THERE ARE STILL PERSONNEL WHO ARE FOREIGN TO THE ACTION STILL INSIDE HERE.

And Colonel Ramírez responds:

Well he says he is worried by the situation. That we must not start now saving on ammunition OR ANY DESTRUCTION THAT YOU NEED TO CARRY OUT. DON'T WORRY ABOUT ANY NECESSARY DESTRUCTION. There must be Action!

General Arias complies. Given the green light by his superiors, in the course of the next two hours he proceeds to bombard the fourth floor of the Palace of Justice with every weapon at his disposal.

CHAPTER 8

The Palace on Fire

---

*In which the Special Forces arrive on
the fourth floor of the Palace of Justice
from the roof too late to do any good;
and General Arias, Commander of 'the
operation to rescue the hostages,' orders
army engineers to dynamite openings
in the roof above the room where the
guerrillas and the hostages are trapped;
and in the end, a fire rages through the
fourth floor, consuming all before it.*

"*One of our major problems was the soldiers who had been posted in the
adjoining buildings as sharpshooters. They were firing right and left
without rhyme or reason and we had constantly to find cover from them
because otherwise we were going to be hit. Indeed, many of the soldiers
who were wounded inside the Palace were hit by their own, by 'friendly
fire.' They themselves admit it.*"—From the recording of an internal
investigation into "The Rescue Operation at The Palace of Justice," conducted by official instructors of the Police Special Forces with surviving
members of the GOES assault unit.

The participation by the Police Special Forces—the GOES—in
the attack against the guerrillas on the fourth floor of the Palace of
Justice, takes place at about 5:30 p.m. that evening of November 6.
It is a fiasco from start to finish. For the young men who take part
in it, the elite of the force, it is something worse.

It is already four o'clock and beginning to get dark when, having wasted two hours trying to break down the wrong door, they finally discover the roof entrance, masked behind a skylight. The door is constructed of solid iron and none of the equipment they have brought with them is capable of breaking its steel locks. They also have no radios, or none that work, but they do have a field telephone, and the Captain in command manages to make contact with Police headquarters to order up some dynamite. The line is bad, or maybe the person on the other end misunderstands; whatever the reason, the explosives they so urgently need are deposited at the opposite end of the Plaza Bolívar where they are left on the steps of the *Capitolio* building.

The Captain in charge is a highly motivated young officer nicknamed "the Hawk," who received his special training from Israeli commandos. The Hawk, a Captain Talero, believes passionately in his mission to get to the fourth floor offices in advance of the guerrillas and so rescue the hostages. While his men huddle in a corner of the roof in the driving rain, unable to draw attention to themselves because of the continuous gunfire coming their way from soldiers posted in surrounding buildings, the Hawk goes half-crazy with frustration. Finally, taking matters into his own hands, he spends all the ammunition in his submachine gun—the only ammunition he was supplied with—in an assault on the steel door. It is almost five-thirty by the time he blasts the door open. Followed by three of his lieutenants he leads the charge down a stairway into a narrow passage, around a corner onto the main passageway of the fourth floor, and straight into the fire of the waiting M-19 machine gun—still located diagonally across the patio on the third floor landing of the northwest stairway.

By 5:30 p.m. it is pitch dark inside the fourth floor. The sole source of light penetrating the dark and the smoke is a single beam shining from the jammed door of one of the elevators directly into the eyes of the advancing Special Forces, blinding them to their surroundings. The members of the Special Forces squad have received no briefing, seen no maps, no sketches of the interior of the Palace complex. They don't know where they are, who is shooting at them, nor from what angle the fire is coming. As they hit the ground and drag themselves to the edge of the corridor to look through the balustrade down into the patio below, all they see are the guns of the army's tanks and artillery firing in their direction. "Those armored cars, they were firing at anything that moved," a survivor recalled. The new arrivals assume that all of the gunfire is coming from the army. Lying on his stomach, the Hawk begins to advance down the passage leading north. As he reaches the corner he turns, lifts his head and shouts: "Don't shoot! We're the Police!" But only his companions hear the response: "And we're the Guerrillas!" The Captain is already dead, his head blown away in a burst of machine gun fire from the guerrillas' gun.

Within ten minutes of their penetration inside the Justice Building from the roof, the Hawk is dead, and his second in command, another captain has also been seriously injured. A short while later, when the Army Commander, General Arias, and the Police Commander, General Vargas Villegas, arrive on the fourth floor to command the attack in person, the survivors of the Special Forces attempt to recover the body of their slain leader. But one after the other, three more members of the unit are cut down and seriously wounded by the same gun that killed their commanding officer. The body of Captain Talero is never recovered.

Then the building catches fire. Gabriel recalls how it seemed to his group of hostages, locked away in their protected northwest corner of the building, far from the scenes of life and death struggle on the fourth floor:

"We thought we smelled smoke, but we didn't know where it could be coming from. Almarales said it was the firing of the guns from the first floor. Then the bathroom began to fill with smoke. I felt as though I was going to suffocate. The guerrillas didn't say much. They filled up buckets of water that they placed around the floor and they instructed us to lie down with our faces against the floor because the smoke would rise. Then a young woman guerrilla called Mónica came running into the bathroom calling for Andrés Almarales. She was crying: '*Commandante, Commandante,* they've put a torch to the building! The building is on fire! They want to burn us out!'"

The fire that began at about 5:30 p.m., in the southeast corner of the ground floor Library, spread swiftly through the entire southeastern wing of the building. Later the army would claim that the M-19 had started it. They were burning the files of their paymasters, the drug barons, the army said. In fact, though no one knows with absolutely certainty what happened, the results of the tests carried out later by ballistics experts and investigators demonstrated the most likely cause to have been the recoil effect of the army's rockets. Tests proved that if fired by a soldier standing within twenty feet of the wood-lined walls of the library that housed Colombia's legal archives, the intense heat generated by the rocket's rear blast could have ignited the wooden panelling. In any event, in a shelved area stacked high with old papers, files, books and newspapers, the quantities of explosives used virtually guaranteed a conflagration.

Rising through the building the smoke at first fills the offices on the lower floors, where those who have been lucky enough to avoid the guerrillas on their first sweep through the building are still in hiding. Faced with the prospect of being burnt alive, or perishing from smoke inhalation, many of these people now emerge onto the passages where, between 5:30 and 6:30 p.m., soldiers advancing up the stairs to the fourth floor find them and bring them out to safety. When the smoke penetrates to the bathroom of an office on the second floor where Clara Castro, wife of the Minister of the Interior Jaime Castro, has been hiding since noon, she abandons the comparative safety of this inner sanctum and manages to telephone her husband, whom she locates in the Presidential Palace. Moments later, the army starts trying to find her. From his post in the Defense Ministry, Colonel Ramírez gets on the radio to Colonel Plazas who is directing the attack by artillery troops on the fourth floor.

> RAMÍREZ: Paladín 6 (General Samudio) says that in the sector where Arcano 6 (General Arias) is, the second floor, in the southeast, there is the wife of the Minister of Government, and will you try to shout to her and let her know that she can come

out, that she's not in any danger. At least try to find out where precisely she is and let me know. Over.

PLAZAS: You say the second floor? At the moment I'm on an upper floor but we'll try again. What's her name? Over.

RAMÍREZ: Actually I don't know her name but it's reported here that Arcano 22 is on the second floor. He's talking from the second floor. So the order from Paladín 6 is that you should try to establish contact with her, verbally, without precipitating any kind of situation, and if possible she should get out, or at least give her the prerogative of choosing. Over.

PLAZAS: QSL. (O.K.) I'll pass the order to Arcano 22 who is on that floor. Over.

Clara Castro was found and rescued by the soldiers. Others were not so lucky. Shortly after this conversation Colonel Ramírez talked to another of the officers inside the Palace of Justice again:

RAMÍREZ: A woman just called here, the wife of a magistrate called Carlos Urán, and gave the details of one of the offices where there are some people, and the telephone numbers of those offices. Are these details any help to you?

RESPONDENT [UNKNOWN]: It helps. Over.

RAMÍREZ: Office 313. Six people. All *doctores*. [Magistrates].

But the soldiers never made any attempt to reach Office 313, where Associate Justice Carlos Urán, Justice Horatio Montoya Gil and four other judges still in hiding would eventually find their way, several hours later, through the dark and the fire, to end up with Gabriel and Judge Gaona and the hostages in the northwest bathroom. Nor did they ever try to make their way to the adjacent offices—315, 316, 317, and 318—all of which held judges and staff of the court who had been stranded by the fighting. From all of these offices calls for help were received by the Defense Ministry, but their occupants were ignored by the army and abandoned to their fate.

Sometime after 6:30 p.m. General Arias sums up for the Defense Ministry the state of the operation to date:

> ARIAS: At this moment we are evacuating approximately 20 hostages that we found on the third floor, so we hope we can rescue them all; it was one of those situations where they were barricaded [inside their offices]. The first floor is controlled, the second floor controlled, on the third floor we have to finish the evacuation and clean up what's left of the subversives; in the fourth floor, the explosives didn't work. They only opened a couple of very small holes, so we haven't been able to clean up there yet. They are barricaded in there behind cupboards and file cabinets, and it's been a bit difficult; there have already been seven wounded among the GOES, so now we're waiting for this evacuation to finish up so we can put in an artillery unit, because the GOES has been very diminished at this time by their losses, physically and also their morale. Over.

His correspondent in the Ministry of Defence, who needs some good news to keep the peace within the Cabinet, pushes Arias to find the Chief Justice.

> THE MINISTRY: Do you know anything about the President of the Court? Is he among the 20 you're evacuating?

ARIAS: Negative, negative. So far we haven't heard anything. So far we've evacuated about 14 people, there are still some people to get out.

THE MINISTRY: As soon as you get any information transmit it to Paladín 6 [General Samudio, Army Chief of Staff] so that he can contact Corage 6 [General Vega Uribe, Minister Defence.] Over.

ARIAS: QSL.QSL. [OK OK] The hostages are being handed over to Arcano 2 [Colonel Edilberto Sánchez, of Army Intelligence] who is doing the identification.

But the army has other priorities, other, more urgent problems to deal with. In the Museum on the Plaza Bolívar, Colonel Sánchez is highly encouraged by the discovery that several guerrillas have infiltrated the latest group of hostages to escape the burning building wearing clothes taken from the dead or from hostages.

COL. SÁNCHEZ: [Speaking to the Defense Ministry]. Hey there! To raise your spirits, inform all units that the subversives are asking for civilian clothes from the personnel that remain as hostages in order to enable them to evacuate the building... We've already sent two individuals to the Police to do the necessary and later they'll be sent to our QPH [XIII Brigade Headquarters].

Later, the Army would consistently deny that any of the M-19 guerrillas had left the building alive. None of those detected by Colonel Sánchez were seen alive again.

"Informing on the situation," General Arias calls in to report to the Army Chief General Samudio: "Basement, first and second floors, completely liberated and the third floor, partially. Because of the fire that they instigated in the Library the southeast section is in flames; but we don't need to occupy that part...Paladín, I report, on the fourth floor it has not been possible to liberate it completely because the GOES who held that mission suffered four casualties, among them an officer. So they were unable to take the floor, and the personnel that we had on the terrace had to be evacuated because of the fire which was started by the bandits in the Library...."

From the operational headquarters in the Museum, where army intelligence agents are busy collaborating with the police to identify the living and the dead, the wounded and the subversives, Colonel Sánchez is now able to report that they have brought out one hundred and twenty-eight hostages and arrested five guerrillas. The casualties include five policemen, one soldier, and five guerrillas. There are also, he reports, three civilian casualties, caused by the guerrillas when they stormed the basement, and one badly wounded civilian who has been sent to the military hospital where intelligence agents are trying to establish "to what group he belongs." In addition four soldiers and three police Special Forces have been wounded.

"Tell me something," General Samudio asks General Arias, "what do you know about the President of the Court and those who were with him?" "Negative, negative" Arias replies. "Among the personnel who have been evacuated, one hundred and twenty-eight people more or less, his presence has not been verified. Over." "*Bueno.* Proceed," replies Samudio, laconically. And General Arias does proceed. Responding to pressure from his superiors, he intensifies the attack on the fourth floor conference room where the guerrillas and their hostages are now cornered. There will be no further enquiries concerning the whereabouts of the Chief Justice. From now on, from the point of view of the army, it is as though the President of the Supreme Court and all of his colleagues have simply vanished. As if they have vanished into some mysterious, undiscoverable space within the smoke-filled darkness of the vast building which is now almost entirely occupied by army troops.

For even as the flames continue to consume the third floor, the attack on what General Arias calls "a last pocket of resistance in the fourth floor, northeast corner," persists. "We have total freedom now for the action of the tanks," the General reports confidently, and orders the artillery to fire their rockets from the ground floor courtyard. To the artillery commander, Colonel Plazas, whose men have been coming under fire from the guerrillas under Almarales' command at the opposite end of the courtyard, still impregnable in their northwest retreat, he now insists on a greater effort: "Push on," he tells Plazas. "Don't risk your people too much where you don't need to do so, but push on. We need to use the rockets now. So use them. We are totally committed now and this situation has to be cleaned out." Soldiers would later testify that between 6:30 and 8:00 p.m. the tanks fired six rockets onto the fourth floor at intervals of ten minutes each. Not all of them exploded and General Arias is dissatisfied and calls for army engineers and explosives experts. He wants them to bring dynamite and set charges in the roof to blow open a crater in the ceiling above the conference room. He also calls for one hundred and fifty pairs of night vision infra-red glasses for the soldiers fighting on the fourth floor in the dark and the smoke.

As he directs the battle for the liberation of the fourth floor, Arias has no time for any thoughts about the presence of the justices held hostage by the guerrillas in this "last pocket of resistance." That the hostages do in fact exist, their identity and, in general terms, even their number, is well known to the Minister of Defense, General Vega Uribe, and to his Army Chief of Staff, General Samudio. Perhaps General Arias never does learn the exact identity of "the personnel foreign to this situation" whom he knows to be sharing the conference room that he is now "committed" to destroying. But that he knows there are hostages trapped inside that doomed space, behind the barricades and the blazing guns of the guerrillas, there can be no doubt.

After seven consecutive hours of continuous fighting, hundreds of troops, rockets, grenades and explosives are now thrown into the effort to overcome the fifteen surviving guerrillas commanded by Luis Otero. According to the Army's own, internal reporting system, the various commanders on the scene continue to communicate with one another, back and forth, about the details of the weapons and explosives needed to accomplish their goal, about why the dynamite has not arrived yet, and where the engineers should be picked up to be brought to join General Arias on the roof. But the name of the Chief Justice was never mentioned again. Not once.

* * * * *

"We are at the point of death. They are only twenty meters away. This is like participating in a war in which everyone is destined to die." It was 7:30 p.m. on the night of Wednesday, November 6 when Judge Reyes talked by phone to a reporter for the *El Tiempo* newspaper from within the fourth floor conference room. It was his last communication with the outside world. Moments later the fire burned through the telephone cables and all further communication with the building was severed.

By 7:30 p.m. the fire in the first three floors of the southeast block of the building was burning out of control. Firemen called in to try and control it were unable to fight the flames because of the intensity of the battle still raging throughout the burning building. The army, worried about the danger to the tanks and the troops still milling around the courtyard, decides reluctantly to withdraw from the building. When the tanks emerge onto the square reporters swarm around Colonel Plazas, who clearly sees himself as the hero of this hour. Confident and exhilirated, he gives the press an account from his perspective on the front lines of the struggle. The situation inside the Palace of Justice, he says, is now under complete control. The gunfire they are hearing at that very moment? Oh well, there are a couple of small groups still holding out on the second and third floors, but it's nothing to worry about. The subversives have suffered a great many casualties, a great many, and all of the hostages—well, almost all of the hostages—have been rescued.

The reporters are extremely anxious for news of the Chief Justice and they press the Colonel for details: Does the Colonel know that the Chief Justice has called for a cease-fire? Does the Colonel know where the Chief Justice is at this very moment? "I don't know who is inside and who is outside," the Colonel replies. The reporter insists. "Well then," he asks, "what decision has the army taken? What is the Army going to do next?" "Why, defend the democracy, professor!" the Colonel snaps peevishly. "That's what the army's for—to enforce respect for democracy!"

After the withdrawal of the tanks, General Arias gets ready to blow up the roof. "The idea," the General informs his superiors, "is to locate the office where that garbage are firing from, to place a charge immediately above their heads, to create an opening, and then let them have it—with grenades, sub-machine gunfire, and whatever else. Over."

"I am sending you two more charges of fifteen pounds each and four charges for the crater bombs and forty pounds of TNT," his respondent tells him, warning him to be careful with the crater bomb charges: "They're pretty powerful, and the distance kept by the soldiers should, for security's sake, be greater than for the normal demolition bomb."

Between eight o'clock and eight thirty p.m., a series of powerful explosions shakes the center of the city. During the battle of the past eight hours, nothing quite like this has been heard before. Inside the cabinet room the lights flicker above the table, over the heads of the somber members of President Betancur's government. They sit on, continuing their desultory discussions over options they have no intention of acting upon, and which, in any case, no longer exist.

Flames light up the sky above the roof of the stricken Justice Palace. Firefighters, who have been standing disconsolately at the corner of the square, unable to do their job, now mobilize. There are a large numbers of soldiers, some of them wounded, trapped on the burning roof. The great fire-ladders go into action and, with enormous difficulty because of the flames and the wind, the firemen send up cage-like lifts to bring General Arias and his troops out to safety. There are also two women whom they manage to rescue, cleaning women who have been discovered by the Special Forces hiding in a broom closet between the roof and the fourth floor.

As for Chief Justice Alfonso Reyes Echandia, and his eight colleagues on the Supreme Court, his six associates from the Council
of State, together with twenty-odd other civilian hostages and all
of the M-19 guerrillas, those who survive the bombing, the
grenades and the submachine gunfire that the Army pours directly
into the conference room through the craters they have blown in
the roof, are all burnt alive in the conflagration that now engulfs
what remains of the fourth floor of the south and east wings.

The clearest images of their final moments come from the testimony of a soldier who, equipped with infrared eyeglasses, wit-
nessed the end of the battle through a skylight in the roof. From
his vantage point he could survey the length of the fourth floor
corridor, looking north, to the barricades outside the corner conference room, and he had a partial view along the northern portion
of the corridor running from east to west. He testified that as he
scrutinized the scene below him he saw the last of the volleys from
the guerrillas' guns firing across the barricades; then he caught
sight of the figure of an unarmed person emerge onto the corridor
from an adjacent office and start to crawl along the floor. As he
watched the progress of this figure, dragging itself along the passageway by its elbows, a hail of bullets struck it, flinging it to one
side, outside the soldier's field of vision.

That was all he saw because right then General Arias came to
stand beside him, took the glasses from him and crouched down to
watch the scene below for himself. The time, he thought, was
about nine o'clock, nine-thirty. But although he couldn't see any
more, the soldier said, he could hear: he heard the sound of the
flames that were now reaching to the roof and the cracking, splintering of wood; he heard the footsteps of people below him running. He heard, above all other sounds, above the continuing rattle
of the guns, the screams of the people trapped in the consuming
flames.

PART II

CHAPTER 9

Night

In which, in a secluded, marble-lined bathroom in another wing of the Palace, the surviving hostages and guerrillas plot to get word to the outside world of their existence; the President and his ministers receive an optimistic briefing from the Minister of Defense —and then go to their homes to sleep, and are awakened to the thunder of the cannons of the army's tanks, assaulting the Palace of Justice once again.

"Many survivors have testified to the great dignity with which all of those present conducted themselves at all moments of the tragedy. Justices, cleaners, assistants, chauffeurs, secretaries, lawyers—even the guerrillas themselves—behaved with such serenity that only rarely did anyone suc-cumb to an outburst of desperation."—From "The Report on the Holocaust at the Palace of Justice" published by the Special Commission of Inquiry established by President Betancur to report to him on the tragedy. (Bogotá, June 1986.)

On the night of Wednesday, November 6, bombs, bullets, and the all-devouring flames, took the lives of fifty-seven or fifty-eight people trapped on the fourth floor of the Palace of Justice. According to the official autopsy reports many of these bodies were so badly incinerated in the fire that it was impossible to estab-lish with precision the exact cause of death. It was also impossible to establish the identity of many of the bodies that were recovered in the ashes after the siege ended. Nevertheless, the remains of several of the bodies, including that of Chief Justice Reyes and many of his colleagues, showed that they died from gunshot wounds. When, later, ballistic tests were conducted on the M-19's weapons, the investigators discovered that none of the bullets lodged in the hostages' bodies had been fired by the M-19 guns which the army had found in the rubble of the fourth floor and which they turned over to the ballistic experts of the city morgue for testing. Since none of the weapons of the troops who fought on the fourth floor were subjected to any tests, in the absence of tangible proof, the investigators were left to deduce that many of the hostages must have been shot and killed by army fire while attempting to escape from the flames.

* * * * *

In the northwestern area of the building meanwhile, on the opposite side of the Palace courtyard, amazingly, the remaining guerrillas and their hostages, under the command of Andrés Almarales, have survived. Throughout that night of November 6, from behind their strategic gun emplacements on the stairs, some ten or so young guerrillas, alternately wielding guns and firehoses, managed to keep control of all access to the second, third and fourth floors in the building's north and west wings. After the flames die down, leaving the south and east wings of the great building gutted, the army's remorseless attack resumes. In order to "preserve the institutions," as President Betancur put it, between 2:00 a.m. in the pre-dawn hours of November 7, and 2:30 p.m. on the afternoon of the following day, the Colombian Army relentlessly presses its advantage. To finish off their despised enemy, to recoup their wounded, institutional honor, and to forestall any possibility of being called upon to negotiate with terrorists by the civilians in the Presidential Palace, the generals and colonels in charge of "defending the democracy" will continue to lay waste to the Palace of Justice. As the siege continues into the second day, in order to open an unobstructed field of fire for their tanks and rocket launchers, the army will dynamite ceilings, floors and internal walls around what is left of the Palace complex. Once the structural obstacles in the path of their high-tech arsenal have been demolished, the soldiers will be able to fire freely into the guerrillas' last hold out: the secluded, mezzanine bathroom, tucked away behind the M-19's stairway fortifications.

In May 1986, before the ruins of the great building were cleared to make way for the construction of the newest version of the Palace of Justice [the second reconstruction in forty years], I visited this bathroom. It was a narrow, windowless, rectangular space, twenty feet long by ten feet across, with a low ceiling, marble-lined walls and a concrete floor. It contained two urinals, four toilet stalls, and a row of marble basins. On the night of November 6 and the morning of November 7, at the time that it was being subjected to the remorseless pounding of the army's assault, this bathroom held a population of about seventy hostages, three badly wounded guerrillas, laid out on planks over the basins, and two young women whose only function was to keep loading and reloading the guns for the guerrillas fighting outside on the stairs. In the immediate aftermath of the battle to retake possession of this room the army had cleaned up much of the mess. Yet when I stepped across the threshold, six months after the tragedy, blood was still spattered across the ceiling and down the walls, and I counted seventeen jagged bullet holes that had torn through the metal divisions of the toilet stalls.

I have pored over the plans of this room and its structural surroundings with Felipe. I have followed, with him and Juan and Mauricio, step by step through their reconstruction of the battle that was fought within and without its confines. But until I met Gabriel I did not understand how seventy people had managed to survive inside this claustrophobic space, hour after hour, with their humanity and their sanity intact. Gabriel's factual, low-key description of what went on inside that room testified to the fact, that when face to face with imminent death, what kept the people in that room sane was solidarity, compassion and simple decency. "Humanly," says Gabriel, the reawakened memory of pain flickering behind his eyes, "you just have to feel sorry for everyone. For the women, for the wounded. One of the young guerrillas had been shot in the stomach. He was in great pain, and some of the secretaries took turns through the night trying to nurse him." For the first time since we began to talk several hours earlier, Gabriel dropped his eyes and an uneasy silence filled the space between us. He fought, without moving a muscle, to get his emotion under control, while I resisted the impulse to break the tension by asking a question. In that moment, Gabriel, I felt, was very far from this impersonal hotel room, where he sat on the edge of his chair, an untouched cup of coffee growing stone-cold in front of him. He had slipped away and was back inside the hellhole of that bathroom again, facing death. And there was nothing to say. Nothing. "It stays with you," he muttered finally, "all of it. Many times when I'm at home alone, or at work, whole scenes of what went on there come back to haunt me. And I try to imagine what might have been if they had agreed to negotiate. Try to imagine some different solution... Not even the guerrillas ever imagined that it would turn out the way it did."

*　*　*　*　*

By nightfall on November 6, for Andrés Almarales, now, by default, the sole surviving *Commandante* of the M-19's attack, the situation was a living nightmare. To begin with, he was every bit as isolated as were the hostages. Every now and again, when one of the young men or women fighting on the stairway to keep the Army pinned down in the courtyard appeared at the bathroom door, looking for a freshly loaded gun, or a drink of water, Andrés urgently sought news: "Where is Luis?" he would ask. "And Jacki? What has happened to the *companeros* on the fourth floor? What about those in the basement? In the south?" And the reply was brutal, it never varied: "*Muertos mi Commandante.*" Of the thirty-five young men and women who stormed the building on that Wednesday morning, so eager for a high-noon confrontation with the Colombian government, only the handful now fighting for their lives on the northwest stairway remain.

Then, too, Andrés Almarales, who came to the Palace of Justice to lead the negotiations, and who can barely fire a gun, is quite unsuited both by experience and by temperament for the role that has been thrust on him. For this congenial, middle-aged man with his wide circle of friends encompassing people from all walks of Colombian life—people as diverse as Gabriel García Márquez and the current Minister of Justice, Enrique Parejo—to find himself in the role of hostage-taker and keeper of a group of innocent people, most of whom he essentially respects, some of whom, in other phases of his chequered life, have been former collaborators and even friends, is, on the face of it, absurd.

There had been occasions when Andrés could have said no to Álvaro Fayad and Luis Otero and the *compañeros* on the M-19's National Command. There was the day when he discovered that the antitank rockets that had been promised from Panama, through the Medellín drug cartel, had not materialised. At the time, from his clandestine camp deep within the mountains, M-19 Supreme Commander Fayad had sent word to the Bogotá command to say: "Don't make a move until you receive the rockets we've been promised by the 'Extraditables.'" "Fuck the rockets," Otero had said. "Those people have no intention of helping us. We'll make our own explosives. We know how to make a Claymore mine..." Andrés had been dismayed but he held his peace. Five hours, Luis had forecast, was the maximum that they would need to confront and hold off an Army counterattack. Everyone had agreed. By nightfall, they told each other, the President and the government would be pleading for negotiations. A great, historic, nation-wide debate, broadcast to every corner of the country, would be about to begin. The country would never be the same again.

So the Panama-Medellín drugs-for-arms connection had failed to deliver. The Claymore mines that Luis had insisted could defend the building from anything the Army would use had proved worthless. And now Andrés stands in the dark, ankle deep in water, in the suffocating heat and smoke of this confounded bathroom which is looking more like a deathtrap with every passing hour. Gabriel's description of him, slumped in the doorway, evokes the image of a man whistling in the dark to keep his courage up. He tells the hostages not to worry. He insists that their position, protected by the machine gun blazing away on the stairs just above the entrance to the bathroom, is physically impregnable. He repeats the M-19 credo that sooner or later the President must capitulate and order the army to halt their attack, because no Colombian government can possibly afford to let the nation's leading justices be slaughtered by the soldiers of the nation's army. But the rhetorical phrases, the reassuring words no longer convince.

* * * * *

Between eleven and eleven thirty p.m. on that Wednesday night of November 6, almost twelve hours since the first volleys of gunfire from the Palace basement reverberated through the Palace, alerting the court's employees to the M-19's assault, the gunfire of the soldiers gradually diminished, then ceases completely. The Commander, General Arias, has called for all the officers to meet him behind the Congress building, on the opposite end of the Plaza Bolívar, for a review of their strategy. He wants to plan a coordinated, final assault on the last outpost of M-19 resistance in the Palace of Justice.

Within the bathroom, in the sudden, astonishing silence after the brutal barrage of the past eleven, consecutive hours, the collective spirit of the hostages quickens, and the first, faint glimmerings of hope begin to circulate around the filthy, smoke-filled, overcrowded room.

Throughout the endless hours of their captivity, one man among the hostages has emerged as a leader. Supreme Court Justice Manuel Gaona Cruz is a self-made man in his early forties. He is a man from the provinces, who paid his way through law school by selling shirts from a barrow in the Bogotá open street market where poor people from the south of the city come for their shopping. Gaona knows his country and his countrymen. Manuel Gaona is a realist. He knows that for all the fine rhetoric of the politicians about "the nobility of the institutions" and "the sacredness of the rule of law," the truer attitude of successive

Colombian governments towards the members of his profession is one of barely disguised indifference. So from the first moment that the M-19 invaded the Palace of Justice that morning, Manuel Gaona realized that by equating the status of Colombian Supreme Court justices with that of foreign diplomats in the analogous case of the Dominican Embassy, the M-19 have made a fundamental political error. Gaona knows what the M-19 leaders should have known, namely, that it was only the presence of North American and European diplomats within the Embassy which, on that occasion, had averted the same savage military response that has exploded over the Palace of Justice and all of its innocent occupants today.

When the siege began, Gaona had been relieved to find someone like Andrés Almarales in charge. During the first couple of hours of the battle between the army and the M-19, the hostages had spent considerable time discussing amongst themselves the various menacing scenarios whereby the guerrillas would succeed in forcing the government to submit to the series of "nonnegotiable" demands they had brought with them to the Palace. But as time wore on and the army's counterattack escalated, the focus of their concern shifted. After spending several hours locked up with Andrés Almarales and a bunch of mostly polite, mostly middle-class young men and women, almost no one was too concerned any longer for their safety at the hands of their captors. The spectre of murdered hostages, their bodies flung one by one from the Palace windows onto the Plaza below as a ploy to force the government's hand, simply did not apply.

To Justice Gaona, the presence of Andrés is particularly calming, for it indicates that the M-19 are serious in their intention of sitting down with the government to negotiate their grievances. Why else would they bring one of their senior, most qualified negotiators on such a violent incursion? Gaona expects that the M-19's demands will start out to be outrageous, but he also expects they will settle for a good deal less. They have always done so in the past. So having concluded that Andrés Almarales lives up to the impression he has always had of him, that of a decent, if limited man, and someone with whom it is possible to discuss rationally even in the midst of a perilously irrational crisis, Gaona is quite content to wait. Throughout the tedious, frightening hours of that Wednesday afternoon, while the army focuses its firepower on the the opposite wing of the building, Gaona's serenity and self-confidence sets a standard for discipline and tolerance under stress that has profound effects on the morale of his companions.

But as the craziness erupting all around the building culminates in the unforeseen disaster of the fire, the situation deteriorates. Hour by hour, Gaona senses that Almarales is becoming disoriented, that the situation is slipping out of control. Trapped in the dark, almost asphyxiated by the smoke, and deafened by the incessant explosions of the guns, the whistle of bullets biting into concrete columns and splintering wood, it becomes clear to Gaona that if any solution is to be found, some initiative will have to come from the hostages.

Now, in the eerie silence that has fallen over the building since the withdrawal of the army, Gaona approaches Almarales to insist that he must find a safer place for the hostages before everyone inside the bathroom expires from smoke inhalation. Almarales responds by deputizing one of the young guerrillas to go and seek an alternative, and within moments the messenger returns to report that there is a similarly protected bathroom on the mezzanine one floor below, where the smoke is less dense.

It is close to midnight as the hostages leave the bathroom. Slowly, led by one of the guerrillas, with Andrés bringing up the rear, they begin to descend the stairs in single file. Emerging from the confines of the bathroom in which many have been imprisoned for almost twelve hours, they are exposed, for the first time, to the devastating impact of the fire. Across the courtyard, as far as they can see, the whole roof of the building is in flames. "That" says Gabriel, "was when I first thought: 'we're not going to get out of this alive.'"

On the third floor landing they pass two of the guerrillas who are plying hoses, trying to prevent the fire from spreading in their direction. Then, as the long line of people starts slithering and sliding in the dark down the wet steps suddenly, from the courtyard below, a single gun begins to fire in their direction. "We froze," Gabriel remembers. "The word came back: Hold it! They must have seen us. We waited in absolute silence for a full five minutes. Then Almarales passed down word that we should remove our shoes, and barefoot, holding our breath, we slowly crept down to the second floor bathroom. When we got there we felt a little calmer. We were no longer in the center of the fire and everyone, including the guerrillas, settled down to get some rest."

*　*　*　*　*

It rained torrentially during the night, and by one o'clock in the morning, having completely gutted the southeast wing of the building, the fire began to subside. Inside the Presidential Palace, from whose windows the President and his cabinet have watched the lurid glow filling the sky above the burning building, the civilian leaders of government receive the Minister of Defense, General Vega.

Vega says his commanders on the scene are optimistic, confident that the end of the long ordeal is in sight. There have, he claims, been no casualties among the hostages to date. Most of them have been successfully rescued in the course of the last few hours and are already safely reunited with their families. All is now calm within the great building, the General insists. Owing to the fire, which was ignited by the guerrillas in the Palace Library, the Army has temporarily withdrawn their forces to allow for the smoke and heat of the conflagration to subside, and no further military action will be undertaken before daylight.

Since nothing he has said is contested, General Vega procedes to wrap up his report with some additional, factual information, of a kind that is guaranteed to give the civilians confidence and that he hopes will despatch them to their homes in a more tranquil frame of mind. In the course of retaking the basement, he says, and also on the fourth floor, the soldiers found large amounts of M-19 ammunition, which the guerrillas had been forced, by the speed of the army's counterattack, to abandon. The army is confident that the last, small focus of fanatical resistance, concentrated in the northwest wing, must soon run out of ammunition. Come morning, the General says, the Army confidently expects to bring their operation to a successful conclusion.

Some members of the cabinet press General Vega for information regarding the whereabouts of the Chief Justice. There were, the General said, a small number of hostages still being held by the guerrillas in one of the bathrooms, in the vicinity of the northwest stairway. The Army believes that the Chief Justice was probably among them. Owing to the fire it had so far been impossible for the army to penetrate to the bathrooms. Nonetheless the ministers could rest assured that the Army's prime objective was to rescue these few remaining hostages safely. And General Vega assured the President and his cabinet that, like all the other objectives of the operation to date, this one too would be accomplished at the earliest opportunity.

President Betancur, and even the most skeptical members of his cabinet, were immensely relieved. It was agreed that the emergency session that had been meeting continuously for the last twelve hours could be dissolved. "After the final briefing by General Vega we went to our homes to get some sleep, relieved that there had been no casualties caused by the army's incursion onto the fourth floor of the Palace, and satisfied that the end of the long ordeal was finally in sight," the Minister of Justice recalled bitterly some months later. At 1:00 a.m. it was agreed that the cabinet would reconvene at nine o'clock that morning.

*   *   *   *   *

At one o'clock that morning, at around the same time that the ministerial limosines are queueing up outside the other Palace to drive the ministers to their homes, one of the guerrillas enters the bathroom carrying a small transistor radio on which he is listening to the latest news bulletin. Gabriel remembers that the batteries were weak, and he recalls the instantaneous and absolute silence in the overcrowded room as hostages and guerrillas held their breath to catch every syllable of the broadcast. The newscaster was reporting that the military operation to take back control of the

Palace of Justice was nearly over. Almost all of the people who were trapped in the building when the M-19 invaded had been successfully rescued and there were no further hostages left alive in the still burning building. A small band of guerrillas still remained to be cleaned out, the reporter allowed, but the government was confident that the crisis was all but over and the cabinet had suspended its emergency session for the night.

When the broadcast ends there is a moment of stunned silence; then all at once the hostages explode with rage and frustration. Many find it impossible to accept what they have just heard. They look around the crowded room at all the well-known faces— among them five Supreme Court Justices and three Councilors of State—and in their desolation they conjure up the image of their families, sitting at home listening to the radio. The realization dawns of the devastating effect that the broadcast they have just listened to must have had on every family member and every close friend. Until this moment, each of the hostages has managed to cling to a private illusion, that out there in the city that appears to have abandoned them, some one person whom they love—a husband or a wife, a child, a lover, a parent—must be beating on official doors, clamoring for some intervention, some action on their behalf. Now this last small hope of eventual deliverance evaporates.

Andrés Almarales reacts very differently. The broadcast has shaken him out of his torpor. Now he knows what has to be done. Until this moment he has never totally lost hope that the government must, in the end, initiate a dialogue for the release of the hostages and the safe conduct of the surviving guerrillas from the building. Throughout the last thirteen hours he has clung, against all of the evidence, to the M-19's formula: so long as the guerrillas hold onto their hostages it can only be a matter of time before they succeed in forcing the government's hand. The possibility that the government and the general public might somehow be convinced that there were no more hostages had never crossed his mind. Somehow, he now realizes, they have to make contact with the outside world.

So Andrés Almarales and Manuel Gaona hold an urgent conference and they agree to try to telephone for help. Judge Gaona
takes out his diary and finds the home telephone numbers of half a
dozen important people in Bogotá. He tears out some sheets from
the back of the book on which to write: his list includes the Bishop
of Bogotá, the dean of the Law School, and the President of
Betancur's Peace Commission. Almarales adds the names and
home telephone numbers of a couple of well-known journalists,
and Judge Gaona also writes down the names and the rank of the
most important hostage members of the court. Almarales gives
both pieces of paper to one of the young guerrillas and sends him
off to make the phone calls on the hostages' behalf. His instructions are to tell the first person he can find about the actual situation within the Palace of Justice, and to request that person to pass
on the information to the government, together with an urgent
plea from the hostages for a cease-fire, for a delegation from the
Red Cross to tend to the wounded, and for a delegation from the
President to coordinate the M-19's withdrawal from the building.

The guerrilla leaves the bathroom to find a telephone and
within five minutes he returns to report that all of the phones are
dead. It was, Gabriel recalls, one of the worst moments of the
entire siege. "You see," he says quietly, "we had begun to hope, to
believe in a solution."

But Almarales refuses to give up. "You have to let them know
you're here!" he tells Gaona. "If the army believes that there's no
one left alive but a handful of guerrillas we're all done for. Go out
onto the stairs and start shouting. Give them your names. Identify
yourselves. You have to let them know that you're still alive! Shout,
shout for all you're worth. It's your lives that are at stake!"

"So we left the bathroom" says Gabriel, "and went out to stand
on the landing above the stairs, and we began to shout: "WE ARE
THE HOSTAGES! THERE ARE SEVENTY OF US! WE ARE
THE HOSTAGES! PLEASE DON'T SHOOT! PLEASE
DON'T KILL US! WE ARE THE HOSTAGES OF THE
COURT! PLEASE DON'T FIRE!" Gabriel shrugs his shoulders.
"We got tired," he says. "We would shout for five minutes and then
rest for five minutes, and all the time Almarales was urging us on,

'Insist!' he kept saying, 'Keep it up! Your lives depend on it!' When we stopped to catch our breath there would be dead silence. Nothing was moving. Then, after half an hour, we got our response—it came in a hail of bullets."

* * * * *

Shortly after 2:00 a.m. the army launches another all-out assault on the Justice Palace. The attack begins when one of the tanks takes up a position on the far end of the square, and from the base of the steps leading to the Congress building, fires three times, point blank, at the facade of the Justice Palace. A shell pierces the outer wall of the building, just west of the main doors, blasting a jagged opening in the granite facade through which a thick column of black smoke escapes and hangs heavily in the wet night air. Then the tanks and armored cars, accompanied by fresh troops, re-enter the smoking building, intent on storming the guerrillas' last hold out.

"By this time," says Gabriel, "we were able to recognize the sound of the tanks, and besides, the entire building shook with the impact of the explosions of the rockets and the shells. We retreated into the protection of the bathroom and all of the guerrillas returned to the stairs to go on fighting."

The army's pre-dawn assault on the bathroom failed yet again to dislodge the young woman firing the M-19's big machine gun from the stairs. At about three o'clock in the morning, driven out by the intensity of the heat and the smoke and unable to see anything in the dark, the soldiers withdraw. Once again, an exhausted, uneasy silence descends on the building.

CHAPTER 10

The Nightmares and the Ghosts

*In which the citizens of Bogotá confront
their worst nightmare; the Minister of
Justice reminisces about his old school-
friend, M-19 guerrilla leader, Andrés
Almarales, and evokes the ghosts of the
1928 massacre of the banana workers
in his home town of Cienega.*

Bogotá, 2:00 a.m. Thursday morning: the second day of the siege.
When the army shells the Palace of Justice any horror is possible.
As the reverberations of the tanks' pre-dawn bombardment resonate through the narrow streets, all across town the lights go on
again. People awakened by the explosions, seeking a friend,
reaching for a human voice with whom to share their terror, grab
for their telephones.

All day, all night, the Bogotános have waited in vain for some
word from President Belisario Betancur. Statements of his refusal
to negotiate—"no reward for terrorism"—and calls on the M-19 to
release their hostages, surrender to the army, and submit themselves to trial by civilian courts, have been broadcast on all media
since nightfall. But ever since the crisis broke there has not been
one word; not a single official communiqué in the voice of any recognizable government spokesman has broken the dense silence of
the Presidential Palace. Earlier, on the late night television news,
scenes of the conflagration that has already consumed most of the
Palace of Justice had taken over—brutally and briefly—from the
football fields and the Miss Colombia extravaganza. Suddenly and

inexplicably the scale of the tragedy invades the living rooms of Bogotá as a sheet of swirling, orange and blue flames engulfs the screen. Images of these flames, leaping high into the air above the roof of the stricken building, contrast with the sight of the men of the Bogotá Fire Brigade, standing in silent groups in their familiar yellow and orange coats amidst the tanks and armored cars at the corner of the Plaza Bolívar. With their great hoses still uncoiled, their hands idle, they stand forlornly beside their unwanted trucks, waiting for a lull in the fighting to leap into action and commence their life-saving task.

These images on the small screen evoke a Hollywood disaster movie, or some terrible phenomenon of nature like an earthquake or a volcano. Only this great building exploding in front of the cameras is no mock-up construction on a back lot in Los Angeles. This building is integral, central to the daily life and history of the city. In a way it is sacred to the city's sense of its own identity. So to most Bogotános, everything about these late-night scenes that have erupted into people's homes like an apocalyptic footnote to this grim day is incomprehensible. At 2:00 a.m., with the sound of the latest explosions still hanging over people's heads, the question that has been burrowing in the recesses of everyone's mind, ever since the dramatic plea from Chief Justice Reyes for a cease-fire went unanswered all those many long hours ago, begins to circulate along the telephone lines of the frightened city. Where, people ask each other, is the President? What has happened to the government? And all around the city, reluctant, hesitant rumors of a military coup begin to circulate. The President, so the rumors have it, has been taken to an army barracks... the government is under arrest... the army has taken over.

These rumors come loaded with an ancient, historic dread, one that is never too far below the thin layer of what passes for security in Latin America. The nightmares of contemporary Latin Americans come inhabited with images of the sixteen years of brutality in Pinochet's Chile, of the horrors of Argentina under the dictatorship of the Generals in the seventies and early eighties. The nightmares of Latin Americans are easily evoked. So it is only logical that now, in 1985, fears of a military coup should be abroad in the Bogotá night. In Betancur's Bogotá it is no secret that this particular President has long been at odds with his military chiefs. Here in Colombia, goes the thinking, like their hemispheric counterparts, the local men in khaki have probably had enough of the chaos and complexities of civilian misrule. For thirty years and more, somewhere in the vast Colombian hinterland, too many young soldiers have been dying in daily hit and run confrontations with the insurgency forces of half a dozen guerrilla groups, in an undeclared, un-honored, and dirty war against subversion. Now, in retribution for old grievances, and the perceived humiliations of their ghettoized status at the hands of a frivolous, callous society, surely the military must have seized upon this opportunity to crush their hated enemies of the M-19, and to ride their tanks to power over the ashes of the Supreme Court. How else can one explain or understand what is happening, in the heart of the city, under the very windows of the government and the Congress?

It is presumably this fear that also lurks behind the timidity of the civilians, sequestered in their inertia in the Presidential Palace; the sub-text that underlies the repetitive declarations of respect and admiration for President Betancur from the members of the cabinet. These individual and collective declarations of solidarity and support for the leader who refuses to lead form the entire substance of the official minutes of the Cabinet's emergency session on November 6. This official document is remarkable chiefly for what it reveals of the government's daylong ignorance of developments in the battle between the army and the M-19 to which they have given their uncritical support. A truer picture of the atmosphere within the cabinet room—one that permits a brief glimpse of the confusion, the tensions, the tedium and frustrations of that dreadful afternoon and evening—emerges from the accounts of some of the telephone conversations that individual members of the government held with political colleagues during the crisis. One such, between the leader of the dissident wing of the Liberal Party—the late, assassinated Luis Carlos Galán—and the Minister of Justice, Enrique Parejo, took place at around seven o'clock on Wednesday evening. In his account of the content of their talk to the Commission of Inquiry, Galán relates Parejo's description of the row in the cabinet room just moments after the military had sabotaged Parejo's attempts to establish a line of communication between the government and the M-19 leaders. According to Galán, when Parejo objected to the military's untimely intrusion onto the fourth floor of the Palace, "President Betancur approached the Minister to ask him to calm down, saying that it was better to wait until they knew exactly what had occurred in order to look for other alternatives. According to what the Minister also told me," Galán went on, "the President had said that there was already too much tension, and that it was better not to aggravate things further."

As the endless first day of the siege merged into the night, these ministerial fears of the military had taken precedence over all else. By nightfall, many in the President's cabinet had convinced themselves and each other that the decision of the President to give the Generals a free hand was the only, the correct, and the necessary course. "Throughout the afternoon and the night of November 6, as also during the morning of November 7," the Secretary of the Presidency Victor G. Ricardo, told the investigators, "the leaders of both houses of Congress, the entire Conservative membership of Parliament, representatives of the business associations and the unions, arrived at the [Presidential] Palace to present their expressions of solidarity and support for the decisiveness of the President of the Republic in standing up to this terrorist attack." Faced with the ultimate threat to the continuity of their hold on power, the establishment has closed ranks.

Yet when, at 2:00 a.m that Thursday, the sounds of the army's latest onslaught on the Palace of Justice invades the ministerial bedrooms, for the men and women who have only just left the cabinet room, lulled by General Vega's briefing, the illusion that the worst is over is suddenly very difficult to sustain. In that bleak, vulnerable hour, glimmers of a truth that the members of the government have tried to avoid, seep inside the privacy of their homes. Six months later, speaking of his recollections of that night, Enrique Parejo recalled his own, horrified awakening. The sense of personal and collective betrayal was with him still. "I switched on the radio when I got home," he said, "and as I listened to the sound of the army's guns I said to myself: 'We have been lied to. We, the members of this government, have no idea what is really going on.'"

We had been talking in his office in the Justice Department for over an hour when he told me that. It was a small, dark, rather shabby room, cluttered with piles of books and papers, an unusual setting for a minister of state. But then Parejo is an unusual man. He was the odd man out in the Betancur cabinet—the only one among his colleagues who tried, repeatedly, to withstand the pressures of the military and intervene on behalf of the hostages. Later, he would be the only one to resist the pressures to conform to the Official Version of those critical hours of governmental inactivity. When I met him in the spring of 1986, the Commission of Inquiry had not yet published its report and Enrique Parejo was under enormous pressure to change his line. Pressures that included the routine, the inevitable death threats. But for Parejo, the risks were not new. He had taken over the ministry in 1983 as a result of the assassination of his predecessor, Rodrigo Lara Bonilla, and had quickly proceeded to incur the personal hatred of the drug cartels by signing extradition orders against some thirteen of their members. He was also deeply suspect in some military circles because of his openly proclaimed loyalty to his boyhood friend, Andrés Almarales, to whom he had frequently offered a refuge in his own house when the amnestied M-19 leader had needed one, during the confusing and dangerous days that led to the rupture of the truce.

That day Parejo talked a lot about Almarales, speaking of him with a spontaneous warmth and respect that took me by surprise. "*Mi compadre*," he said, referring to their joint origins in the small town of Cienega, and revealing, with that one untranslatable word, how deep the bond can be in this inchoate land between those who grow up together in some far-flung village or township. Listening to him reminisce about their shared past in that strife-stricken coastal town, I began to understand how a Colombian cabinet minister and a Colombian revolutionary leader had indeed managed to sustain a life-long friendship.

"I always maintained a great admiration and respect for Andrés," Parejo said that evening. "I have always admired and respected the courage and the honesty of those who fought for their convictions when they could see no other option, because they genuinely believed there was no other way. Whenever and wherever I met him—and during the truce we saw a lot of each other—we always embraced each other warmly. And I was also extremely curious about the people around him, some of whom were very brilliant. He came often to my house—of course he wanted my support—and we would talk at length about his ideas and about the goals of the M-19."

They must have made an incongruous couple: this modest, dapper, courteous man with the white skin and European features, slight, elegant and cleanshaven, who sat across the desk, choosing his words with thoughtful precision, a formal, reserved man, whom his critics called uptight and hot tempered—and the shaggy, dark-skinned, heavy-set extrovert, with his intense, compelling vitality, and that volatile, gambling streak that was so intrinsically a part of his charm, and that was fated to lead him into disgrace and a grim and sordid death. But in the small-town society of Cienega, where Parejo's family would have been well established socially while Andrés' father was still laboring in the banana fields, for the two small boys who sat beside each other in school, money and social position were not important. Their friendship predated the consumer society, and was forged in times of social upheaval. "We were all young *Gaitanistas* then," Parejo said, evoking the abiding influence of the great, lost, leader of the forties, Jorge Eliecer Gaitán, whose life and violent death left such an indelible influence on the generation that followed him. In the 1950s, what counted for a future cabinet minister and a future revolutionary, was that from an early age they had seen deeply enough into the Colombian malaise and wanted to do something to change it. They were *inquieto*. They shared unquiet spirits. And both came to the same determination to use the law as a stepping stone to political action, to dedicate their lives to working for a better, and more humane country.

Then, of course, these two *compadres* shared another obsessive memory. They were both haunted by another ghost from Colombia's history: the specific, localized legacy of the tragedy that had scarred the lives of their families and neighbors, yet which, for the rest of their countrymen, survived, if at all, only in the pages of the fiction of Gabriel García Márquez. It had grown late and very still in the gloom of Enrique Parejo's office when he began to speak, in his quiet, measured voice, of the 1928 massacre. Suddenly sixty years of history dissolved, and the anonymous victims of that hot Sunday gathering in the square of Cienega were sharing the room with us. "Many of those gathered in the square that Sunday never even heard the order to disperse before the soldiers began to fire" he says. "No one really knows how many people died that day. My parents used to tell me that during the night, they could hear the mule wagons carrying the corpses out of town. The muted sound of the mule wagons, they said, dragging their burden along the deserted, silent streets, went on all through the night."

Almost sixty years after the blood of the banana workers had soaked into the dusty square on that hot Sunday in Cienega, their unquiet ghosts seemed to keep company with the tragic events at the Palace of Justice. The ghost of Gaitan too had played a role during the crisis. And not only because Andrés Almarales and the founders of the M-19 had all adopted him as their political inspiration and mentor. Within the Presidential Palace, whenever the temptation to call a halt to the conflict surfaced, however tentatively, in the tense atmosphere of the cabinet room, the generals needed only to evoke the spectre of a second "*Bogotázo*"—as the ferocious riots that swept over Bogotá in the aftermath of Gaitán's assassination are known—to bring wavering ministers back into line.

CHAPTER 11

The Messengers

*Or how Colombia's most famous cit-
izen, Nobel Laureate Gabriel García
Márquez, becomes a messenger-boy for
his friend, the President, and reaches
across the world from Paris to try to
offer President Betancur a way out of
the impasse in which he and his government have become mired; and the
guerrillas and the hostages, trapped in
the Palace of Justice bathroom, also
send a messenger out into the world to
bring back help.*

*"At dawn all was desolation and ruins. Amid the rubble lay the inciner-
ated remains of hostages and guerrillas, their weapons, also calcified,
beside them. Few of the bodies retained their human form. The air
exuded an unbearable, penetrating stench, record of the destruction of
human life."*—From The Report of the Special Commission of Inquiry
on The Holocaust at the Palace of Justice

At around 3:00 a.m., on the morning of November 7, after the
army had been forced to withdraw once more, driven from the
building by the heat and the asphyxiating smoke and Violetta's big
gun, still operating with deadly efficiency from the stairs, silence
descended again over the Justice Building. Leaving only a a single
guard posted on the stairs to keep watch, the guerrillas were able
to retreat to the bathroom to get some rest. Some of the hostages

193

fell asleep too, sitting up, packed together like sardines on the wet floor. A chauffeur for one of the justices, who had been wounded during the initial guerrilla assault on the basement, had somehow lost most of his clothes. It was cold during the night and he began to tremble, until one of the guerrillas gave him a pair of insulated army issue running pants and a green sweatshirt which he gratefully accepted.

During this first, lengthy pause in the fighting, the guerrillas and the hostages began to talk. The line between captors and captives, now essentially sharing a common fate, had begun to blur.

"We started a discussion with Andrés Almarales," Gabriel recalls. "We beseeched him to surrender and not to allow us all to be killed. But Almarales told us that we didn't understand. He said: 'we didn't come here to kill anyone.' And for the first time he started to explain to us why they had come to the Court and what they had wanted. He said: 'we came to present our case against the President and the military. We wanted all the justices to serve as judges.' He said that the President had betrayed the truce accords which the government had signed with the M-19. And he told us that they had been prepared to withstand a battle with the army for a maximum period of eight hours, after which time they had expected to sit down with the judges to outline their positions. He told us the name the M-19 had given to their operation: 'Antonio Nariño for The Rights of Man."

Manuel Gaona immediately picked up on this and began a debate on the M-19's concept of human rights. 'How can you people call yourselves defenders of human rights when you do what you're doing to us?' he asked. Whereupon, says Gabriel, "there was a tremendous discussion. Everyone attacked Almarales. There was a very courageous, strong young woman, a secretary, she was from the provinces, and she screamed at him: 'You're an assassin! How can you keep us all locked up here. We're all going to die!' And Almarales never could provide a concrete answer. He couldn't justify what they were doing. He just kept on repeating 'this is different. It's different. We haven't killed anybody. We didn't come here to harm anyone!'"

Then he abandoned the discussion to go outside and inspect his area of control and a depressed, resigned silence settled in once more inside the bathroom. "Of course," Gabriel continues, "we knew that they were 'protecting us'—as they put it—because we represented their only chance of getting out alive. We knew they would never let us go because in the end we were their passport to freedom."

At 5:00 a.m. the guerrilla with the transistor radio came back into the bathroom to tell Andrés there had been a new announcement from the Army. "*Operacíon Rastrillo*," the start of the final offensive to clear the building of the last holdout of terrorist resistance, was scheduled to begin at 6:00 a.m. Immediately Almarales became agitated. "He was extremely nervous," Gabriel recalls. "He explained to us what "*Operacíon Rastrillo*" meant. He said it was the tactic the army used in the countryside, in the villages, when they went looking for guerrillas. 'It means,' he said, 'that they go from door to door, from house to house, shooting first and asking who's there later.' That was how he explained it to us. And he told us we must start shouting again. We had to let them know who we are and how many of us there are.

"So once again Manuel Gaona led the effort. He and the other judges took turns going to the door of the bathroom and shouting: "I am so and so. Justice of the Supreme Court! Or Justice of the Council of State! Please. Hold your fire! You are going to kill us!' But there was no reply. Nothing. And finally we got tired of shouting. Tired of pleading for our lives. And at 5:30 a.m., when the gunfire started up once more, Almarales said, 'If this is "*Operacíon Rastrillo*" we've had it. They'll just come in here and sweep everything in front of them.'

"We were terrified. We began discussing among ourselves what to do. And the guerrillas began coming to Almarales saying: '*Commandante*! They're already on the second floor! They're on the third floor! They're on the fourth floor!' Then Almarales told us that they were maneuvering a tank into position on the far side of the courtyard opposite the first floor bathroom, and he said 'Quick, quick! We've got to get up to the next floor.' So once again, but very fast this time, we raced up the stairs and we all reached the bathroom between the second and third floors. That's where we remained. Until the end."

*   *   *   *   *

At 6:00 a.m. with the sounds of the Army's *"Operación Rastrillo"* already echoing through the city streets, a prominent Bogotá reporter answers the telephone by his bedside. Over a transatlantic connection from Paris, he recognizes the voice of Colombia's most famous citizen, "Gabo," alias Gabriel García Márquez.

The reporter is not surprised to find Gabo on the line. Both the writer's personal friendship with President Betancur and his close associations with a number of the M-19 leaders are well known. As is the fact that throughout the ill-fated peace process and truce, the President had entrusted him with a central, if secretive role in some of the most delicate negotiations between the Colombian government and the guerrillas. Speaking in code to circumvent a military phone tap—a code which the reporter immediately understands—García Márquez now proceeds to transmit an urgent message on the President's behalf. The reporter does not for one minute question the validity of the mission entrusted to him.

"Listen," García Márquez says, "I have just been speaking to Mrs. Thatcher, who called me on behalf of Brigitte Bardot... You understand me?" Translation: I have just been speaking to the Colombian Ambassador in London, who called me on behalf of B.B., (Belisario Betancur). And the message from the President that has travelled in this bizarre fashion—from the Presidential Palace, just a few blocks from the reporter's apartment, via London, to Paris, and back again to Bogotá—is that the Colombian President is now anxious to negotiate the withdrawal of the guerrillas from the Palace of Justice. President Betancur urgently needs someone to contact the M-19 command structure in the Bogotá underground to find out their terms for abandoning the building. "You had better move fast, there's not much time," García Márquez warns the reporter. "Brigitte needs the answer before 10:00 a.m."

When the reporter hangs up the phone at six o'clock on the morning of Thursday, November 7, the second day of the siege, he knows precisely how to fulfill the assignment entrusted to him. His contacts to the leadership of the M-19 are excellent. However, at 5:30 a.m. that morning the army placed the entire city under a state of emergency. Armored cars, tanks and troops are watching every major intersection, and intelligence agents are busily at work picking up suspected "Emme" sympathizers, searching known "Emme" households, watching press offices, and the offices of any lawyer with left-wing clients. So to get word to the Central Command of the M-19 in the underground is not simple. Nonetheless, "there always exists a chain of communication and I knew my way into that chain," the reporter says cryptically; before the ten o'clock deadline two messengers from the M-19 command arrive at his office, bringing with them a concrete proposal for President Betancur.

The M-19's formula for ending the siege is simple and brief. The reporter writes it down on a single piece of paper while they spell it out for him. The M-19, the messengers say, want to leave the Palace of Justice with dignity. They request a safe passage for all of their members to Cuba, or to Nicaragua, and they want a delegation to go to the Palace of Justice to receive the hostages and to accompany the guerrillas safely to the airport. The members of this delegation should include the Archbishop of Bogotá, Monsignor Carillo, the President of the Peace Commission, John Agudelo Ríos, and a reporter. "If those three people go to the Palace of Justice" the M-19 spokesman says, "then you can tell the President that the problem is over."

The reporter calls the Presidential Palace. He is prepared to follow through on his assignment in good faith. He is even enormously relieved, because like most people in the Bogotá press he has friends among the hostages, and he believes that the piece of paper he is bringing with him to the Presidential Palace is close enough to an admission of defeat by the M-19 that it will be easy for the President to accept. Yet, by ten o'clock that morning, the chief protagonists in the drama have been so relentlessly forwarding their own agendas that by the time the reporter delivers

the M-19's response to the President's request for a speedy resolution of the crisis, new realities, and a very changed psychological
climate now prevail.

* * * * *

At 7:30 a.m. that morning, the commanding officer inside the
Palace of Justice, General Arias, had given his situation report to
the Army Chief of Staff, General Rafael Samudio. Ninety minutes
after it began, *"Operacíon Rastrillo"* has been halted in its swift
advance through the building. Once more Violetta's marksman-
ship, firing the big M-19 machine gun to deadly effect, has frus-
trated the army's best attempts to storm the staircase. One army
lieutenant has been shot in the leg, and over the short-wave radio
General Arias confirms to General Samudio that, whereas the
Army has successfully reoccupied the first, second, third and partially the fourth floors, they have not yet managed to come any
closer to dislodging Almarales' small force on the stairs outside the
bathroom.

"We tried another approach up the stairs but it was not possible because the resistance in that area continues to be very heavy.
Above all, owing to the position of their guns on the landing
they're protected... we've fired four grenades already but it's been
impossible so far to break through. We've made three attempts to
break the resistance on these stairs, both from the upper floors,
firing downward, and also from below firing upwards. We also
attacked with one of the armored cars, but unfortunately that
ammunition, because of its powers of penetration, only explodes
after it has passed through the building to the street beyond, so we
halted that fire."

"Tell me something," General Samudio asks, "Where do you
think that they are holding the justices?" To which Arias replies:
"Well, if they are holding them they must be in the northwest
sector, that's to say, in some place next door to where the strongest
resistance is coming from." Samudio has no immediate reaction,
he simply instructs Arias to continue with his report of the operation to date. The General goes on to talk about the difficulties of

operating in the overwhelming heat and smoke; he mentions the fact that the fire has broken out again, that a conference room in the southwest wing, just beside the principal entrance, is once more in flames, and he has sent for the fire brigade to try and cool off the blaze.

In the course of this report to his superior officer, when referring to the fourth floor, General Arias did not mention the piles of incinerated corpses which his soldiers found when they reached the fourth floor landing in the early hours of Thursday morning. The subsequent testimony to the tribunal of Sub-Lt. Orlando Ramírez Cardona of the Presidential Guard, who led a detachment that reached the fourth floor at the very start of "*Operación Rastrillo,*" describes the scene:

> Question: Tell the court, if you please, everything you were able to observe on the fourth floor?
>
> Reply: There were incinerated corpses. There were quite a number in the area overlooking the Carrera 7. There were also some on the south side and a few in the north section of the Palace. They were mostly piled together, in heaps, though it was difficult to make them out because they were totally incinerated. Most of the corpses were huddled together, and where I saw most of the bodies heaped up was on the section over the Carrera 7, in the middle of the passageway. But I want to be clear about one thing: given the circumstances it is totally difficult to establish between... correction... to establish the difference between certain wooden objects and the corpses, because they were practically all melted down into one solid black mass on the floor...

General Arias, however, confined his report of the situation on this floor to the discovery of three M-19 weapons that his troops recuperated from the ashes.

Then General Samudio returned to the subject of the hostages. "One further thing, Arcano," he asks, using the Commander's code name, "has there been any evidence, voices, shouts, or anything at all from the hostages?" "No," Arias replies, then he adds: "Sometimes those people do shout that they need the presence of the Red Cross, but then immediately they follow up with renewed gunfire. But so far we have heard nothing clearly from the hostages."

Samudio: "Anything more?"

Arias: "Negative Paladín 6."

* * * * *

By eight o'clock that morning, the reporter and the M-19 Command outside the Palace are not the only ones trying to reach the President to break the military's monopoly of control over the situation inside the Justice building. A new initiative to break the military stranglehold was brewing, one launched by the hostages themselves. Gabriel insists that the idea originated with one of the associate Justices, Carlos Urán. The assistant to the President of the Council of State, Carlos Urán is a quiet-spoken, thoughtful jurist in his late thirties. Happily married and the father of four young daughters, Carlos has a great deal to live for. Shortly after the apparent failure of *"Operación Rastrillo,"* when the army appeared to have pulled back once again, Carlos comes up with a plan which he presents to Almarales in the following terms: He asks the guerrilla leader to allow him to venture out into the battle and attempt to reach the ground floor. If and when he succeeds, he will then insist that a member of the government come immediately to the Justice Palace to talk to him. Once he has fully informed the government of the true state of affairs in the besieged bathroom, and has communicated the M-19's request to be permitted to abandon the building in return for handing over the hostages, he will immediately return to the bathroom to report back to Andrés Almarales and to his hostage colleagues.

Since the intensity of *"Operación Rastrillo"* had slackened significantly, the success of such an initiative appeared more likely. But although Andrés Almarales approved of the idea in principle, he also worried that Carlos Urán might be the wrong person to carry it out. For in yet another of those curious, paradoxical relationships that have converged in these critical final hours of his life, Andrés and Carlos had once been friends. Together they had edited a publication—"*Mayorías*"—which, in the 1970s, was the official voice of the Popular Alliance or ANAPO, from whose ranks so many of the founding members of the "Emme" had emerged. Their former political collaboration and friendship would have been known to the army. Furthermore, Carlos, a serious scholar and historian as well as a lawyer, had recently published a book about the military dictatorship in Colombia. One which has made many senior officers quite unhappy. So Andrés, fearing for his former friend's life, turned down Carlos Urán for the role of messenger.

Manuel Gaona instantly volunteered but Andrés rejected him too, feeling that what was needed was someone with impeccably conservative credentials. When an elderly justice of the Council of State, Judge Reynaldo Arciniegas, spoke up to say that he had a personal friend in the High Command, a member of the staff of General Samudio, Andrés accepted immediately, convinced that he had found the perfect candidate. So Justice Reynaldo Arciniegas, a kindly, somewhat timid and politically naive elderly gentleman of frail health, a man of courage certainly, but quite lacking in experience or even awareness of the potentially brutal and devious ways of the ambitious and powerful of this world, assumes the task of carrying out Carlos Urán's plan.

Smitten by a sudden, wild surge of hope, their spirits buoyed in anticipation of finally getting their message heard, the hostages are galvanized into action. "Someone produced a piece of paper," Gabriel remembers, "and we all wrote our names on it. Our names and our positions. Everyone's name was there. The idea was to get the paper into the hands of someone in authority who could do something to call a halt to the fighting so that the guerrillas could talk to someone. That was the main thing. And we also asked if they would please send a representative from the Red Cross—not the Colombian Red Cross, but the International Red Cross—

because they are more neutral. And also a negotiator from the government. Carlos Urán had said: 'This is going to be a massacre,' and we knew that we had to reach someone whom Almarales could talk to. Andrés also said that we must tell them that there were wounded people who needed medical attention. And he said that we should also request some food.

"When Judge Arciniegas was ready to leave, Andrés said he should carry a white flag. So Manuel Gaona took off his jacket and his shirt and handed him his white undershirt. And that's how he left the bathroom. Holding Manuel Gaona's undershirt in one hand and the slip of paper with all of our names, and the messages for the government, in the other. We could hear him shouting, all the way down: 'I am so-and-so of the Council of State! Please don't fire! Please don't kill me!' All the way down the stairs we heard his voice, going very slowly, one step at a time. He was shouting the whole time: 'Please! Halt your Fire!' Then we heard the voice of a soldier shout back: 'Come out with your hands up!' There was an absolute silence then, that lasted for about ten minutes. And once again, the crash of the guns...

"We shouted at the guerrillas: 'Don't shoot! Don't return their fire!' We told Almarales: 'Please! Stop them! We've just sent someone out to halt the fighting. How do you expect to have a cease-fire if every time they shoot you return their fire?' And Almarales did pass the order. He did tell them to stop. Only to fire in self-defense, or if they saw someone coming up the stairs. And we heard them, the guerrillas, yelling insults at the soldiers: 'Hold your fire you sons of bitches!' But it was hopeless. Once again the Army attacked us with everything they had. And the guerrillas started coming to Almarales: '*Commandante*! They're on the third floor! They're firing from the fourth floor! They've got us surrounded! They're on top of us!' Almarales kept up an appearance of calm, but you could see they were getting desperate. And an hour passed, and an hour and a half, and Arciniegas didn't return."

*   *   *   *   *

It was just after 9:30 a.m. when Judge Arciniegas reached the ground floor of the Palace of Justice and delivered his sheet of paper with the names of all of the hostages to the Commanding General, Arias Cabrales. This slip of paper was never heard of again.

The General and his staff listened to the Judge's story, and duly noted the information he offered regarding the numbers of the hostages and their location. They listened politely to all of his requests—for a cease-fire, for a negotiator from the government to arrange for the guerrillas to withdraw, for the urgent presence of a delegation from the International Red Cross. Then Justice Arciniegas, delighted and relieved to have accomplished his mission so easily, turned to return to the bathroom. But at that point the officers explained, courteously, with great concern for the judge's well-being, that this was not possible. Not yet. They were regretful, but very frankly they could not take the responsibility for his safety at this particular time.

They were full of assurances. After all, the good Judge had accomplished his mission, now the Army must fulfill theirs. There was no need for him to worry any further about his fellow hostages. Now that the Army knew who the hostages were, and where they were hidden, everything would be done to rescue them and bring them to safety.

There was, however, the General explained, one further service the judge could most usefully render to his friends. Would he be kind enough to spend a little while helping the officers who were in charge of their rescue? There were a few details about the location where they were imprisoned about which the Army was still a little confused. Would the Judge mind spending a few moments with the General's staff to answer some of their questions before being driven to his home to get some rest? The Judge was delighted to be of service in any way possible.

Questioned by General Arias' staff, inside the army's temporary administrative headquarters on the corner of the square, Justice Arciniegas gave the army all the information they requested: the precise location of the bathroom, the number of guerrillas still fighting,—there were, he thought eight, seven or eight—their weapons, the precise location of the machine gun manned by Violetta on the third floor landing. He told them that he had been quite impressed by many of these young people of the "Emme." They were, he said, full of idealism, and they had treated the hostages quite exceptionally well. He also told the army that the guerrillas were worried because they were running low on ammunition.

He forgot all about trying to contact the civilian government, just up the street. He never asked why the guns were still blazing away inside the ruins that he had just left. Or where the Red Cross delegation was. Or who would be arriving from the government to talk to Almarales. He was advised to call his house and ask for someone to come and pick him up. So Justice Arciniegas went home, to his pleasant, suburban house, too far from the center of town to be troubled any further by the sound of the explosives and the gunfire from the Palace of Justice. Once home, he went to sleep, an exhausted but contented man, peaceful in the conviction that he had managed to carry out the mission that had been entrusted to him with complete success.

* * * * *

It was not yet quite ten o'clock, the conference between General Arias' staff and Justice Reynaldo Arciniegas was still in progress, when the reporter called the Presidential Palace and was put through to the Minister of the Interior, Jaime Castro. "Yes, yes, we've been in touch with Gabo," Castro said, "and we've been expecting your call. I'll send my car for you right away."

Yet when the reporter arrived in the ministerial car and stepped inside the Presidential Palace to deliver his message from the M-19, something about the place, a mood, an atmosphere, struck him as odd. President Betancur's nine o'clock cabinet meeting was just breaking up as he arrived and there were lots of people—civilians and military—milling around the corridors and the halls. It was all fairly chaotic, but there was something else going on in the Palace that morning which the reporter could not quite fathom. He sensed a jaunty optimism in the air. He found it puzzling and it troubled him. Yet more startling discoveries were to come.

In the cabinet meeting just ended, President Betancur had opened the proceedings with a description of his dawn visit to the Barracks of the Thirteenth Brigade in the north of the city. At 6:00 a.m. he had gone to offer his personal gratitude and appreciation to all the officers and men for their loyal conduct in the prosecution of their dangerous task. He had also paid visits to the bereaved families of the policemen of the Special Forces, slain on the previous evening upon entering the Palace building from the roof. Then he had watched the dawn break over the city and had been profoundly moved by the splendor of the Bogotá sky.

According to the minutes of that 9:00 a.m Cabinet meeting taken by the Secretary to the Presidency, *Señor* Ricardo, the Chief of State was insistent that, "the government is doing everything that it should be doing, the Armed Forces and the Police have made no mistakes, and they have acted with magnificent coordination. Furthermore, the Colombian Red Cross has received, and will continue to receive, full guarantees from the government for its humanitarian labors." This latter statement, while never contradicted, might have surprised the Colombian Red Cross, to say nothing of their colleagues in the Bogotá fire brigade.

The Chief of State's contribution was followed by the Minister of Defense, General Vega, who presented his colleagues with "a detailed report on the situation in the Palace of Justice, and an evaluation of the necessary actions still to come." Insisting that the Armed Forces and the Police have "sought at all times to avoid any loss of life among the hostages," the General claimed that "they have acted throughout with great firmness, but also with prudence." Indeed General Vega stated categorically: "If the protection of the lives of the hostages had not been the fundamental objective of the military operation, the Palace of Justice could have been retaken from the guerrillas in a matter of minutes."

Perhaps it was the General's "detailed report," or maybe it was his repeated claims of "prudence," that got to Enrique Parejo. Reading *Señor* Ricardo's account of the cabinet meeting of that November 7 morning, one can only guess, since the sole mention of any contribution by the Minister of Justice is reported in these few words: "The Minister of Justice," says Ricardo, "proposes that contact should be sought through the Red Cross to initiate the dialogue which was agreed to last night and which could not [then] be realized." There is not a whisper in the official minutes about the investigations that Parejo demanded that morning, both of the true circumstances of the army's incursion the night before onto the fourth floor, and of the circumstances surrounding the unauthorized removal, the day before the attack, of the police security which had been established, by prior order of the Security Council, to patrol and protect the Justice building.

To get any idea of what really went on during the cabinet meeting that morning, it is necessary to turn to other sources. Parejo's own testimony to the Tribunal of Investigation five months later reveals a different story from that documented by the Secretary to the Presidency. The Minister of Justice must have made himself quite unpopular with his colleagues that morning. In contrast to the statements of support with which—at least according to the official record—the rest of the ministers bolstered the President and each other, Enrique Parejo complained bitterly about the lack of information they were receiving concerning the military operation. He reminded his colleagues that many of them had agreed with him as recently as last night. Then they had not believed the military when they asserted that "the powerful explosions we were hearing... were not endangering the lives of the hostages... because they were taking place in a wing of the building opposite from that in which the hostages were held."

The discussion initiated by the Minister of Justice was cut short by the President who wanted the cabinet to read and comment on the text of an official statement which the Chief of State wished to release to the press. President Betancur was planning to address the nation on television at the successful conclusion of the siege, and it was agreed that 4:00 p.m. would be a reasonable hour for him to go before the cameras. When the meeting returned to the unfinished business of the hostages and the guerrillas, the ministers concentrated their efforts deciding what kind of message to send to Almarales via the Red Cross. The goal was perceived to consist in how to "open a dialogue" with the guerrillas without interfering with the ongoing military operations. It was unanimously decided that the military operation should not be interrupted for the purposes of delivering this message. Rather, while the military were pursuing their own objectives, the government would ask the Red Cross to simultaneously take a message and a walkie-talkie to the guerrillas. The message would let them know that if they surrendered their lives would be protected and they would be guaranteed a fair trial in a civilian court of law.

At ten o'clock, when the meeting breaks up, the Ministers of Defense, of the Interior, and of Justice, are instructed to work on the text of the message that the Red Cross will bring to the guerrillas. The Ministers of the Interior and of Foreign Affairs are to put the finishing touches on the President's statement for the press. The Secretary of the Presidency is told to request the presence at the Presidential Palace of the director of the Colombian Red Cross.

*   *   *   *   *

Moments later, Jaime Castro, the Minister of the Interior, leaves the cabinet room to greet the reporter. Taking him aside, Castro settles into an easy chair to read the M-19's proposal. It takes him less than a minute to scan its contents. "We don't need to do anything like this," he says dismissively, tossing the piece of paper back to the reporter. "Tell them all they have to do is to surrender."

This is so far from the reaction that the reporter had been led to expect from a government which he assumed to be at its wits' end, desperate to find a solution to the raging mayhem that has been going on within earshot inside the Palace of Justice now for twenty-two hours, that he starts to argue. But the Minister is adamant. No discussions. No negotiations. The government, he says, has decided to send the director of the Red Cross into the building with a message for Almarales to surrender and a walkie-talkie so that he can communicate his decision back to the government. If the guerrillas accept the President's offer there will be a cease-fire. They can take it or leave it.

He takes back the piece of paper from the reporter to look once again at the suggestions for the delegation the M-19 has requested. "Agudelo Ríos?" he says, naming the president of the government's own Peace Commission, "He's discredited. The Archbishop? He's closer to those people of the 'Emme' than he is to us. No, no." The reporter says there are other people the government could send whom the guerrillas would respect, and he mentions the Attorney General for one. But Castro will have none of it. "The Attorney General? He's got no credibility." "Well, then call Gabo," the reporter insists. "He'll have ideas." "Gabo," says the Minister of the Interior, "is a charlatan. If you want to help, get your friends in the M-19 central command to record a cassette tape instructing Almarales to surrender, and we'll send it to him with the fellow from the Red Cross."

And then he discloses a confidence. "I'll give you a scoop," he says. "Five minutes from now, the military is going to take delivery of some special paralysing gases from the Israelis. They're waiting for them at the airport right now." The Minister checks his watch. "Five minutes from now. You'll see," he says confidently, "this whole problem will be solved."

The reporter knew about the Israeli gases. And he knew that the Army did not need to send to Israel or anywhere else for them because they were permanently stocked in the army's arsenal. He also knew that they could only function in an enclosed space, like an apartment house or an office building. In the open spaces of the Palace of Justice, with its large inner courtyard open to the sky, the Israeli gases would be useless.

Just then, President Betancur comes to the door of the room and asks to see the text of the M-19's proposal. The reporter watches while the President stands in the doorway, glances briefly at the single sheet on which the M-19's conditions for withdrawal are written, and gives it the thumbs down sign. Then President Betancur too begins to enthuse about the government's coming victory. "We're going to devastate them," he says. "Those guys are not going to know what hit them. They don't imagine what we've got prepared for them!" Recalling the scene several months later the reporter still shook his head with disbelief.

It was nearly eleven o'clock when the reporter left the Presidential Palace. Over the ubiquitous walkie-talkies, news of a military breakthrough had begun to percolate through the halls and offices. Twenty-five hostages, the army said, had just been rescued. Andrés Almarales had been wounded. Almarales was on the first floor. Almarales had been captured. "Now?" Castro called out to the reporter as he started to leave, "which one of us is right? You see? They're caving in already!" On his way out, through an open doorway, the reporter heard the voice of the Minister of Justice. Parejo was agitated and the reporter overheard him say: "Call up Almarales! Get Andrés Almarales on the phone for me. He's a friend of mine."

The reporter left the Presidential Palace with a heavy heart. On that November 7 morning he felt, as he had often felt before, that his was a nation trapped in its own myths. Murderous, killer myths, that blocked any possibility of coming to terms with the country's true realities, experiences and complexities. He passed through the ornate, gold/black, wrought iron filigree of the Palace entrance, crossed the manicured lawn, past the meticulously tended flower beds and the classical statues, and out through the heavily guarded exit to the pitted pavement of the street. It was a short journey, yet it highlighted for him the chasm between two worlds, two diametrically opposed realities. Behind him, in the building he had just left, the optimism of the President and his ministers belonged—or so it seemed to him—in some fantasy world of their own creation. One that was wholly remote from the reality of this fatal moment in Colombia's history. The President and his Minister of the Interior did not want to see the true situation. The rule of government had ended. They themselves had contributed to its demise. And the reporter worried, that while the President and his ministers continued to tell each other fairytales about miraculous gases and glorious victories, inside that other Palace just down the street, unknown numbers of innocent lives were going to be sacrificed in this unnecessary war so that the Colombian authorities could save face.

CHAPTER 12

The Personage

In which the army reaps the benefit of the hostage's messenger; while the government decides to send a message of its own to the guerillas; and as the generals become afraid that an order to halt the fighting will follow, so it comes to pass that they arrange to delay "the personage" bearing the government's message, just long enough to launch a massive, final assault on the crowded bathroom.

"The tanks were firing closer now. After Judge Arciniegas left. He must have told them where we were. They had to know where we were now. Because the tanks sounded as if they were firing right beside us and with every new bombardment the whole room trembled."

It had grown very quiet in the hotel room. Gabriel was speaking in ever shorter sentences and even in the stillness of the room I had to strain to hear him. He no longer bothered to search my expression for a reaction. He was beyond caring whether I believed his version of the last four hours of the battle or not. He sounded tired and he seemed to have gotten very small. Small, and very young, he sat there staring at the floor. As if the despair that had overtaken the hostages inside the besieged bathroom after Judge Arciniegas failed to return was crushing him once more.

The hostages had watched Judge Arciniegas leave their prison, bravely waving his slip of white paper with all of their names and signatures in one hand and Manuel Gaona's T-shirt in the other; bearer of all their hopes of eventual rescue. The idea that this good and respected man might abandon them was inconceivable. Perhaps Andrés Almarales had considered the possibility of such an outcome. The others needed so desperately to believe that their horrendous plight was the result of some dreadful mistake—a misunderstanding that needed only to be corrected. But when Judge Arciniegas did not return to rejoin them, and when instead the army stepped up its bombardment of the crowded bathroom, the hostages were finally disabused of their last illusions. From then on, inside the filthy, overcrowded, claustrophobic space, hostages and guerrillas shared a common sense of alienation and betrayal.

Before their conference with Judge Arciniegas the army had not known the exact location of the bathrooms. After twenty-two hours of combat they still did not know either the layout of the building or the number of surviving opponents that they faced. Following on the army's conversations with the Judge that all changed. What did not change, in spite of the receipt, by General Arias personally, of the signed list containing the names of all sixty-nine hostages still trapped in the bathroom, were the army's operational procedures for fulfilling their objective: namely to annihilate the last of the seven or eight M-19 guerrillas still on their feet.

Shortly after 9:30 on that Thursday morning, after General Arias had despatched Judge Arciniegas to be interviewed by Colonel Sánchez in the Army Intelligence center located in the Museum, the General began calling for his favorite weapon. It had worked the night before in "cleaning out" the fourth floor, it would be put to equally lethal use again to wipe out the remnants of the M-19's depleted force. In the General's own words, it would provide the necessary "to accomplish our mission."

"Is there any personnel out there with the capacity to lay some explosives?" General Arias asks, speaking to the command center. "The grenades we have are no use and neither are the machine guns on the armored cars, and we haven't got enough room to fire the rockets." Assured that "the material [TNT, dynamite and plastic exlosives] is clean and ready to go," he orders army engineers to bring it to the ground floor where they are to meet him beside the elevators: "all the way back and to the left, next to the stairs where we're having the problem."

After his talk with Arciniegas, the General's first objective is to silence Violeta. Now that he knows precisely where she and her troublesome 50mm machine gun with the revolving barrel are located, barricaded behind sandbags on the third floor landing just a short flight of steps from the entrance to the bathroom, he instructs the engineers to blast an opening in the floor of the fourth floor mezzanine immediately above her head. While the engineers are preparing the explosives to plant the charge as instructed, the chief of Army Intelligence, Colonel Edilberto Rubiano Sánchez, speaking excitedly from the Army's command and intelligence center in the Museum, comes on the line: "To stimulate your morale," he says, "according to some hostages who've just escaped from somewhere in the basement—just ten minutes ago—they say that in that area where you're having so much trouble there is a revolving machine gun, and that there's a small group up there of five subjects and a woman. They gave us her name, they say she's tough this woman—Violeta Román Paéz—and another they call "the Captain." Apparently that's the group that is commanding the entire subversive operation. It's a group of five (people) who are holding you up."

"Affirmative," General Arias replies, "it's the same woman who gave us so much war yesterday, between the second and third floors. It must be the same bitch because she has great mobility and aggressivity... in any case, we're almost ready to finish up here, the engineers are just laying the charge now..."

But blasting away Violeta proves to be more complicated than the general had anticipated. The first two plastic explosives fail to make the desired impression in the thick granite floor of the stairway, and it takes a third attempt before army engineers, using vast amounts of dynamite, succeed in blasting a huge crater, several feet in diameter, in the fourth floor mezzanine landing just above her head. Shortly afterwards, two soldiers appear in the main entrance of the Palace of Justice before the waiting newscameras, carrying the mangled remains of Violeta's machine gun between them.

*   *   *   *   *

It is impossible to establish the precise hour on that Thursday morning when General Samudio calls up General Arias. But sometime between 10:30 and 11:00 o'clock the following conversation takes place. It begins with General Samudio's customary request for a situation up-date. General Arias talks about the different explosives he is experimenting with, he passes along Colonel Sánchez' information about "the five individuals who apparently control the entire operation and who are guarding the hostages." Each time he makes a break in his report, Samudio laconically instructs him to "Continue." Arias complies. He says that they have occupied the second and third floors, "with the exception of the opening to the staircase and the access to that mezzanine." He goes on to say: "It appears that on the third floor, in that same corner," [stairway mezzanine] there is a machine gun, according to what a magistrate, one Arciniegas, whom we just rescued a few minutes ago, [sic] says. So in any case," Arias goes on, "we're going to force the entrance with explosives again,... so as to continue the operation and try to get those people out. Apparently there are a lot of them locked in the women's bathroom. Over." Once again Samudio's bored, gravelly voice intones the familiar: "Continue." And Arias changes the subject. He informs Samudio that yet another police lieutenant has been wounded, and evacuated, and then he tries to sign off: "That's all for the moment Paladín 6." At which point Samudio reveals what is on his mind, and the conversation takes a new tack.

> SAMUDIO: Tell me something. Did you speak with Judge Arciniegas?

> ARIAS: Affirmative. I spoke with him because we received him when he came down the stairs and I also sent him to the Two, [Army intelligence in the

Museum—Colonel Sánchez] so he also spoke to him and gave him this information that I'm giving you.

SAMUDIO. Concretely, I'm asking you: Did he ask for the Red Cross?

ARIAS: Negative. Simply when he came out, he was ordered to come out with his hands up, and he came out with his credentials. Anyway his face was known to us, and immediately he said to us that he was a good friend of General Vega Torres, and he said they had allowed him to leave, that in the entrance to the stairs there were some people barricaded with automatic rifles, who are the ones that are holding us up. He also informed us about the hostages on the second floor.

SAMUDIO: How many hostages does he calculate?

ARIAS: I think he's a little exaggerated in his numbers because he speaks of fifty, and we evacuated 148 yesterday, plus some that we got out this morning, who came out from the basement - mainly service personnel from here, none of any importance. I don't think there are as many as he says. Over.

SAMUDIO. Was he in some special place alone or did they let him go?

ARIAS: He was with the personnel. They let him go down the stairs to where the personnel who are controlling the stairs are. Then they started to shout that they wanted the Red Cross, that the Red Cross should come, so we said they should send someone down. They said they were going to send a judge, and we coordinated that they should send the people down, one by one with their hands above their heads, but the only one who came was him. And so we rescued him. But he didn't mention any conditions or demands. Over.

SAMUDIO: Correct. Did he say if they needed medical assistance or hygiene?

ARIAS: Negative. He only referred to three of the opposite side who are wounded, one in an arm, two with leg wounds, one serious. And when he spoke to Arcano 2 (Colonel Sánchez) he stated that they wanted a journalist and the Red Cross.

SAMUDIO. OK. Continue.

ARIAS: That's all the information Paladín 6.

End of conversation.

It is difficult to believe that General Samudio was so much in the dark about the Arciniegas mission. According to Judge Arciniegas' own testimony, and to the testimony of Colonel Sánchez, before leaving the Museum on Thursday morning the judge spoke to his good, personal friend, General Vega Torres. General Vega Torres was, at the time, an aide on the personal staff of General Samudio. In the first few days after the tragedy Judge Arciniegas spoke freely to the press. "I beseeched the General—who was accompanied by two army colonels who knew me, and there were other officers there—I begged them not to kill those innocent people," the judge told *El Espectador* a week after the tragedy. "I said they had to have respect for those people's lives. I told them the guerrillas wanted them to send a journalist and someone from the Red Cross. I said that as far as the rebels were concerned they were very anxious to talk to someone. They replied that I should be calm, that I was not to worry. They said they would study what should be done."

Shortly after that interview Judge Arciniegas complied with the advice of his good friend General Vega Torres, not to give any further interviews to the press, nor to elaborate in any way on his experiences after leaving the Palace of Justice. "Your personal health is what counts now," General Vega is reported to have advised the elderly Justice, as the army, citing "intelligence" regarding the M-19's intention to take revenge for the death of Andrés Almarales and their other dead *compañeros*, insisted on providing round the clock, personal security for him and his family.

Yet on that Thursday morning, just around the time that General Samudio was talking to General Arias, there is, in the corridors of the Presidential Palace, a development underway which could also have had a bearing on the Army Commander's acute interest in the subject of the Red Cross as it relates to the 'rescue' of Judge Arciniegas. The government's decision at the close of the cabinet meeting, one hour earlier, to send a message to the guerrillas via the Red Cross has been making the generals extremely nervous.

Between ten thirty and eleven o'clock that morning, the Director General of the Colombian Red Cross, Doctor Carlos Martínez Saenz, is received by the Secretary to the Presidency, *Señor* Victor G. Ricardo in the Presidential Palace. On his arrival, Doctor Martínez accepts a formal request on behalf of the President to perform an "important, humanitarian task." He is to go to the Palace of Justice to deliver—to Andrés Almarales in person—a communication from the government offering guarantees of personal safety and trials in the civilian courts to all of the guerrillas in return for their surrender. Together with this letter, Doctor Martínez is delegated to take with him to the Palace a couple of walkie-talkies: one is for Andrés Almarales, so that the guerrilla leader and the Minister of Justice can finally communicate and "have a dialogue;" the second is for himself, so that he too can communicate with the government from within the Palace of Justice.

The "humanitarian" task assigned by the government to Doctor Martínez Saenz represents the closest that the members of the cabinet of President Betancur ever came to intervening in the conflict at the Palace of Justice. All the evidence indicates that even at this late hour, had their initiative been pursued with urgency or commitment, had the government, or more specifically, had President Betancur, truly wanted Dr. Martínez Saenz' mission to succeed, the tragedy which ultimately overwhelmed the hostages could still have been averted. But there was no such commitment. There was certainly no urgency. The evidence is conclusive that like all of President Betancur's actions throughout the crisis the decision to send the Red Cross representative into the Palace, "without interfering with the military operation underway," was primarily conceived as a political initiative, one taken in response to those few critical voices around the cabinet table, and the more numerous sounds of dismay and criticism being voiced by leaders of the opposition.

In his testimony to the Special Commisssion of Inquiry, the late Luis Carlos Galán gave evidence that he had spoken to President Betancur at 8:00 a.m. on Thursday morning to suggest that he should call for a cease-fire. "I stated to him that while I agreed that the government could not negotiate, I was in favor of trying everything possible to save the lives of the hostages. I told him he should seek to establish a humane dialogue....The President told me that he had presented my point of view to the cabinet, and in consideration of my opinions, and for other reasons, it had been agreed to diminish the military presure in order to permit the entry of the Red Cross to the Palace to rescue the wounded and to bring out the corpses... later, [at the conclusion of the cabinet meeting, or after ten o'clock that morning] he told me that it had been decided to ask the Red Cross to bring a walkie-talkie to attempt to hold a humane dialogue with the guerrillas. While waiting for news of these developments, I was surprised to hear from the radio that a high official of the Red Cross had only begun to approach the Palace two hours later."

The President's statement to Luis Carlos Galán regarding the decision to "diminish the military presure" was never implemented. On the contrary, the minutes of that morning's cabinet meeting, at which the decision to involve the Red Cross was discussed, reveal the precise opposite. It was decided at that meeting that there would be no interference with the military operation; the Red Cross representative would enter the Palace and deliver his message to the guerrilla commander while the conflict continued to rage. One can almost hear General Vega Uribe selling his colleagues in the cabinet on this "two-track approach," "the carrot and the stick," and similar clichés. And like guests at some grotesque Mad Hatter's tea party, the cabinet went along, without protest, without ever pausing to consider the absurdity of the arrangement that they had solemnly set in motion.

But perhaps most baffling of all, once the decision is taken to send the Director General of the Colombian Red Cross to the Palace, the government appears to have lost all subsequent interest in the fate of his mission. In the minutes of the government's next cabinet meeting, at one o'clock that afternoon, there is not a single mention of the Red Cross representative. Both the messenger and his message have vanished into the smoke and din of the battlefield, never to be heard from, never to be spoken of again.

The government's Red Cross initiative typifies the deep ambivalence and paralyzing contradictions which characterize the actions of the government of President Betancur throughout the twenty-seven hours of the siege. Nothing in the instructions given to Doctor Martínez offers the slightest clarification of his intended role. When asked, by reporters, Doctor Martínez himself has no clear idea what his role is supposed to be. Instead he seeks instant refuge in his own, highly personal concept of "institutional neutrality." "The Red Cross" he says, speaking to a journalist moments before entering the burnt-out building, "does not mediate. Ever. The Red Cross cannot be a mediator of conflicts. It is neutral." At another point in the impromptu press conference that he gave in the Plaza Bolívar while waiting to enter the Justice building, Doctor Martínez also said that the Red Cross was always on the side of the legitimate authorities.

Until the call came summoning him to the Presidential Palace, the Director General of the Colombian Red Cross had been noticeably absent from the crisis. The alacrity with which he accepted the assignment, and the lack of curiosity on his part as to how he will to carry it out, might lead one to suppose that, much like the ministers who entrusted him with it, Doctor Martínez is largely ignorant of what is going on. This absence of personal interest or concern might seem curious in a man whose own staff have been haunting the Plaza Bolívar with a deepening sense of frustration for most of the past 24 hours. But then again, like Justice Arciniegas, Doctor Martínez is a Colombian bureaucrat, and a member of a caste and a generation in his country who are, by temperament, character and education, virtually incapable of questioning 'the authorities.' A lifetime of subservience to the status quo has robbed this decent man of any capacity for independent thought. Faced with an event as politically controversial and violent as the tragedy unfolding in the Palace of Justice, the Director General of the Colombian Red Cross is unable to express any opinion, make any demands, or take any independent action on behalf of those he has been deputised to help. As Gabriel noted, when the guerrillas specified that they wanted a representative of the International, rather than the domestic, Colombian Red Cross, "because they were more impartial," the guerrillas knew what they were talking about.

From 10:30 a.m. Thursday morning until almost noon, Doctor Martínez patiently waits inside the Presidential Palace for the letter from the President and for two walkie-talkies. It takes this long for the two paragraph text to be composed by the ministers and then it must be read and approved by the President. But the President is very busy. According to *Señor* Ricardo's notes, he should have been receiving one of the official delegations that have come in solidarity to offer their support for the exemplary manner in which he is defending the honor of Colombia's institutions. In actual fact, at 11:30 a.m. that morning, the President was attending an extremely uncomfortable meeting with four Supreme Court Judges who escaped the conflict by being absent on the previous morning when the M-19 attacked. Now, on behalf of "the many judges, councilors of state, and employees of the court who are in danger of death," they have come to see the President to make an urgent request for the government to adopt "a more flexible approach, disposed to initiate a dialogue." To the consternation of his visitors, the usually loquacious Betancur maintains an unbroken silence throughout the entire meeting.

After his meetings, the President finds the time to read and approve the text of the letter for Almarales. But then there is a new problem, a further delay: The army has no walkie-talkies to spare inside the Presidential Palace and has to send out for them. To speed things up, perhaps if the good Doctor would not mind going to the corner of the Carrera 6 and Calle 11, where a soldier will meet him and bring them to him? Doctor Martínez duly goes to stand on the windy street corner, one block east of the Palace of Justice, where he waits for another thirty minutes.

In the Presidential Palace meanwhile, the Minister of Defense becomes personally involved in a strategy session with his staff. Now that they are able to pinpoint the exact location of the bathroom for the first time since the conflict began, it occurs to the

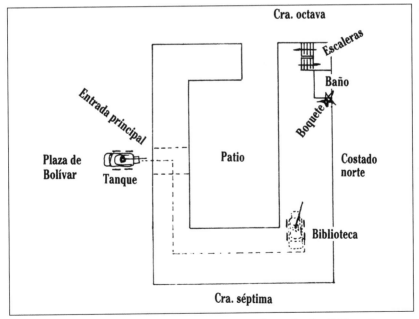

Overview of the bathroom's location within the building demonstrating the position of the tanks firing from the ground floor library.

generals to consult the construction plans of the Palace of Justice. The engineers who maintain the building are sent for to bring a set of the building's plans to the Presidential Palace. The Minister of Defense then sits down with his staff to analyze the structural obstacles standing between the army and their objective.

The bathroom had no door. The entrance faced north and as it had been designed for privacy the approach to the room could only be reached along a narrow, L-shaped passage leading off the mezzanine landing overlooking the stairs. It was this landing, and all access to it from the stairs, which the handful of surviving guerrillas, some seven or eight men and women, still managed to control.

The facing [south] wall of the bathroom was completely protected by a bank of elevators that stretched flush with the bathroom wall across its full width. To the west, were the stairs, to the north, the bathroom adjoined the concrete exterior wall of the building. The east wall, which flanked the western limits of the once great Palace of Justice library, also incorporated the main air

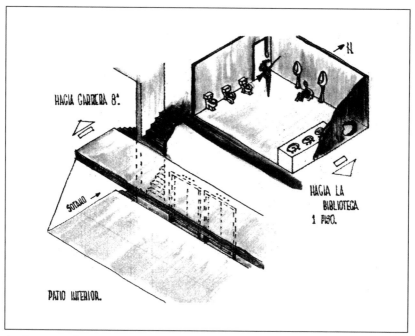

Artist's rendering of the interior of the bathroom. The view is from the south and [partially] the east.

duct for the building. As a result it was constructed in two, parallel sections, enclosing a three and a half feet wide space between them.

It would have appeared, from the physical structures surrounding this room, that so long as the guerrillas' ammunition held out the bathroom was impregnable. Not so, said the generals. They and their staffs studied the plans and concluded that there were two ways to get at their enemy. One approach entailed attacking the bathroom from above, by dynamiting an opening in the ceiling through the floor of the bathroom on the floor above. The second way would entail breaching the east wall from the burnt out library.

General Arias is not dismayed by the need to demolish one entire adjoining wall in order to penetrate beyond the air duct to the bathroom wall proper. He devises a strategy requiring large amounts of explosives. His list includes another 60 pounds of TNT, four 40-pound dynamite charges, and several smaller amounts of plastics and PVC of 12 and 15 pounds each for the shaped charges. The General's plans include the removal of a number of interior walls on the second and third floors to provide the open spaces he will require for his rocket launchers. He also needs to remove a wall on the ground floor that is blocking the access of his tanks to the gutted library. According to the General's calculations, once he has removed the outer section of the east wall, when he has cleared the way to drive a tank from the courtyard into the library, then he will be able to fire 90mm shells from the cannons of his tanks point blank at the exposed east wall of the bathroom.

According to the later testimony of soldiers who participated in the blitz on the bathroom, the early results were disappointing. In his evidence to the Investigative Tribunal, Sub-Lieutenant Ramírez Cardona described the placing of three plastic charges in the floor of the upper bathroom which had little effect. He also described how one of the engineers attached a whole series of explosives to the outer, northeastern wall of the bathroom. They were "special explosives," he said, not designed to hurt anyone: "generally the explosive used is TNT; its only use is to demolish, to knock down walls and open holes, the explosive has no ammunition."

"Before you placed these explosives on the wall of the bathroom" the investigator asked, "did you know that there were hostages inside, did you know how many there were?"

"I did not know the exact number" Ramírez replied, "but it was known that they had hostages in there..." However, he continued, "it was necessary to knock down a lot of walls between us and the bathroom and the only way [we could do it] was with these demolition charges."

Between 11:30 that morning and one o'clock in the afternoon, the explosions rolled and echoed repetitively around Bogotá. Sometimes they came in a series, three or four close together. Some were louder than others. The after-shock reverberated off the peaks of the surrounding mountains. It was said in the streets and offices of Bogotá that morning that the army was blowing up stocks of ammunition captured from the M-19. Another theory had it that the army was disposing of landmines that the guerrillas had laid to keep the soldiers at bay. No one spoke about the hostages anymore. Most people in the city did not really believe that there were any hostages still alive. How could anyone have survived inside a building that had been devoured by fire and was systematically being demolished while the government sat idly by, and most of the population continued about their business? For in spite of the overpowering military presence in the heart of the city, banks, restaurants, offices and shops remained open. While the Palace of Justice and its remaining seventy or so hostages agonized, the commercial life of the city continued to function.

Since the loss of Violeta and the silencing of her machine gun, the area that the guerrillas continue to control has shrunk considerably. They still hold the crucial approaches to the bathroom—up a flight of ten steps from the level of the mezzanine to the third floor landing, and down a flight of eight steps to the floor below. But as the process of demolition proceeds, the army is increasingly able to roam at will around the second, third and fourth floors. The soldiers are so close now that between the explosions the hostages can plainly hear their voices, shouting orders to each other from floor to floor.

There comes a moment, around noon, when the soldiers start yelling: "Surrender! Give up! You're lost! You're surrounded! Let the hostages go! Hostages! Come out slowly with your hands up!" But Andrés Almarales refused to even contemplate surrendering. "He said, 'if we go out now they'll kill us all.' And we said to him: 'Come out with us! We'll all go out together! We'll go in groups. Small groups, and we'll surround you, we'll protect you.' And Manuel Gaona told him: 'I'm a Supreme Court Judge and in my official capacity I will make certain that they respect your life if we leave together, all of us. We have to leave, now!' But Almarales said 'No.' He said, 'It's suicide. To leave at this moment is just suicide.' He said it would be the same for us as for them. That if we left in a group now they would just kill all of us."

After the failure of the Arciniegas mission, whatever flexibility or creativity Andrés Almarales has managed to hang onto seems to desert him. During this last phase of the battle, according to Gabriel's description, he wanders aimlessly from the bathroom to the landing and back again like a sleepwalker. Confused, exhausted, and conflicted, he clings to the M-19's original belief: if they can just hold on long enough, he insists, the government will be forced, finally, to intervene. At some point during the morning a small walkie-talkie is found, and Almarales becomes obsessed with the idea that they might somehow still manage to reach President Betancur in person. For a few electrifying moments it appears that a breakthrough is almost within their reach when they manage to make contact with a ham radio operator; someone, says Gabriel, "who never identified himself, but who answered them, and said he would try to make the connection, try to get word to the President. That's all Almarales ever talked about. He kept saying: 'we have to get out, we have to negotiate our way out.' To an embassy. Anywhere. Just to avoid a massacre, you see. That's all he talked about. That was what was important, the only thing that mattered was for them to escape from the building. To reach a refuge in some embassy. They were all discussing it, all the guerrillas. But it was far too confused. You see everything depended on making the communication. And the attempt failed. They never did manage to talk to anyone."

Meanwhile, the military have also concluded that there is a limit to how much longer they can stave off government intervention. While General Arias methodically pursues his task of demolishing the interior of the Palace building, the pressures on him to bring the conflict to a swift and bloody conclusion intensify. By mid-morning, in the streets, and on the radio, public pressure for a cease-fire is growing, opposition to the army is becoming more overt, and the nerves of the generals are beginning to fray.

Pressure on the government to intervene is being orchestrated from two quarters: from the underground activists of the M-19 Central Command and, more seriously, from the legal community, who know precisely how many of their colleagues are missing, presumed hostage, in the besieged building. Early that morning, the judges of the Bogotá High Court broadcast a public appeal to the President, requesting, "courteously but emphatically," that, in keeping with Article 16 of the National Constitution, he should call "an immediate cease-fire, and initiate a dialogue to guarantee the protection of the lives of the honorable magistrates and employees who are hostage." Led by colleagues of the Chief Justice in the faculty of the law school, students and relatives of the hostage judges are calling for a major demonstration in the center of town at midday. And the M-19 has begun broadcasting threats of "diversionary actions."

For General Arias, whose prestige is now so publicly compromised in this grotesque battle to dislodge a handful of remaining guerrillas, the fears of his superiors that the government will cave in to public sentiment and call a halt to the fighting add to the pressures on him to bring this embarassing conflict to its speediest conclusion. The greatest irony of all is that it is Doctor Martínez' ambivalent presence, hovering ineffectually in the wings as the tragedy moves inexorably towards its climax, that becomes the catalyst for the final eruption of savagery inside the devastated Palace of Justice. For the army had its own interpretation of his role. The army is convinced that once the Red Cross representative enters the building he will become a spokesman for the M-19. "We have information from a high source that Doctor Martínez will remain inside as a mediator of theirs. Over." "Continue." "Those are the additional instructions. Over." The voice speaking is that of Lt. Colonel Plazas, talking to his superior, General Arias, from outside the Palace of Justice—probably from the army command head-quarters in the Museum on the Plaza Bolívar. From this moment, the pressure will be on to "finish up," to "accomplish our objec-tive."

"I want to tell you something:" General Samudio announces to General Arias. "Those subjects (sic) are right now announcing on the radio—I've just heard them—they are demanding the pres-ence of Vasquez Carrisoza and Jaime Betancur before midday in the Palace of Justice. If this [demand] is not carried out, according to them, they will begin to kill off the hostages one by one and eject them from the fourth floor. They also say that if they are attacked they will have suicide commandos in other locations to assault other instalations. Whether their plans are for real or not" Samudio continues, "our objective must be speeded up. Over." "Understood Paladín 6" Arias replies. "Good," says Samudio, "then I wait for you to succeed, and I wish you luck."

After a few more moments General Samudio is on the line again, looking for troop reinforcements from Brigade Headquarters to patrol the streets.

> SAMUDIO: These individuals have plans to create concentrations of people and demonstrations of support to bring pressure on the government and oblige them to negotiate. In addition, they have even threatened the wives of the magistrates and the councilors of state, telling them they must par-ticipate at midday in a so-called demonstration, so that they can lend their collaboration to the demands on the government to negotiate. Impose at once the plan of occupation and control of the city to impede any concentrations or public demonstrations.

REPLY: The plan to occupy the city has been in operation since 05:30 this morning, I will alert the units of this latest information.

SAMUDIO: We must make a show of force and not permit these he-goats [sic] to take the initiative.

Nevertheless, one hour later a large demonstration is in process on the Plaza Santander, just two blocks from the Palace of Justice, and amid chants of "Army assassins!" the demonstrators are throwing stones at the soldiers. An irritable voice from the ministry of defense is heard complaining on the army's radio link that the situation is growing complicated. Another voice demands to know why the platoon ordered to the scene over an hour ago has not yet arrived. "The judges," says the voice from the ministry, "and some students, are causing us problems."

However, it is the imminent arrival at the Palace of Justice of the head of the Colombian Red Cross that remains the cause of gravest concern to the military that morning. At 12:00 noon, when Doctor Carlos Martínez Saenz is finally set to make his appearance outside the Palace of Justice, General Samudio calls up General Arias. "I understand," says Samudio, "that the Red Cross people have not yet arrrived, so we still have complete liberty to operate; however, we are playing against the clock. Please, hurry up and consolidate. Finish up with everything and consolidate the objective." But the commander with the passion for explosives is not yet ready to consolidate anything. General Arias is still laying dynamite on the floor of the upstairs bathroom.

ARIAS: We've got access now to the fourth floor bathroom, and we're about to use explosives to try and break through the floor so that we can penetrate to the third floor where they're still firing at us and where apparently they also have some hostage personnel.

SAMUDIO: Well, alright then. Do it. But time continues to be critical to accomplish this mission and to take our objective in its totality. I know other units are involved, so if any of you happen to be listening to me—I'm asking you, I demand from you, your maximum efforts. We are running out of time.

The clock on the tower of the National Cathedral in the Plaza Bolívar is just striking 12:30 when the government's chosen representative, Dr. Carlos Martínez Saenz, arrives on the Plaza Bolívar bearing the government's letter and a walkie-talkie for Andrés Almarales. All sixty-nine of the hostages in the bathroom are still alive when he presents himself, as per his instructions, at the military command center in the Museum at the corner of the Plaza. General Samudio's instructions to the staff in the command center have been explicit. When "the personage" arrives, he is to be delayed. The intelligence officers are to take their time checking the credentials and the finger prints of the five Red Cross stretcher carriers who are to accompany him into the building. The Minister of Defense meanwhile, speaking from the Presidential Palace, has passed word to the command center that when Doctor Martínez reaches the Justice building his mission is to remain inside, "as a mediator for them." But General Arias is still not ready to launch his final assault. "Tell him [Martínez] you have to send someone to inform me," Arias instructs the command center staff. "We're at the point of breaking in and we're still receiving fire... So give me more time. They're still firing at us and we're just getting ready to fire a rocket."

The officers on the staff of Colonel Sánchez receive "the personage" at the Museum with the utmost courtesy. The army is expecting him, they say. The army is most anxious to help. However, they explain, the timing is not yet entirely propitious, for at this very moment there is a crucially important military operation underway inside the Palace of Justice. Perhaps the good Doctor would be so kind as to wait for just a few moments? As soon as it is feasible the commanding officer will come from the

Palace of Justice, where he is directing the operation, to fetch him and escort him personally into the building. The army wants to facilitate the humanitarian mission of the government's representative in every way possible.

Doctor Carlos Martínez Saenz is quite content to wait. "My instructions were to get in contact with the military directors in the area and explain to them the reason for my presence. That I was there in the name of the Presidency of the Republic, to bring a message to the guerrillas," he told Colombian journalist Manuel Vicente Peña a few days later. "Do you mean to say," Manuel Peña asked, "that the Presidency had not made direct contact with the military command?" Doctor Martínez was flustered, irritated by the question. "Well..." he replied, "I think it was up to... actually I can't say anything about that. It's impossible, you have to understand: I can't say to the army: suspend your operations!" So Doctor Martínez waits patiently for General Arias to send for him. While he sits in the Museum of the Casa Florero, the Army High Command, alarmed at the prospect that the order for a cease-fire might materialize at any moment, continues to press General Arias for results. From the Ministry of Defense, a new voice can be heard exhorting the commander on the scene to greater efforts:

> ARCANO 5 [From the ministry or the Command Center]: Well, Commander. It is now urgent to get this situation defined. Over.

> ARIAS: Yes, yes. Here we're giving it every thing we've got. We're giving it grenades and rockets, and we've just exploded a large charge so we have to wait to see what it achieved. It only went off just thirty seconds ago and it seems they [the guerrillas] have retreated to the second floor so far as we can make out.

In one of the more bizarre exchanges of the entire tape, the man in the ministry appears to be trying to send a message to Arias to attack frontally and forget about the possible casualties to his own men.

ARCANO 5: Do not forget the phrase: "You noble dead are my beloved sons in whom I have placed all my hopes." Over.

To which Arias, nothing fazed, replies smoothly: "That is the core and spirit of this army to which we have dedicated our entire lives." His caller signs off wishing him "much luck, much agility, and much cunning."

But it was General Samudio, responding to repeated phone calls from the Minister of Defense, who kept piling on the pressure. The following exchange with the commander of the tanks, Colonel Plazas, reveals the mounting frustration of General Arias' superiors.

SAMUDIO: Listen, tell Arcano 6 [Arias] that I've just this moment spoken to Corage 6 [Minister of Defense, General Vega Uribe] and he's extremely worried. Time is critical.

COL. PLAZAS: We're making our principal effort right this minute, Paladín 6, we're making our principal effort on the sector where the hostages are.

SAMUDIO: Well, continue. Press onwards. Keep insisting. The final outcome of this offensive is urgent. Corage 6 is insisting.

Shortly before one o'clock, General Arias maneuvers his tanks into position on the ground floor of the library. The artillery commander calls for a case of shells, "90mm, to penetrate a wall 50 centimeters thick, penetration shells." General Arias sends for additional troops to go to the fourth floor, "urgently." There are now troops on every floor of the building, closing in on their objective. The final assault is about to begin.

CHAPTER 13

Another Page of Glory

In which the generals accomplish their mission to "finish off" the last of their M-19 enemy, and many innocent people die in the process.

"The guerrillas were running out of ammunition." Gabriel's words are tumbling out in a rush now. "The young woman who was loading the guns kept saying 'the ammnunition is running low' and Almarales had started rationing the bullets; they were only loading three or four guns at one time. He had concentrated the guerrillas closer, around the entrance to the bathroom. There was a black guy whom they all called 'Negro,' who had been fighting all night long. Almarales told him: 'If you're going to fire, wait till they're close enough. Let them have it when you know you can toast the sons of bitches.' Almarales was getting excited. He was running out onto the landing to urge them on, shouting, 'Give it to them, Negro! Get the sons of bitches! Let them have it, Negro!'

"Whenever there was a pause, we'd begin to shout again. We shouted and the soldiers responded. They called out to us: 'Hostages! Come out with your hands up! Come out in single file!' And we would answer: 'We can't! They won't let us go!' We yelled. we begged. We shouted: 'We're the Hostages! Don't kill us! Stop your firing! We're trapped! There are seventy of us in here! Stop your shooting! We can't escape!' And then, once more, the clamor of the guns, of the explosions... and the tanks. Right outside the room..."

*　*　*　*　*

It is 12:45 p.m., Thursday. In the graceful, early nineteenth century Town Hall building that skirts the western edge of the Plaza Bolívar, at right angles to the Palace of Justice, General Villegas Vargas, the Commander of the Bogotá Police force, is just sitting down to lunch with the deputy Mayoress when he receives a call from the military command center on the opposite corner of the square. General Arias' staff wishes to inform the Commander of the Police that the army is almost ready to launch the final offensive on the last "nest of resistance" inside the Palace of Justice. Ever since the chaotic, calamitous attack on the fourth floor the previous evening, in which almost one entire squad of the elite, police special forces were wiped out, relations between the two commanders, never cordial at any time, have been strained. With the army monopolizing the command center in the Museum just across the square, General Vargas and his staff have been happy to avail themselves of the hospitality extended by the Mayor of Bogotá to use the facilities of the Town Hall.

Now, through the windows of the Mayor's elegant official dining room overlooking the square, which provide a ringside view of all movement in and out of the main entrance of the Justice building, General Vargas can see a fresh platoon of troops massing on the steps as they prepare to enter the building to give the final push to a military operation that has now lasted for twenty-five hours. A unit of the Bogotá police force has been fighting alongside the army within the building all morning—though "fighting" hardly seems the right word to describe men reduced to seeking whatever cover they can find, to protect themselves from the fallout of the explosions ripping through the building. Excusing himself regretfully from his gracious hostess, the General now prepares to join his men to witness the inglorious end of this tragic conflict.

*　*　*　*　*

One o'clock. In the Presidential Palace, President Betancur calls his ministers together for their second cabinet meeting of the day. He opens the session by reading the text of the message which he intends to broadcast over national television at eight o'clock that evening, and asks for their comments. Then he calls on the Minister of Defense. General Vega Uribe informs the cabinet of recent developments in the military operation to free the hostages. He reports that little has changed since their last meeting that morning because the army is working, through the use of specialized explosives, to open up access to the area where the remaining guerrillas are concentrated. Their goal, as he defines it, is to be able to rescue the last of the hostages without putting their lives in danger.

The Minister of Foreign Relations says that he has a statement which he would like to put in the record for the sake of history, and he proceeds to read from a written text as follows: "The first decision taken by the President of the Republic with the support of all of his ministers—including the minister of the interior—that of refusing to negotiate or to strike a deal, was taken at a time when the fate of the President's own brother, and of the wife of the minister of the interior, were both unknown. This demonstrates the courage, the wisdom, and the dedication to the highest interests of the nation that has governed all of the decisions taken during this dramatic incident. I would also like to put in the record," he continues, "the unity of the members of the cabinet and their total solidarity with all of the decisions taken by the President of the Republic." The Secretary General of the Presidency, *Señor* Victor G. Ricardo, proposes that this statement from the Minister of Foreign Relations be adopted by all the members of the Cabinet. His proposal is passed unanimously. Strangely there is no record that any member of the Cabinet expressed any curiosity regarding the progress of the government's vanished representative, the head of the Colombian Red Cross, Doctor Martínez Saenz.

* * * * *

Attention all units of the Brigade, tell me if you're
QSL (Present and ready).
Acorazado?
Acorazado QSL.
Acero?
Acero QSL.
Ariete?
Ariete QSL.
Acuario?
Acuario QSL.
Arquitecto?
Arquitecto QSL.
Amperio?
Amperio QSL.
Alguacil?
Alguacil QSL.
Acre?
Acre QSL.
Arnés?
Azabache?
Azabache QSL.
Arpón?
Arpón QSL.
Arnés?
Arnés QSL.

It is roll call time inside the Palace of Justice. The last prelude to
the final assault. Ten army units, belonging to the artillery division
of the XIIIth Bogotá Brigade and the Battalion of the Presidential
Guard, and one unit of the Bogotá military police, approximately
two thousand men are standing by, ready to take part in the final
offensive against the last eight survivors of the M-19.

As the moment of the final assault on the bathroom
approaches, it is unclear just how much General Arias' superiors
understood about their commander's plans. The conversations
between the officers within the Palace and those in the central
command and the ministry become ever more cryptic. There are

several requests for a direct telephone connection—the phrase "give me a 500 line," and "I need a 500 here urgently,"—would appear to indicate that at some level the military outside the building were holding discussions between themselves which they did not wish to be overheard or communicated to General Arias. At some point in the tapes there is a reference to the fact that General Samudio has placed restrictions on the use of certain kinds of explosives. It is not clear whether he orders these restrictions out of impatience, as a tactic to force Arias to get down to brass tacks and attack the guerrillas directly by physically storming the staircase, or whether his motive is a last minute concern for the safety of the hostages; or, as was the case during the previous night's blitz on the fourth floor, a concern to avoid casualties among the troops.

As General Arias positions his tanks to fire 90mm shells directly at the bathroom wall, his officers at the scene appear confused about their commander's intentions. As the platoon of fresh artillery troops, requested by General Arias to join the attack from the fourth floor, enters the building, the following exchanges take place on the walkie-talkies between General Arias and some of his subordinates:

FOR ARCANO 6 [General Arias] FROM ACO-RAZADO 6 [Lt. Col.Plazas]. The artillery platoon is entering the building. Over.

ARCANO 6 [General Arias]: Continue.

COL. PLAZAS: Well, I've got the platoon here but there are suggestions that, they're saying here that there are a lot of personnel up there on the fourth floor already. I've got them waiting but there's the problem that there are very many personnel up there. Over.

No response

COL. PLAZAS: [To ARCANO 3, a Brigade officer on a higher floor] I've got the platoon ready, going to the fourth floor. The platoon is coming up.

ARCANO 3: I'm waiting for them, because I'm ready to go to the fourth floor but there's no one to go with me. I'm still waiting.

AZABACHE 6: Your personnel, Acorazado, does your personnel have hand grenades? Over.

No response.

AZABACHE 6: There's a selected target. We have to break through a 50cm wall. [One and a half feet thick.] Since they want to restrict this type of ammunition, I need instructions. Over.

COL. PLAZAS: What are you going to break through with?

AZABACHE 6: With 90mm shells, penetration ammunition. Over.

COL. PLAZAS: Firing in which direction and into which sector? Because we've got troops on all of the floors. Over.

AZABACHE 6: I really don't know in which direction or into what sector because the person who called me was Ariete 6. I need the precise coordinates from Arcano 6, because I told Ariete that I couldn't fire that type of ammunition without authorization, but he is insisting. I need Arcano 6.

COL. PLAZAS: Well I've got personnel on almost all of the floors, excepting the fourth. We're just about to place troops in that sector. So we need to coordinate things first. We need to know in which direction and at what target you're going to fire. Over.

ARIETE 6: For Arcano 6 from Ariete 6. Over.

GEN. ARIAS: Continue Ariete 6

ARIETE 6: I have made no coordinates with Azabache 6 because I'm not in the area, I don't know where he's going to fire and I haven't talked to him.

GEN. ARIAS: OK. Calm down. It's OK.

ACORAZADO 6: For Arcano 6 from Acorazado 6. Ariete is too far out, he's too far out. Over.

GEN. ARIAS: Continue Acorazado.

COL. PLAZAS: The personnel is carrying rockets, not grenades. Over.

GEN. ARIAS: QSL. [O.K.]

COL. PLAZAS: I also recommend, because there is so much troop personnel, that they should not fire the 90mm cannon. In case of need, they should fire the 50mm. We've been restricted, and we're keeping the restrictions on the 90mm cannon, because the target is very circumscribed. Apart from that the troops are very close to it. And besides, the great capacity of penetration of that ammunition could cause us problems in other areas. So we'll stick to, we'll only use the machine guns. Is the platoon on the fourth floor yet?

A VOICE: [Probably Col. Plazas direct subordinate, Artillery Major Fracica]: A part of it, just a part of it, I'm trying to complete. [The positioning of artillery platoon, on the fourth floor] Over.

COL. PLAZAS: I'm going to look for grenades to see if I can send you some. Over.

A VOICE: Acorazado 6?

COL. PLAZAS: Send me a box of grenades here at once and with maximum security, to back up a machine gun."

General Arias' strategy is as follows: First, to break through the east wall of the bathroom with the 50mm shells of the tanks or with the T-M72-A2 shaped charges, fired from hand-held rocket launchers positioned on the second floor. Then, as the inhabitants of the bathroom are forced to flee the room, his artillery troops, stationed on the second, third and fourth floor landings on the stairs, will hit them with everything they've got—machine gun fire, grenades, the lot.

When the artillery troops are finally deployed on the fourth floor, in position to close in on the guerrillas down the stairs; when the box of grenades has been delivered; when two soldiers, armed with rocket launchers, are in position on the second floor, and Lt. Colonel Plazas, commanding the tanks and armored cars in the ground floor library, is ready to open fire with his 50mm machine guns against the exposed east wall of the bathroom, the final assault is at last ready to begin. The time is almost 1:30 p.m. It is 26 hours since the M-19 attacked the Justice building.

* * * * *

Inside the bathroom, Gabriel says that in the end the hostages gave way to despair. "There came a moment," he says, "very close to the end, when we all fell silent. There had been a lot of commotion in the bathroom, everyone talking to everyone else, everyone begging the guerrillas to let us go. We told Almarales, 'we've all got families.' We implored him, people were begging him, for the sake of their wives and their husbands, to show some humanity and let us go. Some of the mothers were weeping for their children... Then suddenly, we each lost all hope. We just sat. In silence. You have the feeling that you're dead already. You sit there quietly, waiting for death. Even Manuel Gaona gave up then. He said, 'I'm not shouting anymore. I'm not going to say anything more. I know I'm not getting out of here alive.' He said to Almarales: 'I come from simple folk. I'm a man of the people. Before I came to the court I was selling shirts in the street on Calle 19. Then they called me into the ministry. I'm one of you. I shouldn't even be here. I have a baby daughter ten months old. If you kill me, what's going to happen to her? What's her life going to be?

"But Almarales refused to let us go.

"The soldiers were almost on top of us when he made a decision. 'Alright' he shouted, 'we're going to play our last card,' and he ordered the men to kneel in a line in front of the entrance to the bathroom, in order of importance. First, the judges of the Supreme Court and the Council of State; behind them the auxiliary magistrates; then the visitors, because there were some visitors who had been trapped in the building when the guerrillas arrived; then the secretaries and the chauffeurs. Everybody, men and women, in order of importance. We all protested. We said 'it isn't possible, how can you put us in the front line like that, exposed to the first salvo of bullets?' He explained to us the reason. It was so that in the moment when the soldiers arrived in the bathroom—'because make no mistake about it,' he said, 'they're coming, they're going to get here,'—and he said, 'the first thing they see, in the instant they reach the door, they must see you. When they see you, when they realise who you are, they won't shoot.' That's what he said. 'And shout. Shout,' he said. 'You must go on shouting.' That's how he explained it to us.

"So Manuel Gaona said, 'well, if it's your last card then it's ours too, let's do it.' And he went to the front of the room and knelt down, in front of the entrance, and everyone else, all of the others, took their places beside him and behind him—men and women, all in their order of importance. And once again we started to shout. Calling on them to stop firing, calling for the Red Cross. And again we heard the army responding. They shouted back: 'Surrender! Come out with your hands up! Come out slowly in single file!' And we yelled back at them: 'We can't! They won't let us!' And Gaona shouted 'I've got a ten-month old little girl. Please don't kill me! I've got to live for her sake!' And nothing. Just more bullets. More war..."

Soldier Rodrigo Romero was one of those who heard the hostages calling to the army. All the soldiers could hear them. In his subsequent testimony to the Commission of Ennquiry, soldier Romero told the investigating judge: "At the beginning we shouted to them that they should let the hostages go, and they shouted back that they needed the Red Cross. Then when they saw that the army would not let the Red Cross in, they went on shooting at us, because, well, the army said they wouldn't let the Red Cross in until they released the hostages, and they wouldn't obey. They just went on shooting at us, shouting 'Down with the army!' 'Down with the black boots!' And the army shouted back that they should come out with their hands up and they wouldn't be harmed. But they answered back that they would fight on to the death. It went on like that..."

Almarales, according to Gabriel, was intent on making "his last show of military strength." For the first time I detect a bitter edge to his voice. "They detonated the last of their explosives, they still had two Claymore mines left; and they flung the last of their grenades out there somewhere. And then Almarales brought the rest of the guerrillas inside the bathroom with us."

Leaving only two men on the landing immediately outside the entrance to the bathroom, Almarales reorganizes his defenses. He brings the last surviving guerrillas inside the room and lines them up beside the urinals, with their backs to the north wall, and their guns trained on the kneeling hostages. If, at that moment, the soldiers had stormed the entrance to the bathroom, they would not have even seen the guerrillas since the urinals were completely shielded from sight at the entrance by the floor to ceiling extension wall. It would have been impossible for anyone coming into the bathroom to have seen the guerrillas until they penetrated beyond this shielded passage into the center of the crowded room.

But that of course is not the route that General Arias has chosen to take. By the time the army is ready to launch its final offensive against the bathroom, the outer section of the east wall, the one shielding the air duct, has already been almost entirely destroyed by plastic explosives. Only a brick wall, 18 inches thick, now stands between the people in the bathroom and the 50mm machine guns of the armored tanks, with which Colonel Plazas is waiting to pound this wall from a distance, calculated later by the investigators and ballistics experts, of between 45 and 105 feet. In addition, soldiers deployed on the second floor, standing between 80 and 90 feet from their target, await the order to attack this wall with hand-held rocket launchers, loaded with A-T-M72-A2 shaped charges, the weapons that the soldiers called "rockets."

"From my position, rockets were fired in order to make an opening in the wall so as to be able to get the hostages out," Sub-Sargent Ariel Grajales Bastidas of the School of Artillery of the XIIIth Brigade told the Special Commission of Inquiry some weeks later. "These rockets were fired from the east side of the second floor inside the Palace of Justice. I fired one of them. The order to fire came from my commanding officer Major Fracica, from the ground floor. But I was not firing at the hostages, only at the wall. I don't know who fired the other rocket. It was fired from a position behind me."

Inside the bathroom the hostages are still shouting for help, still trying to persuade Almarales to surrender, when the army's bombardment of the east wall begins. Gabriel, surrounded by other hostages, is kneeling on the floor towards the back, or southern end of the room when the first rocket strikes the bathroom wall. It explodes on contact, penetrating the brick at the level of a towel rack attached to the wall beside the wash basins. The explosion propels the towel rack into the room, its metal structure penetrated in three places by pieces of the rocket's explosives. The rocket head tears a hole through the brick wall—ten inches long by seven inches across—through which fragments of the weapon's metal casing penetrate to the interior of the room, killing one hostage instantly, and wounding several others.

In the immediate chaos that erupts inside the bathroom after the impact of the first rocket, two of the guerrillas, believing that the army is about to come through the wall, turn their guns in a reflex action onto the area where the towel rack had fallen, spraying the wall with bullets. The hostages instinctively surge en masse towards the door. "We all tried to escape at that moment," says Gabriel. "Everyone. The general reaction was to flee, somehow, from that room. A young woman, one of the secretaries, attacked Almarales physically. She threw herself on him, pummeling him with her fists, calling him an assassin, a murderer. He was shouting: 'Quiet, be quiet, give me time to think! No one leaves! Be quiet! Let me THINK!' And in that instant the second shell came through the wall, followed immediately by bullets, explosives, everything..."

There was such pandemonium inside the bathroom after the first rocket struck that none of the survivors ever understood where the second one hit. Nor could they ever figure out the source of the gunfire that penetrated the bathroom in the immediate aftermath of the second rocket's impact. Some of the hostage survivors were convinced that they had been fired on by the guerrillas. Gabriel believed the army had thrown a hand grenade into the room through the break in the wall caused by the first rocket. "You could hear it," he says, "skittering across the floor, and then Boom! The explosion. And there were bullets. Bullets coming through the wall. The bullets were flying everywhere. Ricocheting off the marble walls. Everyone was falling on top of everyone else, and there was blood all over..."

In fact the second shell hit the bathroom wall just below the wash basins, right beside the master key of the main water fawcett. Immediately an army marksman, standing outside the bathroom, on the second floor, introduced his 9mm automatic rifle through the break in the wall where the second rocket had struck and fired blindly into the middle of the crowded bathroom, spraying the blood of the dead and the dying upwards across the bathroom ceiling.

No one knows precisely how many of the sixty-nine hostages who were still alive when General Arias' final assault on the bathroom began died as a result of the attack. Some reports claim seventeen casualties; others estimate that over twenty hostages were killed. The army, which took charge of removing and identifying the bodies, spread such a murky smokescreen over all aspects of the last hour of the military operation, that when, four months later, Felipe and his colleagues from the morgue were requested by the Commission of Inquiry to reconstruct what had happened, even their painstaking efforts were only partially successful. The investigating judge wanted to know whether "the wounds that caused the death of several people in the bathroom... were caused from positions outside the bathroom, or, if not, then from where?" [sic] In their report the morgue investigators were forced to respond that: "It is not possible to give a conclusive answer as to whether the shots that killed some people and wounded others came from outside or inside the bathroom, since, in the majority of cases, we do not know where the people were when they died or were wounded." However, in those specific cases of the six individual casualties whose deaths the morgue team was able to investigate and document, what they discovered revealed the strategy devised by General Arias in all its devastating stupidity and brutality.

When the firing stopped, two Supreme Court Justices—Judge Manuel Gaona, and his colleague Judge Horacio Montoya Gil—were dead. So were two young women lawyers, two chauffeurs for the justices, and a young Associate Justice, Lisandro Romero, on the staff of the Council of State. Gabriel, who had never taken his eyes off Manuel Gaona, recalls watching him leave the room right after the second rocket struck the bathroom wall. "I saw Judge Gaona leave the room right after the second shell," he says. "He was still alive when he left the bathroom. I saw him go. I saw him go out the door. But later, when I was leaving myself, he was already dead. I saw his body lying there. At the bottom of the first flight of stairs, just outside the bathroom. But I don't know who killed him." And Urán? Carlos Urán? I asked. What happened to him? "He was alive then, too," Gabriel replies. "He was with us in the bathroom until the very end. But there again, I don't know what happened to him. I never saw Urán again."

Manuel Gaona was shot six times. He died as he crouched beside the exterior wall of the bathroom, trying to make his way down the stairs to the second floor landing. Recreating the trajectories of the six bullets that struck him, the investigators concluded that he was shot by soldiers who were standing on the third floor landing, following orders to fire at anything that moved in the vicinity of the bathroom "target."

The same soldiers also flung grenades down the stairs at the other hostages who were trying to get away from the mayhem inside the bathroom. It was grenade fragments that killed Judge Montoya Gil and a young Associate Justice for the Council of State, Lizandro Romero. It was grenade fragments that tore into Carlos Urán's back and legs, though the multiple lacerations he received then were not the cause of his death. Carlos Urán's death came later.

The two young women lawyers, Aura Nieto Navarrete and Luz Stella Bernal, were both killed inside the bathroom. Both of them were shot in the back where they were sitting together, on the floor, beneath the wash basins and just in front of the opening made by the impact of the second shell beside the main water fawcett. The weapon that killed them was fired from close-up—a distance of approximately two feet. A single fatal shot tore through Aura Navarrete's chest. Luz Stella Bernal was hit four times.

One of the chauffeurs was killed by fragments of the first rocket that broke through the wall; the second chauffeur, who had been kneeling on the floor facing the two young women casualties, was hit and killed by the same shooter who had killed them, firing blindly through the opening under the washbasins.

Inside the bathroom, when the marksman with the 9mm automatic rifle withdraws his gun from the opening beneath the washbasin and the shooting stops, there is a brief, appalled silence. A moment's pause, during which Andrés Almarales forgets about every other consideration except for the one imperative: to halt the carnage. Ordering the guerrillas to hold their fire he starts screaming at the army: 'Let the women out! The women are leaving! Hold your fire! The women are coming out!'

Slowly, skirting respectfully around the dead and the wounded, the women begin to leave the blood spattered room. There is little joy in their release, yet in the eyes of their male colleagues who stand to watch them go, this somber procession of thirty-one mostly young, mostly poor, secretaries, assistants, and cleaning women, who have all survived the monstrosity of the siege with their humanity intact, has a heartbreaking dignity. In somber silence they move slowly, in single file, their hands held high above their heads. A few weep, but most are beyond tears. One young secretary, the same one who had earlier attacked Andrés Almarales and called him a murderer and an assassin, turns back as she reaches the exit and grabs him by the arm: "They're going to kill you, Andrés," she says. "Come with us. Come. Come out now." But Andrés Almarales only shakes his head. "We're *machos*, daughter" he replies; "We only have one life, and we'll stay here to die like *machos*." Then, when almost all the women hostages have left, the two young M-19 women who have spent all day and all night loading the guns, ask Almarales for his permission to leave also. "Good luck go with you, *compañeras*," he says. "Call my family and greet my wife for me if you manage to make it. And good luck go with you, *compañera*, lots of luck." So, they too join the queue of the departing hostages, to step out onto the landing dressed in the same civilian clothes that they wore on arrival in the Palace with Alfonso Jaquín, twenty-seven hours ago. There the army is waiting for them.

Then Andrés decides that the wounded hostages must leave. All those who could stand or drag themselves across the floor and out of the room. There were four hostages who could not make it on their own. In the absence of the Red Cross they are carried across the entrance to the landing by their colleagues. And then everyone leaves. Initially, when Andrés Almarales had called for the wounded to be evacuated, he had said to the room at large, "The rest of us, the men who are unhurt, we'll stay and die like *machos*."

But no one was listening to him any longer. "I told myself," says Gabriel, "'I'm going. If I stay here I'll be in bits. I'm going, going, going...' So Gabriel, like everyone else, walks out of the room with the others, behind the wounded.

* * * * *

The Director General of the Red Cross is still waiting for permission to go to the Palace of Justice to deliver the government's message to Andrés Almarales when the hostages begin arriving in the Command Center in the Museum. "Now," says Lt. Colonel Plazas, who has come to fetch him, "the Commanding Officer, General Arias, can receive you. He is waiting for you inside the Palace of Justice." Clutching the walkie-talkie for Andrés Almarales, and the letter from President Betancur for the guerrillas, and accompanied by five Red Cross stretcher bearers, Doctor Martínez prepares to carry out his "humanitarian mission." The time is 1:50 p.m.. He has been waiting patiently inside the Museum for nearly an hour and a half.

In his testimony to the Special Commission of Inquiry, Doctor Martínez had no complaints to make about this lengthy and fatal delay. To the contrary. He insisted that, "I was given all the guarantees, I met with the fullest support from the Armed Forces, who requested me to have a moment's calm before attempting my entry into the building since, at that time, a major operation was in progress which made it impossible for them to mobilize any of their personnel. At the same time I was informed that the Commander of the Brigade, General Arias, who was leading the troops who were trying to gain entrance to the building, had been informed of my presence, and had ratified the order imparted to me to await a more prudent moment."

So when the army have reached their objective, "two officers of the highest rank," Lt. Colonel Plazas—fresh from his military victory— and the Commander of the Bogotá Police, General Vargas Villegas, accompany Doctor Martínez and his staff to the main entrance of the Palace of Justice. There they shake hands, and inform him that General Arias is waiting to receive him on the third floor. "They told me that the responsibility from here on was mine alone," Dr. Martínez told a reporter a few days later. They also tell him, that "the success of my mission depended exclusively on its acceptance by the occupiers."

In his testimony, several weeks later, Dr. Martínez was emphatic that, on arrival inside the building, he had made use of a megaphone to announce his presence to "the entrenched occupiers," advising them that he was the bearer of a message from the government. "The only reply we received to this invitation," he complained then, "was a burst of machinegun fire, which forced us to take refuge.... I want to make perfectly clear," his testimony concluded, "that my sincere interest in carrying out this mission was totally obstructed because the occupiers at no time wished to accept the government's message, nor the elements, [the walkie-talkies], nor the medical supplies sent for the gentlemen magistrates."

This version of the failure of his "humanitarian mission" fits right in line with the version spread abroad in the press by army spokesmen immediately after the battle ended. It also shares many aspects of the testimony of Colonel Sánchez—the same officer who, together with Colonel Plazas Vega, had delayed 'the personage' in the Museum Command Center. Testifying under oath to the investigative judge two months later, when Colonel Sánchez was asked to tell everything he knew about Judge Arciniegas' mission, he managed to infer that Doctor Martínez' visit to the Palace of Justice was the direct result of General Arias' positive response to the elderly Judge's mission. Colonel Sánchez then went on to describe what happened to Doctor Martínez at the Palace of Justice and to explain his failure to deliver his message from the President to the guerrillas. According to the Colonel, Doctor Martínez arrived at the Palace of Justice, "about an hour and a half" after Judge Arciniegas left the building, "in order to take contact with the the subversives... to mediate some form of arrangement to end the problem. He and his collaborators," the Colonel continued, "went to the Palace of Justice and tried to enter. But unfortunately the response of the subversives was to shoot at them, thus impeding the completion of their mission. Later they returned again and tried to enter once more, and again they had no further success and were forced to withdraw."

General Arias, for his part, testified that the imminent arrival of Dr. Martínez and his five assistants at the Palace of Justice, had obliged him to leave the scene of operations inside the Palace to go and await their arrival in the Museum. After about an hour, the General said, since there was still no sign of them, he returned to the scene of the battle, leaving instructions for the Red Cross delegation to be brought to meet him in the Palace of Justice as soon as they arrived. Then, General Arias said, the "stubbornness, and the manner in which the subversives chose to respond,"—by firing at the delegation—made it impossible for Dr. Martínez to carry out his mission.

The truth about Dr. Martínez' arrival inside the Palace of Justice is quite other. Shortly before he gets there, General Arias has called General Samudio to let him know that "in the mezzanine bathroom where we had the conflict, according to the personnel here, there are only seven guerrillas left... so we have no problem anymore, according to the people here, with any other personnel apart from the guerrillas." In other words, the hostages who have been providing a human shield for the guerrillas, those who survived the siege, have been escorted from the building. There are no further impediments to "accomplishing our mission."

It is dark inside the Palace of Justice when Doctor Martínez arrives. A ferocious gun battle rages on one of the upper floors. In spite of instructions from General Samudio to "be sure 'the personage' is protected," when Doctor Martínez and his staff enter the building General Arias leaves them to find their own way to the third floor where he impatiently awaits the final 'liquidation' of the last of the guerrillas. Feeling their way in the dark up the south stairway, almost deafened by the clamor of the guns echoing around the ruins, Doctor Martínez and his five companions eventually reach the third floor, where they find General Arias at the head of the stairs. There, side by side in the dark, the Director General of the Colombian Red Cross and the Commmander of the XIIIth Brigade wait for the conflict between the guerrillas and the army to conclude. Shouting to be heard above the gunfire, Dr.

Martínez tells General Arias, "You know I bring a message from the President of the Republic for those gentlemen." And the General shouts back, "Of course I know, but how are you going to insert yourself into the middle of that?" pointing helplessly towards the fighting raging on the mezzanine below.

It takes another twenty minutes before the M-19 finally run out of ammunition. The soldiers only enter the bathroom after the guerrillas' last bullet is spent. They find the guerrillas attempting to hide inside the toilet stalls, crouched for protection behind the battered metal doors and partitions. In a final spasm of butchery, the soldiers lift their guns over the tops of the partitions, and fire the last fusillade of the long battle, blindly, frenetically, into the toilet stalls.

The soldiers find Andrés Almarales slumped on the floor beside the north wall urinal. According to the autopsy report conducted at the city morgue, the shot that killed Andrés is a 9mm bullet, fired on contact, execution style, into his right forehead.

When the carnage is finally over, a squad of exhausted soldiers climbs the stairs to report, "mission accomplished, *mi General*," to their victorious commander-in-chief. The Director General of the Red Cross, "given the impossibility of delivering the Government's message to the guerrillas," removes President Betancur's letter from his vest pocket and hands it over to General Arias. The General takes the letter, opens it, and reads:

> The Government wishes to remind those who still persist in their objective of occupying the Palace of Justice, of the offer made yesterday to *Señor* Luis Otero, that the Public Force, as is their duty, will respect the personal integrity and the lives of all those who desist from their military actions and will guarantee them a trial according to the law.
>
> Should any member of the M-19 organization wish precise details regarding this renewed offer, they can make use of the sound equipment which is put at their disposition, on the opposite end of which [sic] they will find the Minister of Justice.

As he folds the letter and pockets it, General Arias comments laconically, "what a pity there is no one left alive to accept this offer." The time is 2:20 p.m.

"The personnel is totally 'fumigated.' Over," General Arias reports to his superiors a few moments later, and the heavy tones of the Minister of Defense, General Vega Uribe, break into the internal communications system to offer his congratulations to the troops: "I want to express my personal congratulations, and also in the name of all the commanders and members of the General Staff of the High Command, to all of the personnel—without exception —of the Brigades and their subordinate units, for the success of the operation. You have demonstrated to Colombia and to the world the professionalism and spirit of service of our army. All of us, and I most particularly, feel very proud. I lament the death of sub-lieutenant Villamízar, and the wounded, who have written with their blood another page of glory for those who bear the arms of Colombia. Many, many thanks. And once more, my congratulations."

CHAPTER 14

"Operación Limpieza"

In which the army, the government, the Congress, the media, and the Church, come together to clean up the mess, and begin the task of establishing an acceptable, official version of the siege.

After the gunfire stops, when the war between the army and the M-19 is over, Colonel Alfonso Plazas Vega emerges from the destroyed Justice building and announces to the waiting journalists on the square the "total annihilation of the terrorists." The soldiers exit the building. They stream out through the broken doors, down the stone steps, and when they reach the pavement, they hoist their guns high above their heads and flash victory signs at the cameras. Then the Colonel climbs into his tank, and at the head of his column of tanks and armored cars, he drives out of the Plaza Bolívar triumphant, to lead his own victory parade, through the streets of Bogotá, back to the XIIIth Brigade's Headquarters in the north of the city.

Such overt signs of satisfaction with the successful completion of the Army's mission to defeat the M-19 enemy were short-lived. For very quickly, Colonel Plazas Vega's superiors, like their civilian counterparts, must turn their attention to damage control. Within the gutted hulk of the still smoldering ruin, in the overcrowded Command Center in the Museum, and inside the cabinet room in the Presidential Palace, the immediate priorities of this post-battle aftermath are perceived differently. But the goal is the same. For twenty-seven hours, the main players in this drama that has transfixed the nation have been unmasked. Now it is time to draw the curtains, to retreat into the shadows. It is a time when old lies will reappear and new ones will have to be invented. It is time to count the corpses.

During the first three days after the battle ended, between Thursday afternoon, November 7, and the following Sunday, November 10, this is what happened:

As soon as the fighting stops, the government calls on the army to produce the Chief Justice. The army is unable to find any trace of Judge Reyes, dead or alive. While the soldiers look for him amid the rubble, and the intelligence agents initiate a search for eyewitness accounts of his last sighting among the survivors in the Command Center, word is passed to the cabinet and the media that all of the justices have been safely rescued. The Chief of Police, General Mallarino, calls up Judge Reyes' son, Yesid, to prepare him for his father's imminent return. Other calls go out to the wives of other justices, telling them to stand by. General Samudio, meanwhile, instructs General Arias to put *"Operación Limpieza"*—mopping-up operations—on hold for the time being, until the mystery of the Chief Justice's disappearance has been solved. It does not take the army long to find the answer. At a few moments past three o'clock that afternoon, the radio reporting from the Plaza Bolívar is brutally interrupted by news of "a terrible mistake." A reporter sorrowfully corrects his earlier news bulletins to announce "the vile death of the Chief Justice." The army has just learned that Judge Reyes "was assassinated in a miserable fashion, in cold blood, by the guerrilla commandante Andrés Almarales."

* * * * *

In the Presidential Palace, when the news of the death of Judge Reyes Echandia and ten other members of the Supreme Court and the Council of State reaches the cabinet, the immediate response of the assembled ministers is to circle the wagons against a hostile world. The Minister of the Interior, Jaime Castro, succinctly lays out the guidelines for the future: "Last night," he admits, "I permitted myself to make certain observations which I am not going to repeat now, but I was very clear in my stated warning that these were internal. That it was not my intention to make any institutional criticisms. I omitted to say that if it becomes necessary for there to be a debate, which will surely be the case, we must be very clear. We must defend the same position. We must avoid everything that could create elements of discord. What is needed now is that we all act in absolute solidarity."

In line with the minister's warning, his "observations" at the Cabinet meeting on the previous evening, November 6th, are excised from the minutes that have gone into the record. It is not too difficult, however, to guess the identity of the "institution" at which his words were directed. In any event, his words find great resonance among his colleagues. Not only now, but in the difficult days and weeks to come, all official contributions to the public debate and to the future judicial investigation of these events will be a model of "clarity" and "solidarity."

With one, predictable exception. Now and in the future, only Enrique Parejo demonstrates any grasp of the awesome dimensions of the tragedy. When Parejo receives the news from the battlefront, solidarity is not his major preocupation. The Minister of Justice alarms his colleagues with a critique of the military operation that has kept the cabinet "insufficiently informed throughout," he repeats his earlier demand for a thorough investigation, and warns them that the country will not recover from the loss of so many of their finest judicial minds. "History," says the Minister of Justice, "will judge these events with extreme severity. As will public opinion around the nation, and above all in the judicial branch, which will undoubtedly blame the government for its lack of foresight in the management of this crisis."

Parejo's colleagues prefer to take their cue from President Betancur, who calls for "a heroic act of serenity, reflection and meditation," and the ministers express the collective conviction that at the end of the day all has turned out for the best. The Minister of Foreign Affairs, Augusto Ramírez Campo speaks for them all when he states: "I have the profound conviction that everything that has happened was done for the good of the *Patria*...

I am convinced that we have offered a magnificent hommage to democracy." Others express this interpretation of the tragedy in phrases like: "The lives of the justices have been lost but the justice system has been strengthened." (The Secretary of State for Economics). "Assailed by the clamor of the battle the country maintained its forward march." (The Minister of Public Works). "Any war has its price... yet we have won a battle in defense of the institutions and given a lesson that will be of decisive value." (The Minister of Finance). And so forth, and so on. "Once again," Minister of Defense Vega Uribe pointedly reminds the civilians, staring down the table at Parejo, "the Armed Forces have supported the legitimately constituted government."

When all of his ministers have had their say, President Betancur closes the session with a pep talk. "The greatest evil known to humankind," says the President, according to his note-taker, *Señor* Ricardo, "namely terrorism, has been dealt with in an exemplary fashion. Self-criticism," he continues, "is always difficult, because one always sees oneself in a good light. So it is hard to recognize one's own mistakes. Sometimes, as in the poem of Carranza, 'I Hear Voices From On High,' it is necessary to lift one's eyes towards the heavens. Permit me to tell you, my dear ministers," he continues, "that this horrible drama must unite all of us even more. Not just for the sake of the government—but for the country, for our beloved *Patria*. Because the *Patria* is a demanding lover, and one who needs us now. We are going to be even more courageous, more united, and show an even greater solidarity." So saying, to applause from his cabinet, the President of the Republic withdraws with his advisors to his private quarters to redraft the text of his forthcoming television address. Once again, this has had to be rescheduled. Belisario Betancur will finally speak to the nation at nine o'clock in the evening.

* * * * *

Within the ruins of the battlefield meanwhile, the army is engaged in "*Operación Limpieza*,"—mopping up operations. General Arias is also engaged in the destruction of evidence. Although the battle to retake the Palace of Justice has ended in victory, the military is not yet ready to step aside. Their operation is not over. During the remaining daylight hours, behind the screen of army and police barricades and checkpoints that encircles the Palace's great shell of blackened steel and concrete, the killings continue. Any M-19 guerrillas found wounded within the building, like the three young men in the bathroom who had survived the entire siege, are executed on the spot that afternoon. Members of the Bogotá Fire Brigade, ordered into the building at around four-thirty to begin collecting the bodies scattered around the rubble, testified later to hearing isolated gun shots, and one lengthy fusilade—about 10 seconds of intense submachine gunfire they said—reverberating through sections of the devastated building until almost six o'clock that evening. Some of the dazed, naive young soldiers, ambushed by reporters as they stagger out into the square—their sweat-drenched faces still smeared with black smoke—admit, a little shamefacedly, that yes, they did have orders not to take any prisoners.

These post-battle killings are not necessarily limited to the extermination of wounded M-19 survivors. Unsure, to the very end, about the precise number of guerrillas who invaded the Palace, the army is not too particular about the identity of those whom they "finish off" that afternoon. Mistakes are made. By the time that General Arias advises his superiors of the successful conclusion of "*Operación Limpieza*," there have been innocent victims. According to the analysis of his medical autopsy, Associate Justice Carlos Urán was among those killed by the soldiers during the course of their mopping up assignment. Wounded but still alive at the end of the battle, Carlos Urán, struck by grenade fragments in the attack on the stairs, had multiple wounds in his back and legs. Yet the cause of his death was not connected to these wounds. The cause of death was identical in every respect to the manner in which the wounded M-19 guerrillas died: Carlos Urán was killed by a 9mm bullet in the brain, fired execution style, on contact, through the forehead. Carlos Urán's body, furthermore, "disappeared" for twenty-four hours after "*Operación Limpieza*." His name was not on any of the army's lists; he could not be found among the living, the wounded, or the dead. Eventually, late on the evening of the following day, Friday November 8, friends of his anguished wife discover Carlos Urán's corpse in the morgue, in the special section reserved by the army for the dead of the M-19. A label had been attached to his chest which read: "N.N. [unknown] Guerrilla," and it took the combined efforts of the Attorney General and the President of the Council of State to persuade the army and police officers in control of the morgue to release Carlos Urán's body to his family for a decent burial.

* * * * *

On Thursday afternoon at about 4:30 p.m., right after the conclusion of "*Operación Limpieza*," the police invite a small contingent of select journalists to a quick, guided tour through the rubble. 'Police sources' volunteer the information that, at the end, "as they saw the army approaching," eight of the guerrilla leaders locked themselves in a bathroom and committed suicide. According to the police, by the time the army reached the bathroom and broke down the door, all of the guerrillas were dead.

The police also provide a hostage-witness to the killing of Judge Manuel Gaona. After the death of the Chief Justice, Judge Gaona's death is the most sensitive for the authorities. Jorge Antonio Reina, described as a driver for the Supreme Court, goes on the radio to give a graphic description to the Bogotá listeners of how the guerrillas forced Manuel Gaona to lie down on the floor and shot him through the forehead. Reina also talked to the foreign press: "They shot Justice Manuel Gaona Cruz here," he said, touching a finger to his forehead. "They made him lie down on the floor and that's where they shot him even though he was insisting that they should try to negotiate." Reina also described a scene for reporters from Reuters, the Associated Press, *The Washington Post*, *Time*, *The New York Times*, and *Newsweek*, among others, according to which: "The rebels turned out the lights in a room with curtained windows and started spraying the hostages with bullets." This, Reina said, happened after he had watched the guerrillas murder several other Supreme Court Justices. The number of judges Reina personally saw shot in cold blood varies, from one account to another, between three and six. His version of the deaths of the hostage justices is broadcast around the world.

The foreign reporters are nevertheless troubled that none of this information can be independently verified. There are conflicting reports circulating about the end of the long battle. Doubts surface as to whether the guerrillas committed suicide, as the officials insist, or whether in fact they surrendered. Reporters and relatives of the hostages are barred from access to the Museum Command Center at the corner of the Plaza Bolívar, where the police and army intelligence agents are still interviewing the "rescued" hostages. And the police cannot provide a figure for the number of survivors they helped to escort from the ruins at the end of the battle. The radio reporting says the number of people who were rescued was between thirty-eight and forty-eight people. By late Thursday night, when the newspapers go to press, there is still no official figure. The Museum Command Center, where army intelligence and police have been keeping a register of everyone who has emerged from the conflict since it began, remains barred to families and friends clamoring for news of loved ones. Inside, the intelligence services are interviewing, debriefing and interrogating the survivors. Not all of those who emerged from the conflict alive will make it safely to their homes.

*   *   *   *   *

Inside the gutted Palace of Justice, when the army finishes their mopping up exercises, they turn their attention to the dead. Several bodies are scattered through the rubble around different parts of the building and in the basement, but the largest number are to be found on the fourth floor and in the bathroom. Colombia has very specific laws governing the removal of corpses from any public place for shipment to the city morgue. The job must be carried out by professionally trained experts, under the supervision of a civilian judge duly appointed by the Attorney General's office. Before any corpse can be moved, a detailed record must be documented of the physical surroundings, including a photographic record. All of these laws are now broken. General Arias, with the knowledge and approval of his superiors, turns over the task of supervision to army officers assigned to fulfill the role of military judges. He then sends for the Bogotá fire brigade and for members of the Colombian Red Cross to collect the corpses from around the building, bring them to the central courtyard, and there line them up for identification. No photographs are taken at the site where the victims died. Later, no one involved can even remember how many bodies there were in the bathroom when they got there; nor which ones were found outside the bathroom, or on the stairs; nor how many of the bodies found in the bathroom were guerrillas. In short, there exists no official record that documents how or where over one hundred people met their death. To conceal the execution-style deaths of the wounded and of the guerrillas in the bathroom, General Arias orders the firemen to hose down the bodies. In several instances the workers remove their blood-soaked clothing, and discard it on the bathroom floor. The dead are then carefully washed before their naked bodies are packed into plastic body bags for shipment to the morgue.

The single largest group of corpses, however, are the fifty-eight victims of Wednesday night's battle for the fourth floor. Their bodies are almost all so badly burnt by the flames that they are no longer recognizable. According to the subsequent testimony of several morgue workers, when the body bags arrive at their destination some of the immolated corpses identified as men turn out to be women; some body bags contain the remains of two or more different bodies; in others there are only parts of bodies; and in all cases, the personal belongings of the dead—a gold watch, a medal, a pen—small items which could have helped the families to identify their own, have been lost, stolen, or shipped in separate containers.

*   *   *   *   *

At nine o'clock, on Thursday night, President Belisario Betancur speaks to the nation. "The government," he says, "could not negotiate what is nonnegotiable: the respectability of our institutions."

Gazing sorrowfully into the eye of the television camera, speaking slowly, and softly, the President then solemnly describes for his fellow Colombians a scene that never took place. "That immense responsibility," Betancur says, speaking of the constitutional defense of democracy and of the institutions, "was shouldered by the President of the Republic, who, regardless of the repercussions to himself for good or for ill, personally made all of the decisions, gave all of the respective orders, keeping an absolute control over the situation throughout. Everything that was done to find a solution corresponds to his sole responsibility, not to other factors which he can and must control." There are few among his audience in Bogotá that night who believe him, and none who fail to recognize the identity of those 'other factors' to which he has referred. But belief is not the paramount issue. Gathered in front of their television sets, the establishment can finally breathe easy. This President, like all of his antecedents, has "finally put on his trousers." He has brought them back from the brink. There will be no constitutional crisis. But for all those outside the circles that make up the power structure of this caste society, in the sad, broken streets of Bogotá, where armored cars and troops armed with automatic weapons patrol the center of the city all through the night, and where rumors of disappearances and arrests among the rescued hostages have already begun to circulate, this night is one of fear.

* * * * *

During those first hours after the end of the battle, downtown Bogotá is crowded with frantic, anguished people, searching for their relatives and friends. Ignored by civilian leaders, obstructed by agents of the army and the police, they have been abandoned, left to search for nonexistent survivors alone. Following a trail of false hopes and misleading clues, amid chaos and spreading panic, they rush from the Museum Command Center to the city hospitals, from the hospitals to the clinics, from the clinics to the police stations, from the police stations to the military barracks, to the radio stations, the newspaper offices—and back again to the

Museum. For many, the search lasts all through the afternoon and evening; for some it continues into the following day. Until finally, in despair, they find themselves among the innumerable rows of mutilated corpses in the overcrowded city morgue.

*   *   *   *   *

One woman arrives at the city morgue to look for the body of her husband after midnight late on Thursday night. More than five years later, when she tries to describe what she saw there she is unable to do so. "There are no words to describe what it was like," she says. "When you're looking for someone you love, and you carry their image with you, you're looking for his face, for the color of his hair, for the way that it grew... In order to look for my husband, in the midst of complete chaos, I had to begin by reviewing the long lines of corpses... Only a very few were even recognizable as human beings."

At that late hour, only a few of the victims from the fourth floor of the Palace have arrived at the morgue, and Amalia Mantilla, the wife of the deputy to the Chief Justice, and a judge herself, is told to return the next day. She decides instead to look first for her husband's body inside the Palace of Justice.

At nine o'clock on the morning of Friday November 8, using her official, bureaucrat's identity card, Amalia Mantilla becomes the only person intimately connected to the tragedy who succeeds in penetrating the ruins of the building while the army is still in control of the site. "Everywhere you looked," she says, "in every direction, it was a war zone. The entire fourth floor had been demolished. There was nothing left. Not a single dividing wall was still standing, the floor was deep in ashes, rubble, broken glass, and in places, the still glowing embers of the conflagration."

Working, "from my memory of how things used to be," Amalia reaches the place where she believes that Judge Reyes' office should have been, and there, huddled closely together, she sees something that appears to be a group of some eight bodies, men and women, burnt past all recognition. "I will never forget the way in which those bodies were lying there," she says, five years later.

"It was so strange. They seemed to have fallen one on top of each other, in two straight lines. As though they had been standing right beside each other, and when death came suddenly, to all of them at the same moment, they had had no time to make a move. So there they all lay, in a row, one beside the other, very, very close to each other."

There are a number of people wandering around in the devastation of the fourth floor that morning: uniformed and plainclothes police and army, some staff people from the Attorney General's office, even some employees of the morgue. Now, as they begin the search for clues to identify the charred remains of these eight corpses, Amalia recalls a scene "like some gruesome, Persian bazaar. 'Here,' someone would say, 'this watch reminds me of so-and-so' or, 'definitely I recognize that pencil.' They identify the body of one of Judge Reyes' bodyguards. They find a piece of jewelry belonging to a woman whom they are able to identify as Judge Reyes' assistant. And then they find the body of Judge Reyes. The Chief Justice is identified by his gold pencil, and by a section of his law school faculty card that has miraculously survived the conflagration. Tucked away inside his vest pocket it was somehow protected by the weight of his body, lying face down, pressed into the floorboards.

Those who were witness to what happened next, have been too frightened ever to speak about it. But on the day that I met Judge Mantilla, five years and five months after these events, she had made up her mind to tell the story for the first time. "I don't know," she said, "if anything will happen to me for telling you now. But I want to tell you what I saw on the fourth floor of the Palace that morning anyway. It still needs to be told."

They took the body of the dead Chief Justice and they set it down a little apart from the rest, in a place on its own. Then a man dressed in civilian clothes walked over carrying a small jug in his hand. As Amalia watched, the man raised the jug and poured its contents over the body of Judge Reyes. And in an instant his body was engulfed in flames. "I saw it," she says. "I'm not exaggerating. The floor, along a line six or eight feet long, burst into flames, which immediately engulfed the dead body of the Chief Justice."

There was an outcry. Amalia and others screamed at the officials to put out the fire. They reluctantly did so. They smothered the flames in the surrounding ashes.

The army makes one final attempt to prevent investigators from finding out how the Chief Justice had died. When his body finally reaches the city morgue, at around noon on Friday, the chief pathologist gives instructions that there are to be no X-rays taken of his remains. But the staff of the morgue revolts. "If you don't allow us to do our work correctly," they say, "you can take over the morgue and do it yourself." So the X-rays of what was left of the Chief Justice's body are duly taken. And the discovery is made that the bullet which tore through Judge Reyes' chest was not fired by any of the M-19 weapons which the army had collected from the fourth floor.

*   *   *   *   *

On Friday, November 8, *The Washington Post* reports from Bogotá that: "Senior government officials suggested today that the rebels' aim was to destroy records in U.S. extradition requests against about eighty drug traffickers who may have helped fund the guerrillas." On Friday evening, CBS Evening News reports that, "there is speculation here the takeover might have been an attempt to block the government's decision to extradite Colombians charged with drug offenses to the United States." Like *The Washington Post* story, this "speculation" originates in the United States Embassy in Bogotá. The "Narco-Terrorist Drug Link," as motive for the assault on the Palace of Justice, has had its first airing. Like the "In Defense of the Institutions" argument, the drug connection to the assault on the Palace of Justice is slated to achieve immense resonance and respectability. Widely broadcast, it will be accepted and repeated, both domestically and internationally, until it becomes the only "fact" that journalists and readers know or remember about the seizure of the Colombian Palace of Justice.

On Friday morning, November 8, Bogotá's *El Tiempo*—the city's newspaper of record with the closest links to the military—congratulates the army and the government on "The most spectacular counter-guerrilla operation in contemporary times." *El Tiempo* writes of the rescue of "more than thirty" hostages at the end of the fighting, " ...all those who had defeated death, appeared smiling and victorious, just as the Colombian flag too has remained victorious. The flag that survived fire and cannon flies still, undefeated and beautiful, over the Palace of Colombian justice." The paper also provides further graphic, unattributed, descriptions of inhumane treatment and cold-blooded slaughter of hostages by the guerrillas. There are fresh details of the murder of the Chief Justice by Andrés Almarales. Now, so the story goes, Almarales was goaded into murdering the Chief Justice by a young woman guerrilla who claimed it was necessary to make the government take them seriously. *El Tiempo* also has more explanations about the M-19 suicide pact. "Not a single guerrilla survived to the end of the Operation," says the headline.

Yet on an inside page, in the middle of a long, emotional description of the scene when the survivors are led from the ruins, there appears this short paragraph: "Through the survivors a man appears, escorted by soldiers, his hands raised high above his head. Because of his thick moustache all the journalists thought it was Andrés Almarales. But," the report concludes, "moments later the army denied that it was the guerrilla leader. They now confirmed that Almarales had died during the intense gun battles that took place inside the justice building."

At the time no one thinks anything of it. If the man with the moustache and the armed escort was not Almarales, then he must be a guerrilla. To the cameraman who gets the shot on tape, to the journalists standing on the square watching this chaotic final exodus of the last of the hostages, the figure is obviously an M-19 terrorist. There have been several such already: young men have been observed leaving the building under arrest ever since the siege began. Only later, when the numbers don't add up right, do people begin to question what is happening behind the Museum's barred door. Only when no trace can be found of the entire staff of the cafeteria, eight young men and women who vanish without a trace, or of the young woman who ran her own small business selling home made pastries to the Palace of Justice staff, or of two young women visitors who were in the building when the M-19 struck, or of the two female guerrillas, who left the bathroom with the hostages when Almarales decided to let the women go. None of these are ever seen, or ever heard from, again. So it is only then, when the army categorically denies that they have made any arrests, that the relatives and friends of the missing go back to screen the news crews' videotapes; searching for evidence in the raw footage, sifting desperately through those images of young men being rushed from the building, their hands above their head and soldiers running behind, with their guns in their backs.

*   *   *   *   *

Early on Saturday morning, November 9, the city morgue receives an order from a military trial judge requesting the release to the police of twenty-eight bodies for immediate shippment to the city's mass grave. One of the bodies on the judge's list belongs to Andrés Almarales, but with help from the Minister of Justice and the Attorney General, Andrés' body has already been identified and released to his family on Friday night. Another body on the list belongs to a young auxiliary judge from the Council of State. His body, too, has already left the morgue. Of the twenty-six remaining bodies covered by the judge's order, only nine have so far been identified. Without pausing to check with his boss, the Minister of Justice, the Director of the city morgue signs over all twenty-six bodies to the police. By nine o'clock that morning the bodies are loaded onto a truck and driven to the forlorn wasteland in the south of the city where they are dumped into a mass grave in the municipal cemetery.

Later, when questioned by the investigators, the military judge will say that his order originated as the result of a phone call from the Chief of the Bogotá Police, General Vargas Villegas, informing him that the police wanted the bodies disposed of because they had reason to believe the M-19 might try to seize the city morgue to retrieve their dead companions. It might seem reasonable to assume that the seventeen unidentified bodies are those of the M-19 guerrillas who were fighting with Luis Otero on the fourth floor. But the identities of these bodies are lost forever beneath the acid poured on top of them in the mass grave. No one will ever be able to know for sure whether all of them were M-19 casualties or not. When asked to account for "the disappeared," the army will point to these unidentified bodies, and sugggest that among them there must be some or all of the so-called "disappeared." It is furthermore suggested that others among those missing may have been incinerated in the fourth floor blaze. The facts of the tragedy are rapidly becoming blurred. They are being transformed into "mysteries." They are becoming unknowable.

*   *   *   *   *

On Saturday, November 9, *The Washington Post* is warning that a "reinvigorated military could ... make the armed forces more of a power to reckon with in the redrafting of any government peace process." *The Post* says that "the crushing blow the Colombian military was permitted to administer... has lifted Army morale after months of frustration..." By Saturday, November 9, the Colombian Government has received the blessing of the State Department and the White House. President Reagan's Washington stands firmly behind the Colombian Government in its hour of difficulty. Both Bernard Kalb for the State Department, and Larry Speakes for President Reagan, have gone on the record to confirm that the United States supports President Betancur's handling of the situation. By Saturday, President Betancur needs all the support he can get. In Bogotá, on Saturday, a lot of things are starting to unravel for the Colombian authorities.

More than thirty-six hours after the gunfire stopped there are more questions than answers about every aspect of the attack. There is still no official statement on the number of casualties or on the number of survivors. Nobody has any explanation as to why the police security was lifted from the building twenty-four hours before the assault. There is no explanation as to why the army kept up the attack after the building caught fire. The government, in short, has been unable to provide any details relating to the assault.

This is the day when the families, colleagues and friends of the eleven Supreme Court Justices who lost their lives in the tragedy will bury their dead. The legal community is enraged and embittered and does not buy the official version of their colleagues' death. Judicial workers are on strike nationwide. The bereaved families have advised the government to stay away from the funerals. President Betancur sends wreaths to the Church. The families return them to the Presidential Palace. And the twelve surviving Supreme Court Justices announce a boycott of the official memorial service for the victims of the Palace of Justice tragedy, which the government, the military, the Senate and Congressional leaders, the diplomatic corps and the Archbishop, are planning to hold in the National Cathedral on Sunday. Responding to these pressures, at a crisis cabinet meeting on Saturday morning the government decides to go along with the investigation that Enrique Parejo has been demanding all along. The government also decides, that after the President and all the *emminente* have attended Sunday's memorial service in the Cathedral, the Minister of Justice will meet the foreign journalists, who are in a state of near-rebellion. Enrique Parejo gets a rough ride.

For it so happens that on Saturday, the independent newspaper, *El Espectador,* has a story from an anonymous source about the mysterious disappearance of the staff of the Palace of Justice cafeteria. Under the heading "Collective Disappearance," *El Espectador* provides the names of the nine young people who have gone missing: the chef, the manager, the head-waiter, the two asistant waiters, the young woman who ran the self-service counter, the cashier, the kitchen assistant, and the young woman who sold her pastries at the coffee breaks to the employees of the Court. The report points out that one of the strange aspects of this mass disappearance is that the cafeteria, tucked away in the western corner of the ground floor, right beside the entrance from the underground garage through which the guerrillas penetrated the building, was almost completely unaffected by the conflict. "There were even the remains of food found still on the tables," according to *El Espectador.*

When the Minister for Justice meets the foreign press he is unable to comment on the rumors of disappearances and extra-judicial executions. He tries hard, but the reporters do not buy his explanation for President Betancur's failure to return the Chief Justice's call. He cannot say who gave the order for the tanks to break into the building. The Minister for Justice gives the press the drug story. The government now knows, says Enrique Parejo, that "the M-19 went to the Palace to destroy legal records and to kill the judges involved in the prosecution of drug trafficking crimes." When challenged repeatedly by Colombian journalist Manuel Vicente Peña, translating for the reporters for *The New York Times* and *The Boston Globe*, the Minister loses his temper.

*   *   *   *   *

"We've captured a female guerrilla," Colonel Sánchez told General Samudio, speaking from the Museum at around five o'clock on that Thursday evening. "She's been identified, she's fully identified." General Samudio responds: "Well, you know what to do. If the sleeve disappears, make certain you disappear the jacket too." Translation: "If she is 'disappeared' [to be tortured], make certain you dispose of the body."

*   *   *   *   *

She told one of the young soldiers assigned to guard her on the second floor of the Museum Command Center that her name was Irma, and she asked him to please call her family and let them know that she had been arrested. The caretaker of the Museum remembered her. He identified her from a press photograph for the judge who was investigating her disappearance. The caretaker had seen her leave the Museum with several armed men, armed civilians. He remembered her name too, Irma Franco, because he had overheard her give it to the officials when they were interrogating her up on the second floor. Irma Franco, she said, law student.

The assistant caretaker of the Museum also remembered her. The assistant caretaker had seen several people under arrest in the course of the siege. He was responsible for the second floor of the Museum, and the suspicious ones were brought up there, he said. The people in charge had set up their office in the Hall of the Signatories to the Act of Independence. They had even brought some young women to work with them, and the *señoritas* had sat on his chairs, which was never permitted. In answer to the investigating judge, he said he had seen four people under arrest in the passageway, three men and a woman. And three more detained in the "*Nariño* Room," two men and a woman. When the young woman in the check skirt and the boots was taken away it was evening already, the very last of the light. He remembered because he was standing in the entrance to the street.

Irma Franco, law student and M-19 guerrilla, entered the Palace of Justice on Wednesday morning with Alfonso Jaquín, in the vanguard of the M-19 invasion. She spent the entire siege in the bathroom, loading and reloading the guns for the guerrillas fighting outside on the stairs. It was Irma who asked Andrés Almarales for permission to abandon the bathroom and escape from the Palace of Justice with the hostages when Andrés allowed the women to leave. After she was driven away from the Museum on Thursday evening, accompanied by F-2, or more likely by B-2 military intelligence agents, Irma Franco was never seen again.

The disappearance of Irma Franco is documented by a number of different sources. But how many other M-19 guerrillas tried, like her, to escape? Who they were, and what happened to them, is unknown. A little later on that same Thursday evening, Colonel Sánchez announces a second success: "We've just captured another one, who has also been plainly identified," he says. This time General Samudio's instructions are slightly more direct: "You already know the instructions in that regard," he says, "they are *terminantes*."

One week after the battle, on November 14, the remnants of the M-19 command structure issued a communiqué to the press, signed by Álvaro Fayad and Alfonso Navarro among others, claiming that the senior leaders of the attack, Luis Otero, Alfonso

Jaquín, Irma Franco, Luis Otero's second in command, Elvencio Ruiz, and a second young woman, Marcella Sossa, had all been "disappeared" and murdered by the army, together with "seven other fighters." What is known, from the tapes of the military and police inter-communications, is that army intelligence arrested at least seventeen people in the course of the two days of the siege. It is also know that none of the M-19 leaders, with the exception of Andrés Almarales, were ever identified in the city morgue.

* * * * *

The voices on the recording have been distorted. The tape, addressed simply to "*Los Señores* Investigators of the Palace of Justice," is dropped off, anonymously, in the Attorney General's office, during the week following these events.

"The object of this audio cassette," says the voice, "is to make known to the general public, that on the seventh day of this current month, several of the hostages from the Palace of Justice were arrested. They were taken to the cells in the Cavalry School in the North of Bogotá. Up until last Saturday evening, [November 9] these people, who would seem to have 'disappeared' as a result of the Palace of Justice affair, were in the cells of the Cavalry School. There are no 'disappeared.' We saw them there. We know they were there. We escorted them there."

The authors of the recording identify themselves as a group of noncommissioned officers in the B-2 army intelligence service. Throughout the two days of the attack on the Palace of Justice, they were assigned to work under the command of Colonel Edilberto Sánchez in the Museum, receiving and checking the credentials of the hostages as they escaped from the Palace. "Some of these people," the voice on the tape explains, "about twelve or so in number, were unable to explain or justify their presence in the Palace of Justice. And for this reason, and especially if their documents did not justify their presence in the court, these twelve or thirteen people were brought immediately to the barracks located in the Cavalry School, at the *Brigada de Instituto Militares* in the north of Bogotá..."

Among the dozen or so prisoners whom the dissident B-2 agents claim to have brought to the cells of the Cavalry School, there are only four people whom they identify by name: Carlos Rodríguez, the missing manager of the Palace cafeteria; Jaime Beltrán, one of the cafeteria waiters; David Celis, the chef; and a fourth person whom they identify as "Fernando Fernández," which seems to be a mispronunciation for Bernardo Hernández, another one of the missing waiters on the cafeteria staff.

Ever since the M-19 invasion of the building, army intelligence has suspected the presence of a fifth column inside the Palace of Justice. These suspicions are reinforced when, according to the recording by the dissident agents, an arrested guerrilla had led the police to the M-19's safe house on the Calle 6 South, where they found a copy of Luis Otero's plan of attack. Now the military knew that an unarmed vanguard of seven people had penetrated the Palace of Justice almost ninety minutes before the main assault force smashed their way into the underground garage. The question for the army was: How did this vanguard suddenly appear fully armed inside the building? Their suspicions fall immdiately on the young, well-educated members of the cafeteria staff. According to the dissidents, the army believes that in the days immediately leading up to the attack at least two of the cafeteria workers smuggled boxes of arms, explosives and ammunition into the Palace of Justice with the food deliveries. Of course the army cannot be sure. They do not know which of the cafeteria staff—if any—are guilty. And their paranoia about the M-19's proven ability to infiltrate Colombian society at many levels is so acute that their suspicions of fifth column activity within the building extend to certain of the justices. When, in the course of their screening of the hostages, they come across two young women visitors who, in their view, do not have a satisfactory explanation for their presence in the Palace on that fatal Wednesday morning, both these young women are also arrested. Neither of them is ever seen or heard from again either.

The dissident B-2 agents make it clear they believe that all, or most, of the people they arrested were actively involved in some phase or other of the seizure of the Palace. Furthermore these young noncommissioned officers admire their commanding officer, Colonel Plazas Vega, and think that the manner in which he carried off the military counterattack inside the Palace was highly successful. "There are not many Colombian officers," they say, "who are such talented military tacticians." What disturbs this group of young intelligence agents is that over a period of three days they have been forced to watch the prisoners being tortured to death in their own barracks, under the supervision of their own commander. The assignment is straightforward: Get all the information you can out of these "subversives." Use any means you need. And above all, leave no survivors. There must not be a single witness to the fact that there has been torture in the Cavalry School.

Torture in Colombia is not new. These young officers knew about it, but they had not experienced it before. Torture was something that happened in someone else's barracks. Under normal circumstances it was practiced by specially trained units of the *Charry Solano* Intelligence and Counter Intelligence Battalion at their own headquarters on the far side of Bogotá. But these are not normal times. The special circumstances of this occasion, the number of prisoners, the unaccustomed pressures that the military feel, forced to operate amid signs of a growing controversy and in the face of a likely judicial investigation, create the need for speed and special precautions. The *Battallíon Charry Solano* is the obvious place to look for political detainees. So the prisoners arrested in the Museum are brought instead to the Cavalry School. And the torture units from the *Battallíon Charry Solano*, "the highest ranking units that exist in the entire military intelligence service," according to the dissidents, follow right behind them. The dissident agents who make the tape want it known that they have not participated directly in torture sessions. That "the physical torture" has been carried out by specialist units from Intelligence and Counter Intelligence. But they were ordered to watch.

"In one of the interrogations of one of the terrorists where, by direct order of my Colonel Plazas Vegas, we were present, they wanted to make the subversive [the prisoner] sign a statement, in which it was written that they, [the M-19], had received three million pesos from the narco-traffickers for the purchase of war materials which the subversives had used to finance their operation... The subversive, who had refused to give his name, or any other information, responded to the Captain interrogating him with an obscenity—in spite of the fact that he was tied down to a chair. As a result, he was dragged out and since he was half-dead already, because of the tortures he had been submitted to, they drowned him in the water troughs that we use for the animals, for the horses, right there in the middle of the stable yard... This individual went on moving for only a few seconds. With the beatings they had given him on his kidneys, he gave out. They just threw him on the ground then, and he lay there. We think he was the first of these seven who died."

"We admire *mi Coronel Plazas*," they say, "but we did not know that he agreed with these methods of interrogating the terrorists. We admire him a great deal—but in this case we do not agree [with him]. We are not in agreement with torture, *señores. We-are-not-in-a-gree-ment.*" Each syllable is separated out, punched out for emphasis.

On Saturday night, November 9, when they leave the barracks to go home, the group of B-2 dissidents decide to contact the families of the "disappeared" to try to stop the torture. They make the phone calls, anonymously, and they tell the families they must go to the Cavalry School, and demand to see the prisoners. But their efforts backfire. The families are unable to gain admittance to the barracks and they start making phone calls which alert the military commanders. On Saturday night the prisoners are removed from the cells in the Cavalry School. Perhaps they were taken to another barracks. Perhaps, the dissidents say, they are already dead, since that was the order. All that they know for sure is that on Sunday at dawn, when the entire B-2 unit from the rank of Sergeant down, some thirty soldiers and noncommissioned officers, are called back to barracks, the cells are empty, the prisoners are no more. And the B-2 unit involved is hauled before their superiors to be informed that an investigation has been launched to find and arrest M-19 "infiltrators" in their ranks who are "abetting and working for the subversives." "They told us that if any of us thought of taking our denunciations any further, that if any of us had any thought, for example, of leaving the country, or seeking asylum in a foreign embassy, our families would pay dearly." The unit is kept in barracks until late Tuesday.

Between Sunday morning, November 10, and Tuesday night when they are allowed to go home, the dissidents claim to have found out from the comments of some of their colleagues that three more members of the cafeteria staff are under arrest in another barracks. "We have not seen them, physically, ourselves," they say, "but we know from colleagues that they are in another military barracks where they are being subjected to terrible interrogations." The names they have heard mentioned are: "Luz Mary or Luz María Puerta,"—which seems to correspond to Luz Mary Portela, the chef's kitchen maid; "Nora Esguerra,"—namely Norma Constanza Esguerra, the pastry seller; and "Rosa, or Margarita Castilblanco,"—the name of the chef's assistant is Ana Rosa Castilblanco.

Before signing off the recording the dissidents promise to get back in touch, by the same method, if they manage to learn any further details about what has happened to any of these seven prisoners. "It will not be easy," they warn. "If they are dead, possibly their bodies may have been brought back to the Palace of Justice, to make it look as if they died in the battle. Or they may have been dumped in a bath with sulphuric acid, so that not the least shred of anything remains of their bodies. We apologize. It is hair-raising to even talk about it, but it happens *señores*, it does happen. Here in Colombia that is how 'disappeared' people are disposed of."

The recording ends with repeated, nervous requests for the greatest prudence in the handling of the tape. Above all, they plead, it must not fall into the hands of their superiors in the intelligence service who could clear up the distortions and might still identify them. "They say that we are subversives who have infiltrated the service. We consider that we are fighting for the *Patria*, for the Colombian State. We feel that torture offends our national honor. That it wounds our democratic institutions. And there are more than one of us, *señores*, we are more than one. We want to defend democracy, but by just means. We want a clean fight with the enemy. Giving back what they give to us, lead for lead and bullet for bullet. We want to fight for the legitimacy of our institutions. But we want to do it legally. With honor. Not in this atrocious fashion. Not with savagery. Not in such an ugly, brutal way."

Then, in the final sentences spoken on this tape, there is a marked shift in the character of the voice. What comes at the very end is an afterthought, and one can almost hear the unrecorded discussion that must have taken place between the participants off-mike, before they agree to add one final message. When the voice resumes, it has lost its sense of urgency and lost the conviction that was driving it. The voice now sounds flat. Defeated and fatalistic. "We are risking our own lives," the voice says "because we believe these risks are justified if our information can be brought to the attention of the Colombian people. But if this information cannot be communicated in some way to the general public, then we will not go on taking these risks. Then you will not hear from us again. Bueno. That is all we have to say, *señores*. Thank you."

*   *   *   *   *

Before Carlos Urán died on the stairway of the Palace of Justice, he sent a message to his wife that was brought to her by his secretary when she escaped. "Give her my love," he said, "and tell her to take the children and leave this country. Colombia is no longer a country where the values that she and I believe in are possible." Anna María de Urán, a university professor with an international reputation, took Carlos' advice. With her four small daughters she left Colombia, to protect her family and herself from the repression that her husband had foreseen must follow in the wake of the Palace of Justice tragedy.

*   *   *   *   *

"You see," says Amalia Mantilla, when she finishes telling me her story of the aftermath of the battle for the Palace. "It's not just a question of the scandal of the siege itself; that's not the only issue. There are far deeper questions raised by this tragedy. What happened in the Palace of Justice revealed the true character of the political class of this country; it also showed us the character of our armed forces; and it showed us who the guerrillas are. When the M-19 seized the Palace of Justice they proved that they knew precisely nothing about our national reality. Unfortunately, Colombia is a country that suffers from amnesia, from forgetfulness. And we have reached a stage of such insensitivity and callousness towards life that people no longer care. That is the most serious legacy of the Palace of Justice. Life has no value. The law has no value. That, in my opinion, is the true, the most devastating consequence of what happened at the Palace of Justice."

*   *   *   *   *

On Sunday November 10, in far away New York, *The New York Times* devoted an editorial column to the tragedy. Under the heading "Two Tragedies in Bogotá," the editor wrote: "...President Betancur refused to negotiate under the gun.... To have negotiated under threat even about reasonable demands would have betrayed all that this wise and good President has accomplished. By undermining his own authority he would have compromised the peace process even more certainly than with this bloodbath."

*   *   *   *   *

On Sunday, November 10, in Bogotá, the bells in the Clock tower of the National Cathedral tolled, and for the second time in a week the life of the pigeons of the Plaza Bolívar was disrupted. They rose with a clattering of wings, from the floor of the great square, wheeled, and turned, and flew away again. Bogotános, some of whom had walked to the Plaza from the south of the city, bringing a handful of flowers or a homemade paper wreath to lay on the sidewalk in front of the ruined Palace, stayed to gaze silently, in awe and in sorrow, at the ugly, blackened remains of Colombia's Supreme Court.

The chauffeur-driven official limousines began arriving early in the Plaza for the solemn eleven o'clock memorial mass for the victims of the Palace of Justice. Security was tight. The members of the government, their wives and their children came. The leaders of the political parties and their wives and children also. The Army High Command attended in full dress uniform, as did the commanders of the National Police and the Bogotá Police. The members of the Diplomatic Corps with their wives all attended. The leaders of the unions and the leaders of the business and employers' associations came. The prominent, oligarchic families were all represented, as were the media chiefs and the official, established artists and intellectuals. And all the members of Congress and the Senate. Colombian Television taped it all: the solemnity of the ritual, the incense, the choir singing the Te Deum in Latin, the homily by the Archbishop, President Betancur's homily, and the music. The cameras also revealed to the nation that in the place of honor reserved for the relatives of the dead Supreme Court Justices, the chairs stood empty. Only one magistrate's widow attended this official memorial service. There were no judges, no lawyers, no law professors and no law students present to hear President Betancur say from the pulpit that: "The tragedy of the Palace of Justice has fortified the principle of legality."

Epilogue

In November 1985, one week after the tragedy, President Betancur's government established a Special Commission of Inquiry, and so began the legal history of the Palace of Justice case, which continues to this day. The Commission's brief was two-fold: Firstly, to investigate all aspects of what had happened; secondly, to report back to the government, the Supreme Court and the Attorney General with their findings and their recommendations for further action if needed.

Between December 1985 and May 1986 the Commission's investigative staff of ten trial judges amassed over 21,000 files of testimony. These files, and the meticulously researched reconstruction of the last moments of the battle inside and outside the Palace of Justice bathroom by the morgue team of experts, still represent the best documentation available on all aspects of the Palace siege. The Commission's investigative work has been at the heart of every indictment, or attempted indictment, ever since.

The Commission of Inquiry's report, however, when published in June 1986, was widely seen as a whitewash for the Colombian authorities. In the choice of extracts that they chose to publish from the 21,0000 files, the two presiding Supreme Court judges were "selective." In key areas of the investigation, where the findings of their own investigators contradicted the official version of events, they chose to ignore, or in some cases even contradict, the findings of their own staff. Thus the Commission report confirmed the official version that most of the hostages who died in

the bathroom and outside on the stairs, were killed by the guerrillas. And the judges concluded that none of the civilian hostages
had been disappeared; the nine missing members of the Cafeteria
Staff and the two missing young women visitors, must, they said,
have died in the "holocaust" on the fourth floor. Their unidentified bodies must surely have ended up by mistake in the municipal
mass grave.

Only two aspects of the Commission's reporting contradicted
the official version. The Commission found no narco-terrorist-
mafia-M-19 links and said so. The report also confirmed the disappearance of Irma Franco, and the judges requested that the
investigation of her case be thoroughly pursued. They recom-
mended that further investigation be conducted "by the competent
authorities"—namely the military justice system—into the allega-
tions of disappearances and extra-judicial executions among survivors of the M-19 assault force. They also requested that further
investigation be pursued to discover who had given the order for
the lifting of police security from the Palace of Justice twenty-four
hours before the attack.

President Betancur had reason to be pleased with the result.
On the occasion of his farewell speech to the Senate in July 1986
he was able to point out that: "The Special Commission of Inquiry
to investigate the holocaust... has reported, in conscience and in
law, the correctness of our actions... the President and his associates are certain he acted in defense of the fatherland, of the institutions entrusted to him, and of the general well-being."

On June 20, 1986, to the fury and consternation of the
Colombian political establishment, the Attorney General, Carlos
Jiménez Gómez, accused President Betancur and Minister of
Defense Vega Uribe of crimes against international human rights
law and the laws protecting civilians in time of war, and sent the
charges to the Justice Committee of the Colombian Congress.
Three weeks later the Congress unanimously rejected the Attorney
General's case. Claiming incompetence to judge "An Act of
Government," the Congress also said that international human
rights laws did not apply to the victims of the Palace siege, since
the "war" between the army and the guerrillas was not, in any legal

sense, a "formal war." Speaking for the nation at large, Congress had this to say: "In the silence of their own thoughts, the Colombian people have already ratified, in their own way, the political decision taken by the President, not to negotiate."

This decision by the Colombian Congress ensured that no further criminal action would ever prosper in the Palace of Justice case.

Four years later, in 1989, the government of President Virgilio Barco negotiated an amnesty with the surviving membership of the M-19 which included a blanket pardon for the assault at the Palace of Justice and opened the door for the M-19 to enter the new government of President Gaviria as a minority partner.

*　*　*　*　*

Five days after the siege at the Palace ended, on the night of Wednesday, November 13, 1985, the snow-capped Colombian volcano known as the *Nevado del Ruiz* erupted, burying almost an entire town of 40,000 people under an avalanche of mud and rocks and ash. While Colombians reeled from the impact of this fresh calamity, hundreds of bodies from the disaster area were brought to the mass grave in Bogotá, and thrown on top of the unidentified bodies from the Palace of Justice. Whatever answers those twenty-six bodies may have held to the "mysteries" of the Palace siege now lay forever buried.

Not only unidentified bodies, however, have been interred in Colombia in the last eight years. The concept of justice itself, the desire to live in a state of laws seems to have died in the Palace of Justice as well. Or perhaps what has happened is that for too many Colombians, their belief in the possibility of a country where the rule of law means something has died. Ultimately, it is this loss that is the most disturbing aspect of the Palace of Justice legacy. Illegality and mendacity at the highest levels of government may have been nothing new. But it was after the Palace tragedy that the phenomenon of public toleration of the intolerable became widespread. After the Palace of Justice, the contempt in which the ideals of the Colombian Constitution are held by the Colombian political establishment—right across the spectrum from the Conservative Party to the M-19 Democratic Alliance—was out in the open. And the rhetoric, the flag-waving fervor of the speeches to *La Patria*, failed to convince any longer. They only made it worse.

This development can be clearly charted in everything that has happened since: it is there in the Parliamentary debates, in the official statements and speeches, in the editorials of the major newspapers, and in the decisions, actions and omissions of the National Congress and the Senate.

Over the course of the past eight years, many and various efforts have been made to fix responsibility for the crimes committed by officials of the state during the assault on the Palace of Justice. Former President Betancur, former Minister of Defense Miguel Vega Uribe, General Arias Cabrales, Colonel Edilberto Sánchez, the Commander of the National Police, General Delgado Mallarino, the Commander of the Bogotá Police, General Vargas Villegas, and the entire surviving leadership of the M-19, have all been the targets of innumerable law suits. Some twenty law suits or more have been filed by, among others, two Attorney Generals, the families of the victims, the families of the disappeared, The Foundation for the Clarification of Events at the Palace of Justice, and, in the summer of 1992, by one of the new, "faceless judges" of the Public Order Courts, established in the 1991 Constitution to give judges and prosecutors protective anonymity in trials dealing with terrorism and drug offenses.

Not one of these cases has ever come to trial. Not a single official, civilian or military, has ever been punished.

Colombia has moved on. Colombia has forgotten the Palace of Justice siege. The new 1991 Constitution which was supposed to bring judicial reform aimed at strengthening the independence and raising the status of the Colombian judiciary, has done no such thing. Today Colombian judges are as underpaid and as disrespected as ever. Rampant violence against judges and their staffs continues. Judicial independence, the kind which Chief Justice Reyes and his dead colleagues practiced, for which they risked their lives and eventually died, has been supplanted by an increased encroachment by the executive branch into functions normally reserved to the judiciary. In the current government of President Gaviria, law-making under state of siege powers has been expanded, habeas corpus and due process rights for defendants diminished, and the jurisdiction of military courts over civilians has been extended to permit the investigation of civilians by the armed forces. With the full support of Antonio Navarro's M-19 Democratic Alliance, the new 1991 Constitution affords members of the Colombian armed forces the traditional "due obedience to superior orders" exemption from prosecution for crimes and abuses against civilians.

Thus Colombia, a signatory to every major international law treaty, has turned the Nuremberg principles upside down: so long as military courts continue to preside over all offenses by agents of the security forces, the new Constitutional provision of "due obedience" effectively ensures that when members of the army or the police are involved in dirty war crimes—massacres, torture, and enforced disappearances—they will not be prosecuted. This in a country where the latest figures show that ten people die every day for political reasons; one person is forcibly disappeared every two days; and each year since 1985, with horrible consistency, the total number of people killed for political, or presumed political reasons, continues to exceed the total number who lost their lives from repression in Chile during the sixteen years of Pinochet's dictatorship. In 1992, with Colombia the largest recipient of U.S. military aid in the hemisphere ($143 million) because of the "war on drugs," at least 1,000 people were extra-judicially executed in Colombia by the armed forces, or by paramilitary groups operating with the military's support or acquiescence.

Colombia is not a military dictatorship. The Colombian Army has never yet sought to remove a democratically elected civilian government by force. Why then was Betancur afraid to stop the carnage? Did he truly fear that if he opposed the military, General Miguel Vega Uribe would move to arrest him and the members of his government and take over the country?

What Betancur thought, and why he thought it, are questions that he alone can answer. The facts that I have endeavoured to make known in this book, however, prove, if nothing else, that if indeed he thought those things, then he was wrong. President Betancur could have halted the slaughter. Throughout the siege at the Palace the army generals were increasingly fearful of an order from the Presidential Palace forcing them to withdraw before they could "accomplish our mission."

Perhaps the most fundamental question posed by the tragedy at the Palace is this: Why, in this so-called constitutional democracy, which has a tradition of electing sophisticated civilian leaders, a country whose armed forces do not plot military coups, why is this the country where the most brutal 'dirty war' against the government's opponents rages?

What happened at the Palace of Justice was nothing more than an exact replay of what has been happening in the towns and villages of the Colombian provinces since the fifties. The Palace of Justice, with its *"Operación Rastrillo"* and its *"Operación Limpieza,"* with its disappearances, its extra-judicial executions, and its torture, brought the dirty war to central downtown Bogotá. There was nothing new for the army about what happened in the Palace of Justice. Nothing new for the guerrillas either. And nothing new for the government.

Only two things about the siege at the Palace were different from the hundreds of conflicts that erupt every day somewhere in the vast interior of Colombia: the character of the victims and the location. In the Palace of Justice tragedy, instead of anonymous slum dwellers or peasants, the innocent victims of the war were the hierarchy of the country's judiciary. Instead of some invisible slum or remote, isolated rural village, the war at the Palace exploded in the administrative center of the capital city. Suddenly, this war that no one wants to acknowledge even exists was all over the nation's television screens. For the first time, the establishment, on whose behalf the dirty war is fought, were forced to view it in their own living rooms. For the first time, a Colombian government had come face to face with the consequences of its own complicity.

When the Palace of Justice tragedy was over, the war went away again. It did retreat, back to the anonymity of the villages, the slums, the distant ranches and farms. Back to *campesino* country, to

Indian country, where there are no historical monuments or archives or television cameras to worry about, and where the casualties are politically invisible.

In 1993, none of the army or police officers who held command posts during the military operation to retake control of the Palace of Justice are still on active duty.

* * * * *

In 1986, General Vega Uribe retired from active service when the new government of President Virgilio Barco took office. From 1986 to 1990 he served as the Colombian Ambassador in Portugal. Today General Vega Uribe (Ret.) is living in Bogotá.

* * * * *

In 1986, Commander of the Army, General Rafael Samudio was appointed Minister of Defense in the new government of President Virgilio Barco, a post he occupied until 1989. Upon retirement, General Samudio was appointed Colombian Consul General in New Orleans, a post he currently holds.

* * * * *

In 1986, General Jesús Armando Arias Cabrales, Commander of the XIIIth Bogotá Artillery Brigade, and the commander of the military operation to retake the Palace of Justice, was routinely promoted to be the Commander of the Armed Forces. In 1989 he retired from active service over disagreements regarding the government's negotiations with the M-19.

In 1991, President Gaviria's Attorney General charged General Arias with violating the laws of war and the rights of civilians in the conduct of the military operation at the Palace of Justice, and ordered his immediate discharge from the armed forces. The Senate voted to promote General Arias to three stars. The Attorney General was forced to resign.

In the same brief, Attorney General Alfonso Gómez Méndez, a former student and friend of the late Chief Justice Reyes, also brought charges against Colonel Edilberto Sánchez for the disappearance of Irma Franco.

General Arias Cabrales and Colonel Edilberto Sánchez have appealed the charges. The case, still unresolved, has ended up with the executive. It is now up to the current President, César Gaviria, and his Minister of Defense, Rafael Pardo, to take action to obey the law and apply the mandated sanctions against both officers.

Upon his retirement, General Arias Cabrales was appointed Rector of the Military University in Bogotá, a post he currently holds.

* * * * *

In 1986, General Delgado Mallarino, National Commander of the Police retired from the police and was appointed Colombian Ambassador in Bucharest.

In 1989, General Mallarino was charged with military insubordination for his role in the attack by troops of the police Special Forces, (GOES) on the fourth floor of the Palace of Justice, in contravention of an agreement with the cabinet to give the Minister of Justice time to make a contact with Almarales. When the case against the former Police Commander reached the Supreme Court the statute of limitations for this crime had run out.

General Delgado Mallarino (Ret.) has returned to Bogotá to live.

* * * * *

In the summer of 1986, Enrique Parejo, the former Minister of Justice, was appointed Colombian Ambassador to Hungary.

On January 13, 1987, Parejo survived an assassination attempt on the street in Budapest by a Colombian hit man, despatched to Hungary by the Medellín cartel to avenge the extradition treaties for drug trafficking that Parejo had signed during his brief and turbulent period as Minister of Justice.

In 1991 Enrique Parejo resigned from the Colombian diplomatic service to protest President Gaviria's deals with the Colombian mafia in general and the government's deal with Pablo Escobar in particular.

Upon returning to Bogotá he stood successfully for election to the Bogotá City Council. Today, Enrique Parejo is seeking to become the Liberal Party's candidate to the 1994 Colombian Presidential election.

*   *   *   *   *

In 1989, the surviving members of the original, 1985 M-19 leadership signed a general political amnesty with the outgoing government of President Virgilio Barco which included an amnesty for the assault at the Palace of Justice. The M-19 Revolutionary Movement is now the M-19 Democratic Alliance.

In the 1990 Presidential elections, the M-19's Presidential candidate, Carlos Pizzarro, was assassinated. The former revolutionaries went on to win several senate and congressional seats, and the new leader, Alfonso Navarro, held a post in President Gaviria's cabinet as Minister for Health. In the spring of 1991, Navarro resigned his cabinet post to become one of three co-presidents of the new Constitutional Assembly.

In November 1992, when the latest round of negotiations with the guerrillas of the Revolutionary Armed Forces of Colombia (FARC) and the National Liberation Army (ELN) ground to an inconclusive halt in Mexico City, President Gaviria invoked a "State of Internal Commotion" —the new Constitution's term for a state of siege—and returned, once again, to "total war" with the guerrillas. Discredited by their performance in government over the previous two years, in which, as the minority partner, M-19 members of Congress had supported an unpopular economic program and several repressive pieces of legislation, the M-19 resigned from the government.

The "State of Internal Commotion" brought Colombia one step closer to a virtual military dictatorship, albeit one supported and encouraged at every turn by the civilian leadership. In Colombia, the proportion of the national territory over which the Bogotá government ruled never was very large. Today, the government's rule does not effectively extend much beyond the city limits of Bogotá and the grassy plain of the savannah on which the Spanish Conquistadors founded their Holy City of the Faith, Santa Fe de Bogotá.

*   *   *   *   *

In 1992, former President Belisario Betancur was appointed by the United Nations President of the Truth and Reconciliation Commission in El Salvador. Belisario Betancur is not currently involved in domestic politics in Colombia.

*   *   *   *   *

To this day no one knows exactly how many people died at the Palace of Justice.

Notes

Persons interviewed whose names have been changed to protect their identities are listed by pseudonyms followed by an asterisk.

PART I

CHAPTER 1: The material for this chapter, and for the section on the M-19 and on President Betancur's peace process during the first three years of his presidency in the Prologue, is based on interviews by the author with the following indivdiduals in Mexico City in April 1986 and in Bogotá, in April and May 1986 and in April 1991: Rafael,* a member of the M-19 National Direction during the negotiations that led to the 1984 truce with President Betancur and at the time of the Palace of Justice attack; Marina Goenaga, wife of Andrés Almarales; María, his common-law wife; Iván Almarales, son of Andrés and Marina; Eugenio Almarales, Andrés' younger brother; Orlando Fals Borda, author, political analyst and anthropologist, and an editor in the 1970s of the ANAPO newspaper, *Mayorías*, for which Andrés Almarales also worked; Germán Castro Caycedo, author of an investigative book on the M-19's largest, failed, weapons importation from Europe into Colombia, and the first journalist to be kidnapped in Colombia by the guerrillas for the purpose of having him do a television interview with guerrilla leader Jaime Bateman; Juan Guillermo Ríos, investigative journalist, and for a brief period in 1990-91, public relations representative for the M-19 Democratic Alliance; John Agudelo Ríos, President of Belisario Betancur's Peace Commission and one of the main negotiators with the M-19 in 1983-84; Ramón Jimeno, writer, investigative journalist, magazine publisher and author, for the North American Congress on Latin America's *Report on the Americas*, of two analytical reports on the contemporary political history of Colombia, during the first year of President Betancur's Presidency (*Colombia—*

289

Another Threat in the Caribbean? [Sept./Oct. 1982] and *Colombia: Whose Country Is This Anyway ?* [May/June 1983]; Ramón Jimeno is also the author of *Noche de Lobos*, [Ediciones Planeta, Bogotá 1988], an early account of the seizure of the Palace of Justice); finally with Magdalena,* the sister of a member of the M-19 assault force at the Palace of Justice.

Further information on the M-19, and particularly on the 1983-84 peace process and truce is based on interviews by the author with Olgar Behar, in Mexico City in April 1986. Behar is author of *Las Guerras por la Paz* (pub. Bogotá 1985), an oral history of the 1983-84 peace process, and *Noches de Humo* (1989), an account of the two-day siege at the Palace of Justice as told by the only M-19 survivor, Clara Enciso; and with Antonio Navarro Wolf, the last surviving member of the founding group of the M-19, now leader of the M-19 Democratic Alliance, in Bogotá in April 1991.

An important source of background information on Belisario Betancur is *Si! Se Puede!*, by Belisario Betancur (Bogotá, 1982), in which the former president states his political program and philosophy as an independent candidate to the presidency, and the interview by the author with former President Belisario Betancur in Bogotá, in April 1991.

CHAPTER 2: The threatening letters to the individual justices quoted in this chapter come chiefly from the report published in June 1986 by the official Commission of Inquiry into the tragedy at the Palace of Justice.

The quotes here from the Supreme Court's indictment of the Minister of Defense, General Vega Uribe, for torture, are from *Semana*, "*Vega Uribe Al Banquillo*," #166, Bogotá, July 1985.

Interviews by the author for this chapter include:

Yezid Reyes, the son of the late Chief Justice Alfonso Reyes Echandia, Bogotá, April 1986; Lázaro,* Bogotá, April 1991; Germán Castro Caycedo, Bogotá, 1986 and 1991; Manuel Vicente Peña, investigative journalist, whose *Las Dos Tomas* (Bogotá 1986), was the first published documentation of the Palace of Justice attack, on which some of the chronology in this chapter is based; former Attorney General in Betancur's government, Carlos Jiménez Gómez, Bogotá 1986; former Minister of Justice, Enrique Parejo, Bogotá, 1986; Gustavo Gallón, head of the Colombian branch of the *Commissión Andina de Juristas*, Bogotá, 1991; Jaime Cordoba, Assistant Attorney General for Human Rights, Bogotá, 1991.

CHAPTER 3: Most of the information in this chapter comes from the author's interview with Gabriel* in Bogotá, May 1986.

The details of the M-19's plan of attack come from the M-19's communique to the press, *"M-19 se pronuncia sobre asalto al Palacio de Justicia,"* (*El Tiempo*, Bogotá, Nov.14, 1985) and from the original battle plan drawn up by Luis Otero, found by the army inside the M-19 safe house, and published by the Commission of Inquiry; Also of interest is an account of how the attack was planned, published in *El Tiempo* (*"De como se planeó el atentado al Palacio de Justicia,"* Nov. 11, 1985).

CHAPTERS 4 and 5: The information in these chapters is based in part on interviews by the author with Gabriel,* Bogotá, May 1986; Yezid Reyes, Bogotá, May 1986; Juan Guillermo Ríos, Bogotá, April 1986; Manuel Vicente Peña, author of *"Las Dos Tomas,"* Bogotá, April 1986.

The Minutes of President Betancur's Cabinet Meeting on Nov. 6th, 1985, provide critical information on the dynamics during the siege at the highest levels of the civilian government. Extracts first appeared in *Zona* magazine in Bogotá in June 1986. The full text was provided to the author by a source in Bogotá legal circles in April 1991.

The letters from President Betancur to the presiding judges of the Special Commission of Inquiry, Bogotá April 10, 1986 and July 31, 1986, provided an overview of the former President's priorities during the course of the siege. Obtained by the author in Bogotá, April 1991.

The recordings of the military and police communications detail the progress of the siege from the point of view of the commanders of the armed forces and have been extensively used to understand the strategy of the military commanders of the counterattack. Copies of most these tapes, and transcripts of their contents, were provided to the author by a journalist friend in Bogotá, in May 1986, and some missing ones were obtained in 1991.

The transcript of the internal police inquiry into "The Operation to Rescue the Hostages at the Palace of Justice," was made available to the author by a source who had been a friend of the Special Forces Captain who was killed during the attack on the fourth floor of the Palace, in Bogotá, in May 1986. This internal "postmortem" on an operation that cost a number of young policemen's lives, sheds a unique light on the chaotic, improvisational quality that characterized much of the armed forces' response to the crisis.

The information about the arrest and torture of Carlos Rodríguez, the administrator of the Palace of Justice Cafeteria, comes from the transcript of a recording made by a dissident B-2 Army Intelligence defector, noncommissioned officer Gamez, in which he denounced torture and disappearances in connection with the the Palace of Justice siege. It was provided to the author by Amnesty International, in London, in the summer of 1991.

CHAPTER 6: In addition to the sources already cited for previous chapters, much of the material in this chapter is based on the written testimony provided by the President of the Colombian Senate, Álvaro Villegas Moreno, to the presiding judge of the Special Commission of Inquiry.

"Reyes Echandia insistió y BB no pasó al teléfono" (*El Tiempo*, June 20, 1986), describes the Chief Justice's conversations with journalists, politicians, and army and police officers outside the command structure that was running the operation at the Palace, right up to the moment when the phones were cut off by the fire.

The letters to the presiding judges of the Commission of Inquiry, from the former Presidents with whom President Betancur conversed on the afternoon of Nov. 6, 1985, offered a somewhat different version of the substance of these conversations than that given by President Betancur at the time. Later these contradictions were generally suppressed/ignored in the interests of sustaining and corroborating the viability of the "official version."

Throughout this book, the audio tapes of broadcast and non-broadcast material from radio stations Caracol and Todelar, for the two days of the siege, and the video tapes of Colombian television for those two days—including broadcast and non-broadcast material as well as rushes—have been an invaluable resource.

CHAPTER 7: The interview with former Minister of Justice, Enrique Parejo, in Bogotá, April 1986, provided crucial confirmation of dissent within the Colombian cabinet during and after the siege.

The written testimony to the Special Commission of Inquiry by the Minister of Justice, Bogotá, April 14, 1986, and by Police Commander, General Víctor Delgado Mallarino, highlighted important contradictions and tensions between some of the civilians and the President and the army and police, all of which later would be suppressed and denied.

The testimony of the President of the Senate, Álvaro Villegas Moreno, in his written statement for the presiding judges of the Special Commission of Inquiry, was released to the author by a source in the Ministry of Justice in Bogotá, in April 1991. It offers the only evidence that after receiving a false situation report from the military, almost one hour before the start of the artillery bombardment of the fourth floor, and two hours before the fire swept through demolishing everything in its path, at least one member of the cabinet, former Foreign Minister Ramírez Ocampo, received concrete, specific information concerning the situation of the hostages trapped on that floor.

CHAPTER 8: The description of the final hours of the conflict on the fourth floor, is drawn from the transcript of the internal police "post-mortem" on the events of that Wednesday night (see notes for chapters 4 and 5); from the descriptions of their personal experiences by individual soldiers in testimony taken by investigating judges for the Commission of Inquiry by a source within the Attorney General's office: in particular, noncommissioned officer Carlos Julio Rubio Poveda of the Presidential Guard and Captain Roberto Vélez Bedoya, Batallion No. 1 of the Military Police; and from the recordings of the army and police communications leading up to and during the assault on the fourth floor.

In addition, excerpts from the testimony of the tank commander, Col. Alfonso Plazas Vega, to the investigative judge of the Commission of Inquiry: *"Commandante relata combate en Palacio de Justicia,"* published in *El Espectado*, (Nov. 3, 1986) provided confirmation of the army's unwillingness to take the lives of the hostages into consideration.

For the text of the final conversation between the Chief Justice and a journalist, see *El Tiempo* (Nov. 9, 1985).

A separate ballistics analysis done in the Bogotá city morgue for investigative Judge Luis Antonio Lizarazo, dated Feb. 21, 1986, compared the M-19 weapons collected by the army on the fourth floor of the Palace with the results of thirty individual autopsies of the victims who died on that floor. These tests proved that none of the dead had been shot by any of the guerrillas' weapons. The report was provided to the author by 'Felipe,'* in Bogotá, in April 1991.

PART II

CHAPTER 9: Interview by the author with Gabriel,* Bogotá, May 1986.

Interview by the author with the Minister for Justice, Enrique Parejo, Bogotá, May 1986.

Minutes of the Cabinet meeting for Nov. 6 were provided to the author in Bogotá, in April 1991, by Ramón Jimeno.

Unbroadcast video tapes from Colombian television were screened for the author in Bogotá in 1986 and in 1991 by friends in the Bogotá press.

CHAPTER 10: Interview by the author with Enrique Parejo, Bogotá, May 1986.

Letter of the late Luis Carlos Galán, Presidential candidate in the 1986 elections, to the Special Commission of Inquiry, Bogotá, April 1986.

Letter from the Secretary to the Presidency, Victor G. Ricardo, to the Commission of Inquiry, April, 1986, provided to the author by Juan Manuel López Caballero, provides the basic foundation for the "official version."

During the days and nights of November 6—8, 1985, and in subsequent days, conversations in Bogotá with lawyers, journalists, and with various friends and relatives of some of the hostages, provided the background for the descriptions in this chapter of how Bogotános lived through the siege.

CHAPTER 11: Information about the deliberations and decisions taken during the second day of siege by the President and the members of his cabinet came from a variety of sources of which the most interesting were: the official minutes of the Cabinet meetings for Thursday, November 7, released to the author by one of the lawyers representing families of the victim judges, in Bogotá in April 1991; and the letter to the Commission of Inquiry by the Secretary to the Presidencyt, Victor G. Ricardo, (see notes for chapter 10).

The author's meeting with the reporter who was the courier between Gabriel García Márquez and the President, took place in Bogotá, in May 1986, in the presence of the then-Attorney General, Carlos Jiménez Gómez.

The information about the mission of Justice Arciniegas comes from the following sources: author's interview with Gabriel;* the testimony of former President Betancur to investigative judge Alfonso Triana, Bogotá, March 2, 1987, supplied to the author by a source in the Attorney General's office in Bogotá in April 1991, which confirms that the President knew nothing of the judge's mission until the siege was over. Asked by Judge Triana whether he knew what message or messages the judge had brought out with him, Betancur replied: "I don't remember exactly, perhaps it had something to do with a cease-fire." Asked whether there had been any discussion of the Arciniegas incident with the cabinet, or with any of the military commanders, Betancur said he had not discussed the incident with anyone. The testimonies of General Arias, and of Colonel Edilberto Sánchez to the investigators for the Special Commission of Inquiry (acquired by the author through the same source in Bogotá in 1991), both provided contrasting, interesting misinformation regarding the Arciniegas mission. According to Col. Sánchez, for example, the arrival at the Palace of Justice of the head of the Colombian Red Cross, with a message from the government for Andrés Almarales, was a direct result of the "rescue" of Judge Arciniegas.

Additional information comes from press and television coverage at the time. In particular, *"Dramático testimonio de rehén que se salvó al buscar diálogo"* (*El Espectador*, Nov. 14, 1985)

CHAPTER 12: For the details on the Red Cross Director's mission there exists a wealth of information from many sources, of which the most interesting are: the transcript of former president Betancur's interview with investigative judge Alfonso Triana, Bogotá, March 2, 1987, and the transcript of the testimony given to investigative Judge Humberto Moyano Aguirre, by Colonel Edilberto Sánchez, Bogotá, Jan. 17, 1986. Both documents were provided to the author by a source in Bogotá legal circles who had been close to the investigations that had resulted in charges being brought against General Arias and Colonel Sánchez. The transcript of the testimony given by General Arias was also significant. All these official documents promoted the identical, official version, namely: the Red Cross Mission was chased from the lobby of the Palace by "the messianacal fanatics" of the rebellion.

The tapes of the military inter-communications during the period leading up to "the personage's" arrival in the square, provide indispensable factual background.

The text of the interview with Dr. Martínez quoted here was given by Dr. Martínez within the first few days after the tragedy to Manuel Vicente Peña, published in Bogotá in *Las Dos Tomas*.

The unbroadcast videotape of the impromptu press conference that Dr. Martínez gave to the journalists on the square before entering the Palace was screened for me by Felipe,* and was extremely revealing of the social and political attitudes of the Red Cross Director.

The transcripts of testimony by soldiers who participated in *"Operación Rastrillo"* and who gave evidence to investigators for the Special Commission of Inquiry, were provided to the author in Bogotá, in April 1991, by a lawyer for one of the dead justices' families; they served to confirm the individual military actions taken by the soldiers in relation to the strategic overview provided in the communications between General Arias and General Samudio.

The official minutes of the Cabinet meeting of November 7 remain the clearest indication of the low priority given by the President and the majority of the members of his cabinet to the Red Cross Mission.

CHAPTER 13: The details of the last hours inside the bathroom were first described for the author by Gabriel,* in May 1986. His subjective recollections were confirmed and illuminated in the author's subsequent conversations with Felipe,* Mauricio,* and Juan,* in May 1986, and again in April 1991. In 1991 they shared with the author copies of their documents—the autopsy reports, the topographical scale drawings, the slides, the ballistics analyses—all the background materials that they had originally provided to the Commission of Inquiry in support of their findings and conclusions. All the specifics referred to in the narrative—the dimensions of the bathroom wall, the size of the breaches made in this wall, the details of the weaponry used, the distances from which the soldiers fired their rocket launchers, the positioning of the tanks inside the gutted library—come from the information assembled in these documents. Known collectively as "The Morgue Report," these are the documents which form the basis of the reconstruction of the final assault on the bathroom.

The terms of reference for this work of reconstruction, which Felipe* and his colleagues carried out for the Commission of Inquiry, were set out by Investigative Judge Luis Antonio Lizarazo in his order # 088 of March 3, 1986. Essentially what the judge sought, four months after the massacre, was a technical and scientific analysis of all the available evidence that would be capable of addressing the basic question: Who killed the hostages in the bathroom? Was it the army or was it the guerrillas?

To find the answer it was necessary to find out: First, by what method, using which weapons or explosives, the army had managed to break open the two breaches in the east wall of this room. Second, was it possible, given the dimensions and the siting of the openings in this wall, for someone on the outside to fire bullets directly into the room? Third, in what location were the hostages killed? Inside the bathroom? Or while trying to escape down the stairs?

Using all the tools of forensic science—autopsy reports, ballistics analyses, topographical recreations tracing the angles of fire, minute examinations of the scars and the bloodstains left in the stonework of the stairs by the impact of the grenades—and weighing all of these findings, comparing them with the testimony of survivors and of soldiers, and with a visual record of some four hundred slides taken at the site—Felipe* and his coworkers succeeded in reconstructing the basic facts. The author's access to their documents, as also, in May 1986, to their work in process, provided the basis for an understanding of the final, bloody end to the siege.

This is particularly true of the comprehensive and meticulous visual record established by Mauricio* for the Special Commission of Inquiry. His series of topographical scale drawings, recreating the location of the tanks and rocket launchers in relation to the destruction of the bathroom's east wall, were uniquely helpful in giving the author a visual grasp for what happened. These drawings also locate the position of the soldiers who were firing onto the stairs outside the bathroom, in relation to the fatal injuries sustained by the two judges as they sought to escape; they also include meticulous recreations of the angles and the range of firepower available to the guns of the army's tanks as they attacked the bathroom wall; and finally they define the target area of the automatic rifle that was introduced into the room through the opening breached in the bathroom wall under the washbasins, in the aftermath of the second shell.

The most sensitive and politically significant information uncovered and documented by the morgue investigators concerned the deaths of the two Supreme Court Justices. There were many testimonies by survivors who saw Manuel Gaona and Montoya Gil leave the bathroom alive. From their analyses of the evidence the investigators knew that grenades had not been used within the bathroom; consequently the deaths of Montoya

Gil and of Lizandro Romero, and the wounds suffered by Carlos Urán, could only have happened outside on the stairs.

Access to the autopsy reports of those victims killed by gunfire inside the bathroom, and whose deaths were documented in the "Morgue Report"—the lawyers, Luz Estella Bernal Marin, Aura Nieto de Navarrete; the chauffeurs, Luis Humberto García; Luis Eduardo Medina Garavito; as well as those killed by gunfire and grenade explosions outside the bathroom on the stairs—Judge Manuel Gaona Cruz, Judge Horacio Montoya Gil, Associate Justice Carlos Horacio Urán, and lawyer Lisandro Romero Barrio—provided a rather macabre guide to the author's understanding of how the investigators reached their conclusions.

"*Lo Que el Tribunal y el Procurador Desconoció,—Informe de Medecina Legal,*" *Zona* magazine, (July 1, 1986), revealed the existence of the "Morgue Report" to Colombians, and established the fact of its suppression by the Official Commision of Inquiry.

The transcript of the testimony given to investigative Judge Lizarazo V. on Feb. 22, 1986, by Sub-lieutenant Ramírez Cardona, one of the soldiers who laid plastic explosives on the adjoining walls of the bathroom, and who was also one of two soldiers who fired the rocket launchers from the second floor at the east wall of the bathroom, was supplied to the author by a source in the Attorney General's office in April 1991.

The transcript of the testimony given to investigative judge Gustavo Vega Aguirre, in Bogotá, on Feb. 20, 1986, by soldier Rodrigo Romero, comes from the same source, and confirms the army's knowledge of the existence of the hostage population in the bathroom prior to and during their attack on this room.

CHAPTER 14: Minutes of the Nov. 7 Cabinet meeting (see previous chapters) were crucial to the author's understanding of what happened after the fighting stopped.

The written testimony of the Minister of the Interior, Jaime Castro to the Commission of Inquiry, Bogotá, April 21, 1986, offers an eloquent "official version" of the role of the President during the entire 27 hours of the siege, and strikes a note of explanation and justification in the following terms: "I believe that what the government did during those days was consistent with the Constitution and the law and responded to the country's real interests... In Colombia we talk a lot about the danger to our institutions... yet it is true that the most serious threat to our institutions in the last 25 years or more, took place during those terrible days." Minister Castro insisted that: "From my point of view it was clear that [the President] consistently, without any limitation whatsoever, excersized his role as Commander in Chief of the Armed Forces and the National Police throughout, and that [the chiefs of the Armed Forces] obeyed, as is their duty, the decisions of the civil power."

The transcripts of testimonies by members of the Bogotá firebrigade to the investigative judges, made available by a lawyer for the family of one of the slain justices in Bogotá, April 1991, gave the first indication to the author that the rumors of extra-judicial executions might indeed have some substance.

Information relating to the irregularities and breaches of the law committed by the military authorities in the process of removing the bodies from the scene, comes from the interview by the author with Judge Amalia Mantilla, in Bogotá, April 1991; from conversations by the author with the Morgue investigative team, in Bogotá in May 1986 and April 1991, and from access to their official documents; and from conversations by the author with relatives of the dead and the missing during the first forty-eight hours after the tragedy in Bogotá, in November 1985.

In the search for information relating to the disappeared, an interview by the author with Maria Ximena Castilla, lawyer for the family of slain Supreme Court Justice Ricardo Medina Moyano, in Bogotá, in April 1986 and again in April 1991, helped to put the post-battle scene in Bogotá into a context that made sense. Subsequently, additional information was unearthed with the help of lawyers working for the families of the disappeared. The transcript of the testimony of Captain Luis Roberto Vélez Bedoya, questioned by investigative Judge Alfonso Triana,in Bogotá, Feb. 14, 1986, and again on March 16, 1986 (Captain Vélez Bedoya commanded the artillery unit that entered the bathroom after the guerrillas ran out of ammunition) let in a little light on the post-battle killings that took place inside the bathroom. In his first (Feb. 14) session, while speaking under oath, Captain Bedoya said: "Yes, I managed to recognize Andrés Almarales who didn't have a moustache... he was wearing a green shirt-blouse and was seated, slouched, on the left of the entrance to the bathroom, close to the urinals, and there was another one [a guerrilla] beside him, also under arrest." When recalled on March 16, Captain Bedoya contradicted his earlier testimony. On the second occasion he claimed that the court stenographer must have misunderstood what he had said the first time, since, he now explained, "all the guerrillas died during the fighting...."

Evidence of arrests inside the Museum of the Casa Florero come from a number of sources including: the testimonies of the caretaker and the assistant caretaker of the Museum to investigative judge Alfonso Triana, in Bogotá, February 1986; the transcript of the testimony by free-lance journalist Julia Navarrete Mosquera to the investigative Judge Germán Enciso Uribe, in Bogotá, Jan. 7, 1986, and the transcript of testimony of hostage/survivor Jose William Ortiz to Judge Gustavo Vega Aguirre, Bogotá, January 23, 1986. Each of these witnesses spent time in the Casa Florero where they saw various people being arrested.

This series of testimonies was brought to the attention of the author in Bogotá, in April 1991, by a legal source working with the lawyers of the families of the disappeared cafeteria workers.

The interview by the author with Judge Amalia Mantilla, which took place in Bogotá, in April 1991, served to confirm and corroborate much information which, until then, was coming the author's way chiefly from only one source—namely from Felipe and his team.

The transcript of the press conference with the foreign journalists and the Minister of Justice appears in Manuel Vicente Peña's *Las Dos Tomas*.

The tape of the dissident B-2 agents was given to the author by an unattributable source in the offices of the Attorney General, in Bogotá, in May 1991.

Corroborative background material from *El Misterio de los Desaparecidos*, *El Espectador*, Nov. 5, 1986

EPILOGUE: In the search for understanding of the legal history of the Palace of Justice case over the past seven years, the author's interviews and telephone conversations with Juan Manuel Lopez Caballero, in Bogotá in 1986 and 1991, and from New York in 1993, have been of immense value in gaining an overview of the juridical implications of the Palace of Justice case. Others who have contributed to the author's understanding of the legal and political history of this case are: Maria Ximena Castilla, lawyer for the family of slain Supreme Court Justice Ricardo Medina Moyano; Gustavo Gallón and Guido Bonilla in the *Comisión Andina de Juristas*, (Colombian branch); and Robert Weiner of the International Lawyers' Committee for Human Rights in New York.

The texts of the indictments in the following major cases that have resulted from the Palace of Justice siege were obtained by the author in Bogotá, in April 1991, from a number of legal sources and include:

1. The accusation brought against President Betancur and Minister of Defense Miguel Vega Uribe for crimes against International Human Rights Law and the laws protecting civilians in times of war, by Attorney General Carlos Jiménez Gómez. Attorney General Jiménez conducted a seperate investigation at the same time that the Special Commission of Inquiry was holding its investigation of the siege. The text of his accusations were sent to the Justice Committee of the Colombian Congress in Bogotá, on June 20, 1986.

2. The text of the accusation brought to the Justice Committee of the Colombian Congress against President Betancur and three members of his government—the Ministers of Defense, of the Interior and of Justice—for breaches of the Constitution, by Juan Manuel López Caballero, in Bogotá, on Dec. 3, 1986

3. The text of the accusation brought by Attorney General Gómez Méndez against General Arias Cabrales, for "criminal iregularities" committed during the attack on the fourth floor, the attack on the bathroom, and in relation to the testimony of a "public service representative" who testified that he saw two M-19 guerrillas arrested and taken from the Palace building through the garage exit, and one wounded M-19 guerrilla taken from the garage by soldiers in an ambulance.

In the same case, the text of the accusation against Colonel Edilberto Sánchez for the disappearance of Irma Franco. (see notes for chapter 14).

4. The text of the indictment for co-authorship of crimes of terrorism—rebellion, homicide, attempted homicide, kidnapping and false-hood—brought against the entire surviving membership of the M-19's 1985 National Direction by a "faceless judge," in one of the new Constitution's Public Order Courts, in Bogotá, on May 15, 1992.

And in the same case, the charges brought by the "Faceless Judge" against former president Belisario Betancur and former Minister of Defense Vega Uribe, for the crime of "Homicide by Omission," which were sent to the Supreme Court in May, 1992.

5. The texts of both responses from the Justice Committee of the Colombian Congress, rejecting the accusations brought before it by the Attorney General, Carlos Jiménez, and by Juan Manuel Lopez Caballero and Richard Hernández González on behalf of the Foundation for the Clarification of Events at the Palace of Justice, which reject the "Act of

War," thesis out of hand and exonerate the President and the Minister of Defense of all wrong-doing.

In his 1986 brief, Attorney General Jiménez Gómez pointed out that nothing about the conduct of the battle to retake the Palace of Justice differed in any detail from that of the hundreds of battles between guerrillas and army troops that occur daily on Colombian territory, in which defenseless civilians are regularly involved and sacrificed.

"Seen as such," the Attorney General wrote, "an episode which in itself, is, legally speaking, an act of war, acquires even greater significance. It is a case of looking at what happened not in an isolated fashion, but rather of seeing it as one event integrated within a chronic and recurring state of affairs."

The Attorney General also wrote that: "The evidence of this investigation clearly demonstrates that no serious effort was made to save the lives of the hostages. There was no policy to rescue the hostages. So long as it is evident that no such effort was made, the legitimate hypothesis exists that, with a better handling of the situation, the lives of the hostages could have been saved."

The Public Order Court's "Faceless Judge," for his part, in his effort to annul the effects of the 1989 amnesty granted to the membership of the M-19, and to reopen the Palace of Justice Case against the highest officials of the 1985 Colombian government, wrote: "Neither this office, nor the country, nor the world, can deny that the acts committed during the seige of the Palace were equally as terroristic as the seizure itself; and that the holocaust to which the hostages were submitted was an act of savagery, which in itself constitutes a horrendous crime against the laws of a country that calls itself democratic, without any respect for the right to life of individuals, and in violation of all the rules of war...

"The seizure of the Palace of Justice, constituted one battle in the long dirty war fought in our country between the subversives and the government... This office refuses to accept that the State, through its officials, should be as delinquent as the terrorists themselves, and that their omissions should remain immune under the pretext of the [governmental] discretion of their acts."

The sources for the Epilogue further included:

"El Palacio de Justicia y el Derecho de Gentes," by former Attorney General Carlos Jiménez Gómez (Bogotá, November 1986).

Palacio de Justicia, Defensa de nuestras Instituciones?, and, *Defensa o Sacrificio del Estado de Derecho: Reflexiones sobre aspectos jurídicos y políticos de la tragedia del Palacio de Justicia*, by Juan Manuel Lopez Caballero (Bogotá, April 1987).

Equivocos Fatales de la Controversia Sobre el Palacio de Justicia, by the Comision Andina de Juristas, "Secional Colombia," (Bogotá, published in 1991).

"Las dos Constituciones y el rumor de la Democracia Callejera," published in *El Espectador* (Nov. 2, 1986).

"Año de Silencio, El País Político parece decidido a que se olvida lo ocurrido el 6 y el 7 de noviembre de 1985, Informe Especial," published in *Semana* (Nov. 4, 1986).

"Fuerzas Armadas no piden Amnistia: min-Defensa", published in *El Espectador* (Nov. 7, 1986).

El 6 de Noviembre. First issue of a new legal journal dedicated to the memory of the eleven Supreme Court Justices who lost their lives in the Palace of Justice.

"A Society Torn Apart by Violence, Colombia's 'Dirty War,'" by Penny Lernoux, published in *The Nation* (Nov. 7, 1987).

"Justice Blinded," a briefing paper on Colombia's public order courts by the International Lawyers' Committee on Human Rights (New York, Summer 1993).

The 1987 reports written for America's Watch in Washington by Jamie Fellner.

Various writings about the political situation in Colombia during these last seven years, by Alma Prieto and, whenever possible, the columns for *Semana* magazine, by Antonio Caballero, in Bogotá.